I TATTI STUDIES IN
ITALIAN RENAISSANCE HISTORY

Published in collaboration with I Tatti
The Harvard University Center for Italian Renaissance Studies
Florence, Italy

WHAT GOD KEPT FOR HIMSELF

Atheism, Sodomy, and Radical Dissent in Renaissance Italy

UMBERTO GRASSI

Harvard University Press

Cambridge, Massachusetts

London, England

2026

Printed in the United States of America
First printing

EU GPSR Authorised Representative
LOGOS EUROPE, 9 rue Nicolas Poussin, 17000, LA ROCHELLE, France
E-mail: Contact@logoseurope.eu

This research was funded by the European Union's Horizon 2020 Research and Innovation Programme under the Marie Skłodowska-Curie grant agreement No. 795514. Research project: SPACES - Sex, disPlacements and Cross-cultural EncounterS (PoliTeSse Research Centre, Dpt. of Human Sciences, University of Verona; Dpt. of History, University of Maryland). The book is the result of Dr. Grassi's research activities. It reflects only the author's view and the Research Executive Agency is not responsible for any use that may be made of the information it contains.

Library of Congress Cataloging-in-Publication Data

Names: Grassi, Umberto, author.
Title: What God kept for himself : atheism, sodomy, and radical dissent in Renaissance Italy / Umberto Grassi.
Other titles: I Tatti studies in Italian Renaissance history.
Description: Cambridge, Massachussetts : Harvard University Press, 2026. | Series: I Tatti studies in Italian Renaissance history | Includes bibliographical references and index.
Identifiers: LCCN 2025019831 | ISBN 9780674302860 (cloth)
Subjects: LCSH: Sodomy—Italy—History. | Sodomy—Religious aspects—Christianity. | Sin, Original—History of doctrines. | Sex customs—Italy—History. | Trials (Sodomy)—Italy—Case studies. | Sodomy—Law and legislation—Italy—History. | Atheism—History—Modern period, 1500–
Classification: LCC HQ72.I8 G733 2026
LC record available at https://lccn.loc.gov/2025019831

CONTENTS

WHAT GOD KEPT FOR HIMSELF

Introduction

This book explores the relationship between radical religious dissent and sexual nonconformity by analyzing a series of inquisitorial cases that were prosecuted throughout the Italian peninsula from the sixteenth to the eighteenth century. The defendants came from a wide range of social and economic backgrounds. Despite their many differences, however, they were united by a common denominator: they all assumed that Adam and Eve enjoyed sodomy in the Garden of Eden and that the apple symbolized the buttocks (according to a metaphor that the Church would use for the sake of decency).

The aim of this book is to investigate, through these case studies, the role played by sexual tropes in the development of skepticism and unbelief throughout the early modern period, showing that reflections on nonreproductive sexuality and sodomy, in particular, are crucial to this process. Advocating sexual pleasure in general, and especially anal sex, became a philosophical and critical tool used to debunk Christian morality. While scholars have already recognized that this viewpoint was crucial to seventeenth-century libertine circles, the cases analyzed here invite us both to trace these connections earlier and to locate them in oral culture.[1] When these opinions were crystallized in writing by later libertines, they gained a more refined philosophical expression but lost the more irreverent radicalism that had characterized them when they were circulating orally in the sixteenth century and beyond. Those oral exchanges also cut across class lines and, in some episodes, were indifferent to religious boundaries.

I have collected twenty-six cases dating from the second half of the sixteenth to the beginning of the eighteenth century. All of these cases include, among their charges, the belief that sodomy represented the true—albeit unacknowledged—cause of the Fall from Grace. Nine cases were preserved in inquisitorial archives in Sicily, two in Naples, one in the series of the inquisitorial documents stored in the Diocesan Archive of Pisa, and one in the State Archive of Venice. Thirteen cases came from the Holy Office in Rome, although they relate to events that took place in Colle Vecchio, Casale, Poggibonsi, Venice, Aquileia, Pavia, and Rome. Each case has particular social and historical conditions, and each chapter of this book contextualizes those circumstances. Yet many parallels run through these episodes of early modern religious dissent. The ways in which sodomy was figured as the original sin varied considerably from judge to judge and case to case. Sometimes, it was explored in depth as the main charge in the interrogations and depositions. In other instances, it was one among a host of unorthodox opinions. What is relevant here is the striking consistency with which the idea was framed across the centuries. This book attempts to understand why. What rationale connected this reinterpretation of the Fall from Grace to a cluster of dissenting beliefs that we can trace across the Italian peninsula from the late sixteenth to the early eighteenth century?

These radical religious dissenters shared strong anticlerical leanings and caustic criticisms of the main tenets of the Christian faith. They denied the immortality of the soul, the existence of hell and purgatory, the validity of the sacraments. One of them, Marcello Impicciato, went so far as to refute the existence of God himself. Others disavowed the divinity of Jesus Christ and his death on the cross, stating that he was a fraudster and that someone else was crucified in his place. Some believed that "all can be saved in their own law"—that is, that Jews, Muslims, pagans, and even unbelievers could attain eternal salvation if they behaved well. All questioned the authority of the pope, and all denounced the corruption of institutionalized churches. The framing of sodomy as the original sin, which at first glance might appear as a mere sexual innuendo devoid of any particular theoretical implications, contained grains of subversion that not only were consistent with these wider assumptions but constituted their most daring and radical expression.

Forbidden Fruit

In some of the inquisitorial proceedings analyzed in this book, the defendants were extensively questioned about the meaning of their belief that Adam and Eve enjoyed nonreproductive intercourse in the Garden of Eden. They stated that they thought that the apple symbolized the buttocks and that the Scriptures hid this truth behind a metaphor for the sake of decency. God forbade the first couple to have anal sex because he deemed it a divine pleasure that he wanted to keep for himself alone. By transgressing this prohibition, Adam and Eve dared to make themselves like God. This caused their Fall. This sin of disobedience or presumption caused humanity to fall into its current, decayed state. One of the defendants went even further, daring to say that he believed that God put Adam in the Garden of Eden because he wanted to abuse him sexually.

These statements can be understood as the radicalization of a trope that was widespread in satiric, erotic, and burlesque poetry from at least the fifteenth century. Some authors depicted sodomy as a privilege reserved for the ruling classes, who then used religion to terrify the uneducated masses and thus keep them away from what they considered the most refined of pleasures. This leitmotif would later recur in some anticlerical writings of erudite libertinism as one of the arguments used to prove that religions were nothing but the cover of political power. By attributing sodomitic preferences to God himself, however, the dissenters examined in this book projected onto the Creator the faults commonly ascribed to political and religious elites. They turned the Almighty into the first trickster, the progenitor of all the earthly charlatans and swindlers who founded religious traditions and institutions.

Before exploring this use of sodomy as a critical tool in contexts of radical unbelief, it is necessary to contextualize the use of this term within the cultural and social setting of the early modern period. Since the late Middle Ages, antiheretical literature, criminal law manuals, and actual judicial practice had frequently accused radical dissenters of sexual misconduct. Many studies have already explored the "hereticalization" of nonnormative sexual practices, as well as the instrumental use of these images in antiheretical propaganda. Sodomy and religious dissent were inextricably linked in the rhetoric of the guardians of the faith. They extended sexual tropes to demonize all those they claimed were a threat to the stability of Christian society, a list that increasingly included Jews, Muslims, and the indigenous populations that Europeans encountered during their violent overseas conquests beginning in the fifteenth century.[2] These same stereotypes were revived in the confessional wars that pitted Catholics against Protestants.[3] When someone accused of religious nonconformity was also charged with sexual infractions (and vice versa), these accusations incorporated the long-standing formulaic assumptions of the prosecuting institutions, reflecting their conscious will to manipulate the judicial evidence to worsen the defendants' positions before the judges.

Yet unorthodox opinions about sexual morality were also widespread at every level of society in early modern Europe. These heterodox positions ranged from the belief that sex among unmarried men and women was not a sin to more radical stances about the legitimacy of every form of pleasure, including nonreproductive sexual intercourse, both hetero- and homosexual. Those holding such views needed to free sex from the reproductive injunction imposed by theologians and preachers. In some instances, this need led to a radical criticism that aimed at undermining the basis of the Christian religion. While these radical stances were sometimes expressed through vernacular and vulgar expressions of irreligiosity, especially the attribution of every sort of sexual debauchery to saints, apostles, and biblical figures (even to Jesus and Mary), in some instances (as in the cases analyzed in this book) they gave rise to extremely articulated dissenting opinions.[4]

By directly addressing the issue of original sin, the dissenters under examination associated the beginning of humanity in its current state with an act of anal sex and dared attribute sodomitic preferences to God himself. Although they probably did not always grasp all of the deep theoretical implications of their utterances, it is glaring that anal sex—insofar as it avoids the reproductive implications of intercourse—does not allow any projections into the future, be that through the birth of offspring or, in the condemnatory perspective of that time, the spiritual rebirth in an otherworldly dimension after death. It epitomizes pleasures pursued per se. At some level, our dissenters challenged the injunction to sacrifice the present time to the uncertain promise of future happiness in the afterlife. They celebrated, more or less consciously, the materiality of the here and now.

It is worth noting that they did so from an entirely male perspective. To understand the gendered dimension of these episodes of religious dissent, however, it is necessary to put the term "sodomy" in its proper historical context. The term was used to label a wide range of sexual activities, including both homo- and heterosexual anal intercourse. Scholars of medieval and early modern sexualities have long debated the appropriateness of projecting categories such as "homosexuality" and, even more radically, "sexuality" per se onto past societies. Some see the categories as legitimate, and others believe that in using them we risk losing touch with past social actors' perceptions and understandings of matters of sex and pleasure.[5] While views are now more nuanced, this dispute prompted further research into past sexual epistemologies.[6]

The cases under examination here reflect the variety of meanings attached to the term "sodomy" in early modern western European societies. The theme of Adam and Eve's sodomy shows that the term is flexible and not identified exclusively with same-sex intercourse. Some of the dissenters examined here did not specify the gender of their partners in nonreproductive sexual activities, while others plainly defended enjoying these pleasures with both women and men. Still others clearly leaned toward homosexual preferences, going so far as to denounce women-to-men affairs as a mortal sin.[7] Yet the centrality of penetration united both normative and nonnormative early modern sexual discourses, a predominance that clearly reflected a system of values rooted in a patriarchal social organization that understood pleasure from a purely male view.[8] Despite this prevalence, however, some of the cases presented here provide an interesting perspective on the capacity of women to find space for an autonomous interpretation of sexual matters in a dominant male culture. Chapter 8 analyzes a series of investigations that took place in eighteenth-century female religious houses. Unlike the previous cases, these judicial proceedings centered on the spread, in these secluded environments, of the idea that sex was the original sin. Although they did not focus explicitly on sodomy, these cases were collected by the notaries of the Holy Office in Rome in the same archival folders containing the proceedings against the dissenters who believed that Adam and Eve savored anal sex in the Garden of Eden. They refer to the circulation of forbidden books—one of which seemed to contain a passage in which anal sex was identified as the first lapse of our ancestors—within these female communities. Sister Maria Teresa Garzi, a professed nun in a Venetian monastery (1714), and five girls hosted in a Roman boarding school (1756) proudly claimed their right to interpret the texts they read according to their own reason, sometimes going so far as to question the authority of their spiritual guides. Given the outspoken misogyny of the libertine texts that most likely, more or less directly, inspired their speculations, these cases offer the precious opportunity to analyze the process of the reception of this literature by female readers. The interpretative strategies of Teresa and the Roman girls prove that they were able to question the dismissive framework that surrounded the depiction of their gender in contemporary erotic literature, originally reinterpreting the themes of these works in the light of their sensibility and against the normative authority of their male protectors.

The Theory of Religion as a Fraud

In most cases, those who framed sodomy as the original act of human autonomy further believed that religions were hoaxes created to reinforce the political and social order. Many studies on radical dissent and unbelief have shown that this skeptical opinion was relatively widespread at every level of society during the long Renaissance, acquiring an increasing theoretical definition in the seventeenth and eighteenth centuries.[9]

When we trace the first instances of Adam and Eve's sodomy in sixteenth-century southern Italian oral and popular culture and follow its later emergence in the manuscript and print works of seventeenth-century central and northern European learned libertine elites, we see that such beliefs had remarkable staying power. Most of those expressing these views at this later moment either continued to entirely uphold the theory that organized religion was a fraud or were connected in some degree to dissenters who contributed to spreading this belief. François de La Mothe Le Vayer (1588–1672) was among the sources extensively quoted in the first print edition of the *Treatise on the Three Impostors,* which was published in French at The Hague in 1719 along with a biography of Baruch Spinoza as *La vie et l'esprit de Mr Benoit de Spinoza* (The life and spirit of Mr. Baruch Spinoza). This book alleged that Moses, Jesus, and Muḥammad were tricksters who used their charms to deceive and subjugate the unlearned populace. In the Christian West, the spread of this belief had long been attributed to the circulation of *De tribus impostoribus* (On the three impostors), a book that religious authorities chased obsessively and unsuccessfully all over Europe until this print edition emerged in the early eighteenth century. *The Life and Spirit of Mr. Baruch Spinoza* was published as a transcription of the notorious medieval manuscript, but it was a pastiche that blended together texts from the libertine tradition along with lengthy excerpts from works by the representatives of the most innovative European philosophical currents, especially Thomas Hobbes and Spinoza. Le Vayer, who was widely cited in the chapters on Jesus Christ, discussed the theme of sodomy in the Garden of Eden in a juvenile manuscript titled *L'Antre des nymphes* (The cave of the nymphs).

Another author who dealt with the belief that sodomy constituted humanity's original disobedience was the Dutch scholar Hadriaan Beverland (1650–1716), in his *De peccato originale* (On original sin). Beverland was close to the milieu of the Dutch radical Spinozists from which the French translation of the *Three impostors* originated and he himself was suspected of having authored a version of the *Treatise.* Yet Beverland recognized the Italian genesis of the belief that sodomy constituted humanity's original disobedience, a fact that calls attention to the continuities between the sixteenth- and eighteenth-century cases.

For the purpose of this book, however, it is relevant to point out that—from the time of the earliest cases that took place in the Italian peninsula—the belief that Adam and Eve enjoyed sodomy in the Garden of Eden was associated with themes and authors that were crucial to the initial gestation of the idea that religions were nothing but political dissimulations. Some of the dissenters under examination read works by the physicians, astrologers, and philosophers Pietro d'Abano (ca. 1250–ca. 1315) and Girolamo Cardano (1501–1576), whose writings were foundational to certain expressions of seventeenth-century erudite libertine culture and contributed to the development of the theory of the fraudulence of religions in Italy and beyond. Some of our defendants also undermined the authority of religious revelations by stating that they were inventions devised for mere "reason of State," an expression that, at that time, was (mostly improperly) associated with an oversimplified understanding of Niccolò Machiavelli's political theory, which was also destined to become one of the main roots that nurtured the radical criticism of revealed religions in early modern Europe.

One of the cases analyzed here took place in Naples during the trial of the well-known Italian philosopher Tommaso Campanella (1568–1639), who was accused of having authored a copy of the *Treatise on the Three Impostors.* Campanella was prosecuted by the civil and inquisitorial justice of the viceroyalty of Naples for his famous attempted coup against the Spanish monarchy in Calabria. Most of the charges against the Neapolitan apothecary Marcello Impicciato, who was accused of believing that sodomy was what led to Adam and Eve's expulsion from the Garden of Eden, mirrored those leveled against Campanella. While the alarm raised in the viceroyalty of Naples by Campanella's case might have influenced the judges' attitude toward Impicciato, it is also possible that the similarities in the allegations against the two defendants rest on a common cultural background. Given the many parallels, reading the two cases alongside each other provides us with a unique opportunity to understand the larger context in which those ideas were elaborated and circulated, as well as to recognize the distorted lenses through which the guardians of the faith tended to read and interpret them.

Campanella's suspected authorship of a version of the *Treatise on the Three Impostors,* along with the debated imputation of atheism against him, raises many historiographical questions that will be deeply analyzed in the chapters devoted to his and Impicciato's cases. In this context, however, I have also investigated a hitherto understated reference to original sin in Campanella's proceedings, which recalls a sexual innuendo regarding Adam and Eve that, in my opinion, could be related to the belief investigated in this book. This evidence further reinforces my hypothesis that the idea of anal sex as the forbidden fruit and the theory of religions as frauds were two strictly related phenomena and that this reinterpretation of the Fall from Grace represents a yet uninvestigated theme that was mostly transmitted orally within this larger undercurrent of early modern radical unbelief, from its early incubation in the sixteenth century to its most mature developments in the early eighteenth.

Oral and Written Cultures

Libertine writers largely used sodomy as a tool to debunk Christian religion and the validity of a morality based on a reward in the afterlife. Antonio Vignali (1501–1559) and Antonio Rocco (1586–1653) respectively authored two irreverent parodic libels, *La cazzaria* (The tangle of pricks) and *L'Alcibiade fanciullo a schola* (Alcibiades the schoolboy), whose anticlerical polemics were extremely blunt in this respect. Their works, and especially Rocco's *Alcibiades,* probably inspired some of the dissenters examined here.[10] Both Vignali and Rocco claimed that the prohibition against sodomy was an instrument of control, yet neither dared to go so far as to attribute sodomitic preferences to God the Father or depict him as the progenitor of all the clerical impostors.[11] This radicality invites us to rethink the relationship between oral culture and the manuscript and print circulation of dissenting beliefs. The interplay between these diverse forms of communication is crucial to understanding how the opinions analyzed in this book took shape and circulated.[12] Available sources show clearly that the written word played a role in modeling some of our dissenters' sentiments and opinions. In some of the earliest Sicilian cases, witnesses attributed the origins of this idea to friars and their learned discussions, while in some other instances the judicial proceedings depict it as having been discussed by the defendants in front of open books. On the other hand, the suspects were often reported as bragging publicly about their knowledge in their communities, bridging familiar oral communication and formal "public speech" in ways that stirred the curiosity and indignation of neighbors, relatives, and friends. Publicly defending the skeptical opinion that religions were all forgeries created to manipulate and control common people through the fear of retributive justice in the afterlife was probably a way for these dissenters to distinguish themselves from the amorphous mass of the deceived. Especially for those who belonged to the middle or lower ranks of society, it is likely that this attitude also entailed a certain degree of social revanchism.[13]

These cases are further proof that, despite the growing influence of the printing press, the circulation of ideas was still largely oral in the early modern world. People spread rumors and commented on politics and religion in every corner of their towns and cities; with their speeches, preachers and academics played a crucial role in shaping individual and collective consciousness, although at different levels of the social ladder; many literary genres like poetry and theater, since the beginning, were conceived for oral communication.[14] As Filippo de Vivo has perceptively underlined in his book *Information and Communication in Venice*, "what matters is not to evaluate the strength of orality vs. manuscript vs. print, but to see the ways in which each functioned by connecting to the others."[15] Compartmentalizing these forms of communication simply does not fit into the communication strategies adopted in the early modern world. In western European society, reading was far from being an exclusively private, individual affair. People gathering informally and in public spaces disputed about every sort of topic, and in these contexts those who were able to read often shared their knowledge with the less educated, which is clearly the case in some of the episodes of religious dissent that will be described in the pages of this book.[16]

These observations call into question the long-standing debate about the relationships between learned and unlearned in the elaboration of early modern religious dissent and, in particular, atheism. In his book *Unbelievers: An Emotional History of Doubt* (2019), Alec Ryrie has reinterpreted this historiographical debate through the lens of emotions, writing a history of unbelief that debunks the narrative according to which upper-class philosophy and rationalism killed religion in the Christian West. By analyzing early testimonies of unbelief—some of which are remarkably similar to those analyzed in this book—Ryrie concludes that "unbelief clearly existed in practice (in some form, at some level) before it existed in theory." He criticizes the assumption that, while religious beliefs and feelings are understood as being rooted in emotional and irrational grounds, unbelief and irreligiosity are necessarily the product of a sharp, reasoning mind. Unbelief, too, can be chosen for "instinctive, inarticulate, intuitive reasons," Ryrie argues, focusing on a period "before the philosophers made" unbelief "intellectually respectable."[17]

While anger and unsystematic thought characterized the approach of many of the dissenters analyzed in this book, other elements of their attitudes invite us to reconsider the opinion that the relationship between social ranks was shaped by this functional paradigm, with society as a whole providing a rough cultural material that upper-class culture subsequently reorganized into a coherent system of thought. As Federico Barbierato has pointed out in his seminal work on atheism in early modern Venice, the repertoire of erudite irreligiousness met needs that were already widespread in society and provided people from across the social spectrum with "easily recognizable elements to use and adapt to one's own ideas." When reframed with the support of literary authorities, these "took on a greater degree of credibility."[18] This process of reappropriation, however, required a great deal of creativity and implied a certain degree of theoretical speculation.

The case studies analyzed in this book allow us to take a step further in this direction. Rather than supposing a rigid separation between popular and elite culture, I explore the complex interactions between the oral and written transmission of dissenting beliefs, without considering one or the other as the exclusive prerogative of a determined social rank. As the progression of this book shows, it was not the populace that provided the emotional substance and the elites that reorganized these raw materials into a sound discourse. The process of reorganization could take place autonomously at both ends of the continuum of oral and written culture, leading to similar results, despite the radically different motivations that influenced libertine thinkers and dissenting figures like the ones investigated here. Rather than interpreting these diverse expressions of unbelief through binaries like "reason" and "emotions," this book presents them as expressions of a shared cultural background that was expressed in different ways depending on the circumstances and the social actors' levels of education. Some of the defendants analyzed here read books that were foundational to the development of mature libertine positions, reaching similar conclusions to their learned counterparts. They often did this, however, without apparently being aware of the contemporary intellectual debates that were taking place in learned circles. They obviously did not equal those debaters in terms of theoretical speculation but often surpassed them in terms of radicality and irreverence. The fact that the authors who discussed the belief that sodomy constituted humanity's original disobedience in their writings referred it back to an earlier Italian oral culture seems to confirm that this creativity of the oral culture was amply acknowledged at the level of the intellectual elites.

Mediterranean Backgrounds: Skepticism, Sex, and Unbelief in the Long Renaissance

The first expression I have been able to identify of the belief that sodomy was what led to Adam and Eve's expulsion from the Garden of Eden took place in Sicily and involved a defendant who was abducted by Muslim corsairs in his youth and converted to Islam while he was held captive in North Africa. As we will see in Chapter 4, his beliefs were strongly influenced by his biography, and the experience of conversion left an indelible mark on his skeptical approach toward religions even after his return to his homeland, where he converted back to Christianity. Plenty of Christians shared his fate in the early modern Mediterranean world. Historical studies that focus on this area have, indeed, largely explored the history of religious conversion, and more recent contributions have revealed the extent to which this widespread phenomenon helped foster the development of skeptical attitudes toward institutionalized religion among both the common people and the learned elites.[19] What happened at the level of the uneducated masses as a result of the everyday interactions with other cultures—especially in border zones like Spain, southern Italy, or the Balkans—was accompanied by analogous phenomena of contact in the sphere of the learned elites, and confrontations with Jewish and Muslim authors had long vivified the reflections of philosophers, scientists, and theologians in the Christian West since the Middle Ages. The unaligned beliefs of some of the defendants under scrutiny in this research are a testimony to the complex Mediterranean genesis of some radical dissenting opinions that took hold in Europe during the long Renaissance. Inquisitorial guardians of the faith certainly traced the theory that organized religion was a fraud back to experiences of cross-cultural contacts between Muslims and Christians. The legendary *Treatise on the Three Impostors* was believed to have been first authored by the emperor Frederick II and his chancellor Pier della Vigna, and its gestation was attributed to the influence of Muslim intellectuals hosted by the emperor in the Sicilian court as a result of his commitment to interreligious dialogue.[20]

Authors like d'Abano and Cardano, who were read by some of the dissenters examined here, also developed their theories in part against the backdrop of debates that originated at the intersection of Muslim and Christian astrology. A group of Sicilian necromancers accused of deeming sodomy the original disobedience admittedly echoed passages of Cardano's *De subtilitate* (On subtlety) about the mortality of the soul and the eternity of the world (an idea that obviously implied the denial of the biblical myth of the Creation). The author himself attributed these beliefs to an imagined "Averroist" spirit invoked by his father during an episode of psychic communication. Cardano's mention of the Cordoban thinker Ibn Rushd (520–594 AH / 1126–1198 CE), known in the Christian West as Averroes, reveals a well-established tradition of the skeptical and atheistic reinterpretation of his philosophy that was transmitted in the Christian West from the late Middle Ages and constituted an important undercurrent fueling the development of critical approaches toward religions that would flow into the hotbed of mature libertine thinking. Moreover, the idea that Christ did not die on the cross and that someone else was crucified in his place—which was held by some of the dissenters analyzed in this book and also appears among the charges of the Friulian miller Menocchio famously studied by Carlo Ginzburg in *The Cheese and the Worms* (1976)—also originated at the intersection of polemics between Muslim exegetes, Arabic-speaking Christians, and Gnostics around the eighth century of the Christian era.

The analysis of these cases seems to prove that doubt was not just a matter-of-fact approach to religious matters in a world divided by faith but also an intrinsic part of a common cultural heritage.[21] While our sources make it difficult to assess whether the defendants under examination were aware of such connections, the reality is that these individuals bore the fruits of vines whose roots wove together Muslim and Christian legacies alike (as well as Jewish, although to a lesser degree). Traditions of radical doubt cut across the boundaries of the faiths. On the one hand, doubt was a collateral result of interfaith polemics that ultimately ended up undermining the belief in religious revelations per se. On the other, it nourished itself on the attempts made by scholars of the three Abrahamic religious traditions to accommodate their own religious beliefs with the legacy of a naturalistic understanding of the world drawn from the classical heritage and constituting a common background for Jewish, Christian, and Muslim philosophers, exegetes, and theologians.

Two Centuries of Sexual and Religious Dissidence

The evidence we have points to the belief that our dissenters' connection of sodomy with the Fall from Grace was an undercurrent of the theory of religion as a fraud that for centuries flowed through oral transmission across the Italian peninsula before reaching learned libertine circles beyond the Alps. Tracing its fragmented appearances through the centuries allows us to appreciate the extent to which that which remained unwritten in this tradition sometimes outmatched the audacity of print and manuscript texts. It also shows how much reflections on sex, pleasure, and the body have been crucial to the development of radical dissent in early modern Europe. The belief that sodomy constituted the original sin accompanied the transformations of unbelief from Renaissance natural philosophy, magic, astrology, and skepticism to the various expressions of seventeenth-century libertinism. At a later moment, it was also associated with the heliocentric theory, testifying to one of the defendants' interests in the most daring innovations of the rising scientific method.

Despite these continuities, however, this book avoids indulging in genealogical reconstructions that aim at celebrating the genesis of ideas like "tolerance" or "secularization" in Western Christianity.[22] Rather than highlighting the Italian Renaissance roots of seventeenth- and eighteenth-century rationalism, the evidence collected testifies to the persistence of a different mindset, emerging from early modern expressions of irreligiousness and continuing into the seventeenth and eighteenth centuries. This book emphasizes how religious criticism and the quest for sexual freedom coexisted with opinions that are often incompatible with current notions of "secular rationalism," being instead based on rather different understandings of the natural world and human society.

CHAPTER ONE

Atheism and Sodomy in the Garden of Eden

THIS CHAPTER will analyze the relationship between atheism and the belief in God's sodomitic preferences. These two elements were strongly linked together. Their association was crucial to challenging Christian sexual morals, the foundations of Catholic theology, and the social and political control exerted by the Church over society. In these contexts, God was seen as the progenitor of all the earthly fraudsters who used religion as a means to preserve their position of power. Sodomy was interpreted as a heavenly pleasure that was purposely denied to the common people, whom the ruling classes terrified with the threat of the earthly fire at the stake in this life and of the eternal flames of hell in the time to come.

Among the utterances of the belief that Adam and Eve savored anal sex in the Garden of Eden, those of a seventeenth-century Neapolitan apothecary and a Minor Observant friar in Rome depict the key elements of this construct with greatest clarity. Of all the defendants whose cases will be examined in this book, apothecary Marcello Impicciato was the only one against whom the inquisitors formalized an accusation of atheism. He was also the first to attribute sodomitic appetites to God himself, in the figure of Jesus. Franciscan friar Giovan Battista d'Antrodoco, instead, attributed sodomitic preferences to God the Father, believing that anal sex was a heavenly pleasure that the Creator wanted to keep away from his creatures to maintain them in a condition of inferiority. In both cases, the forbidden fruit, commonly identified with an apple, was believed to be a metaphor for the buttocks.

This chapter investigates the cases of these two individuals against the backdrop of cultural constructs that circulated in Italian print and manuscript culture between the late sixteenth century and the first half of the seventeenth. While some of the themes immortalized in Renaissance erotic and anti-Christian literature were clearly indebted to traditions that simultaneously circulated through oral transmission, the inquisitorial evidence collected here also testifies to the circuitous relationship between these oral traditions and the written page. Despite this interdependence, it is evident that when they were recorded in writing these themes gained theoretical complexity but lost some of their radicality. While often testifying to an unsystematic and impressionistic approach to knowledge, their oral transmission in informal and socially transversal settings did not necessarily imply a lack of speculative inferences. It sometimes went far beyond those of learned counterparts in undermining the pillars of the Christian faith.

Marcello Impicciato: The Context

Marcello Impicciato's case took place in the prosperous port city of Naples, a conflicted environment where civil and religious institutions fought with each other and where the local population was particularly reluctant to accept the yoke of the Church and the Spanish Empire.[1] It was in this context that some testimonies of the irreverent belief that Adam and Eve had anal intercourse in the Garden of Eden were caught in the mesh of inquisitorial justice. In December 1577, the Inquisition brought to trial a forty-year-old man named Biagio di Corso charged with practicing magic. His troubles with the religious court started some years earlier, in 1574, when he was brought to the attention of religious judges for criticizing the sacraments. Leonardo Costa, ex-jailer of the Archiepiscopal Curia, said that three of Biagio's fellow prisoners testified that he was living under a false name, and that in the past he had been burned in effigy by the Inquisition of Palermo. During the interrogations, Biagio (also known as Antonio Messinese) tried to exonerate himself, declaring that he had been arrested in Sicily for assault and thrown into a ditch without food for three days. In this critical situation, he had cried out in despair that if this was the way Christians treated prisoners, he would rather live among the Turks. It was apparently for this reason that he was forced to abjure, standing publicly with a lit candle in his hand as a sign of repentance. During the subsequent Neapolitan trial, Francesco Pistone, a detainee and fellow prisoner of Biagio in the jails of the Archiepiscopal Curia, reported that in prison Biagio had talked about Adam and Eve's sodomy, a fact soon confirmed by another inmate. Both declared that they were rather scandalized by hearing this. In the list of the official charges from the trial ("positiones"), this belief was not reported among the main accusations but appeared only as an additional item ("caput additum"). Nevertheless, the judges resorted to torture when questioning the defendant about the matter. Even though this was a second conviction, Biagio escaped the death penalty, and, probably because the preceding sentence was inflicted by a Spanish tribunal, he was eventually condemned to abjure his crimes only moderately.[2] This belief caught the eye of the Neapolitan inquisitors at other times. On December 31, 1588, Violante Scaglione declared that "Adam's apple was Eve's butt, not the pit of the fruit that got stuck in his throat when he was called by God."[3] This became an object of inquiry in other cases that stand out for the radicality of the opinions held by their protagonists.

Atheism

In 1598, the Inquisition began its prosecution of Marcello Impicciato, also known as Garofalo. One witness said that he heard him repeating, "more than a hundred times,"[4] the idea that Adam and Eve committed sodomy in the terrestrial paradise, while another declared he had said it "hundreds of thousands of times."[5] When relating events that had happened about one year earlier in Impicciato's apothecary shop, Giovanni Casaburo declared, "We discussed a lot of things . . . among them that if Adam hadn't sinned, eating the forbidden fruit, we wouldn't have sinned as well. The abovementioned Marcello, who was in his *apotheca,* as soon as he heard what we were saying, replied: 'What apple? Adam and Eve fucked in the ass, and that's why they were rejected from Paradise.'"[6]

Impicciato spent two years in prison waiting for his verdict, and during that time he kept stubbornly denying the charges against him. He was eventually condemned to serve ten years in the galleys, a punishment that, given the harsh conditions, carried a significant risk of death. We know from the epistolary of the local inquisitors with Rome that he pleaded to the judges, invoking some health problems and his age in an attempt to be spared the terrible punishment.[7] We do not know whether the medical examinations that followed his request confirmed his claims. It is certain, however, that he was still waiting for the medical report when the judges decided to forcibly send him to the galleys.[8]

In this case, unlike many others analyzed in this book, the entire trial has been preserved. More than 140 recto-verso pages and the accounts of numerous witnesses attest to the fact that Impicciato repeatedly uttered the statements of which he was accused. As noted earlier, Impicciato was the only one studied here who was explicitly accused of atheism. In the summary of the charges, he is clearly labeled as a "notorious and manifest heretic, apostate, and atheist."[9] These accusations are probably a consequence of his unapologetic demeanor. His violent behavior, extreme provocativeness, and coarse language have no comparison in any of the other cases whose defendants were accused of believing that the first rebellion against God's commands was an act of sodomy. This is worth emphasizing, given that these other trials are not the picture of piety or moderation either. During the judicial proceedings, Impicciato was accused of not showing due reverence to the Blessed Sacrament, hiding himself when the Corpus Domini procession reached his neighborhood.[10] He radically denied the capacity of God to interfere in, or even care about, the worldly experiences of humankind. He reportedly said, "[I wish] you'll all be slaughtered! What's the point of worshipping the Sacrament? Has it ever done you any good? It has worn me out and has always made me lose money."[11] When addressing his friends, he exclaimed, "You don't have any money, let's see if God will send you some from the sky!"[12] In one statement, Impicciato's denial of God was associated with the belief in Adam and Eve's sexual sin. His neighbor Sebastiano Apicella reported, "He said more than a hundred times that the fruit that Adam ate . . . was not a fruit but the ass, because Adam buggered Eve and broke her ass, and besides that I heard him saying three times that *there was no God,* nor hell and paradise, and 'who has ever seen hell and paradise,' and 'if there was a God He would have made me die tonight because of all the blasphemies and injuries I say to Him.'"[13] In the same deposition, Apicella added once more that he had heard Impicciato saying, "*There is no God,* and He cannot do anything to me." Matteo de Luca, for his part, said that the defendant allegedly swore, calling God an "ass" and a "son of a bitch" and, again, repeating that "*there was no God.*"[14]

These accusations went far beyond skepticism, agnosticism, or simple irreligion. The issue of whether or not they can be labeled as atheism as we understand it today, however, remains problematic. Historians of medieval and early modern Europe have long debated whether it is appropriate to talk about atheism when dealing with the premodern world. Lucien Febvre's *Le probleme de l'incroyance au XVIe siècle. La religion de Rabelais* (1942) established the foundation for this long-standing debate. Febvre stated that he believed atheism to be inconceivable in the early modern world. While acknowledging the undeniable existence of the categories of "atheism" and "atheist" in the rhetoric of the guardians of orthodoxy, he argued that they were largely used to label a jumble of inhomogeneous phenomena that significantly departed from orthodoxy but that could not be conflated with our current notions of these terms. Febvre contended that their meaning became consistent only after the development and spread of the materialistic interpretations of Descartes's thought in the seventeenth century.[15]

Many have since critiqued Febvre's interpretation.[16] Some emphasize the extent to which the polemical definitions of atheism by orthodox theologians (both Catholic and Protestant) stimulated systematic reflections that ultimately contributed to the foundation of a coherent notion of the term. This idea, already formulated by Paul O. Kristeller in 1968, was systematized and brought to its most radical conclusions by Alan Kors in the early 1990s.[17] This approach, however, was also not exempt from criticism. British historian of modern unbelief David Wootton has questioned Kors's interpretation for focusing exclusively on philosophical atheism, overlooking other expressions of radical incredulity that, conversely, were widespread at every level of society in most early modern European countries. In this vein, Nicholas

Davidson, relying on the extensive research carried out by historians in Italian inquisitorial archives, concluded that since the early modern period, "elements of unbelief could be, and on occasion were, combined into atheism," which was "both conceivable and actual among the educated and the uneducated."[18]

As noted by Gianluca Mori, this historiographical debate is fundamentally based on the divide between "inclusivist" and "exclusivist" interpretations of atheism. While the former have tended to incorporate into atheism the criticism of positive, revealed religions, along with their ecclesiastical and political structures, the latter limit their analyses to those thinkers who have explicitly denied the existence of God and provided philosophical and metaphysical explanations to justify their statement.[19]

Despite being devoid of theoretical depth, Impicciato's repeated declaration that "there was no God" seems to satisfy the more restrictive interpretations of atheism. Nevertheless, in other passages of his trial he seemed to deny not so much the existence of the Creator as his power over Creation. According to both some witnesses and the final, formal summary of the accusations, Marcello stated, "God can't do anything to me, He can't do anything more than a fly in Apulia, the only thing He can do is to make me die . . . God cannot wish me a good day, I have to earn it myself."[20] Was he alluding to the fact that God was just a human invention and that only a mechanical natural law regulated the cycle of biological life and death on this earth? Did he conceive of God as a malevolent divinity who did not care about his creatures? Or did he imagine God as being weaker than orthodox beliefs presented him as? If this was the case, did not denying God's goodness and omnipotence equal denying his divinity? Unfortunately, the inquisitors formulated their accusation of atheism without getting to the bottom of these questions, so we are left with many doubts as to whether Impicciato's statements reflected an emotional reaction to the vicissitudes of life or implied deeper ruminations about the nature of God and his power. Nevertheless, it is undeniable that most of his statements appeared to be something more complex than a fleeting impiety uttered out of rage and drunkenness. Although they lacked the theoretical coherence of a philosophical rejection of God, they oscillated between an overt denial of his reality and a negative representation of his powers that clearly contradicted all the theological proofs provided at the time to rationally justify his existence.

Marcello Impicciato versus a Loaf, a Beggar, and a Thief Commonly Known as Jesus Christ

The target of Marcello Impicciato's most vitriolic criticism, however, was not God the Father but Jesus Christ. Impicciato denied his divinity and accused him of lacking even the most basic morals. According to the documents, Marcello allegedly repeated dozens of times to his acquaintances that "Christ was born a tramp, and he wandered by begging around." Some reported him saying that Christ "was lashed because he deserved it" and "because he went robbing around" and that he "loved Saint Peter because they wander around together stealing fishes and dividing them up among them."[21]

Impicciato's repertoire of insults against Christ was not the occasional result of his individual creativity; it reflected a coalescing of themes that can be traced back to a long-standing tradition of anti-Christian polemics. Some of these tropes would become a stable element in the early modern genealogy of radical unbelief and irreligiousness, forming a cultural construct that increasingly assumed clear contours in Impicciato's time and later decades.

The idea that Christ was just a poor man and a beggar and that he therefore did not deserve any credit was a commonplace since antiquity. In the early Christian era, the image of Jesus Christ as a trickster was fashioned against the backdrop of classical literary tropes addressed to prophets and fortune tellers. Such tropes were then subsequently reappropriated by early anti-Christian polemicists.[22] The work that, more than any other, has shaped the circulation of these themes and exerted a lasting influence on popular culture and oral traditions was Celsus's *Alethes Logos* (*On he True Doctrine*, second century CE), which we know of only through the mediation of the Christian theologian Origen's polemical treatise, *Contra Celsum* (Against Celsus, 248 CE). Origen quotes Celsus at length, and, despite the polemical intent, his rendition has been deemed sufficiently reliable by scholars who believe that *Against Celsus* faithfully reproduces a large majority of Celsus's text by following its structure and design.[23] In this indirect reconstruction, the account of Jesus's life is strikingly reminiscent of Impicciato's claims. This biography appears in a section where Celsus reports an imagined dialogue that involves a Jew who questions the foundations of Christianity.[24] In discussing Jesus Christ's early life, the Jew provocatively accuses Jesus of fabricating "the story" of his birth from a virgin "to quiet rumors about the true unsavory circumstances" of his origins. The imaginary dialogue continues with the Jew pressuring Jesus to admit that he was "born in a poor country town, and of a woman who earned her living by spinning"; that his mother "was pregnant by a Roman soldier named Panthera"; and that "when her deceit was discovered . . . she was driven away by her husband—the carpenter—and convicted of adultery." Indeed, the Jew concludes, "Is it not so that in her disgrace, wandering from home, she gave birth to a male child in silence and humiliation?" The text also alludes to the beggar-like life conducted by Jesus and his apostles: "Why—though a son of God—do you go about begging for food, cowering before the threats of people, and wandering about homeless?" The leader and his disciples are depicted as having "scurried about making a living as best as they were able, usually through double dealing and in otherwise questionable ways." In a passage in which Christ's followers are depicted as a "robber band," it is said that Jesus was not only a poor man but "also a coward and a liar as well."[25]

Although the multilayered structure of *Against Celsus* makes it difficult to clearly establish whose voice is being represented in the text, research has shown that these passages clearly echo opinions that were circulating at that time in Jewish environments. This is so much the case that Celsus's *On the True Doctrine* eventually became one of the works through which these themes filtered into subsequent Jewish writings. Along with Talmudic references and materials coming from popular culture, Celsus was indeed one of the sources of the *Sefer Toledot Yeshu,* one of the most derisive Jewish anti-Christian works ever written. The *Sefer Toledot Yeshu* is an even more complex text than *Against Celsus.* It cannot even be referred to as a text, for it constitutes a rather complex textual tradition. Although several versions of this biography of Jesus had circulated since late antiquity, Yacov Deutsch has hypothesized that the existence of a complete version, which included the life of Jesus from his conception to his death, can be dated to no earlier than the twelfth century.[26]

Its contents, however, moved beyond the boundaries of Jewish communities and widely circulated in the Christian West during the Middle Ages. In the thirteenth century, the Dominican friar Ramón Martí included a Latin translation of one of the branches of the *Toledot* in his treatise against Jews and Muslims titled *Pugio Fidei adversus Mauros et Judaeos* (The dagger of faith against Moors and Jews).[27] Martí's transcription of the *Toledot Yeshu* was then repeated almost word for word in the main work of the renowned Christian polemicist Alfonso de Espina, the influential *Fortalitium fidei* (The fortress of faith), which was first printed around 1470. Along with this version, other print adaptations circulated in the fifteenth and sixteenth centuries. A Carthusian monk from Genoa, Porchetus Salvaticus (died around 1315) included Martí's translation of the *Toledot Yeshu* in his polemical work *Victoria adversus impios Hebraeos* (Victory against the wicked Jews, 1303). The 1520 publication of this work is of utmost importance. Through it, Martin Luther learned the contents of this irreverent counter-Gospel, which became one of the main inspirations for his bitter anti-Judaism.[28]

The themes of the *Toledot* were therefore widely known and discussed in the sixteenth century. It is quite likely that Marcello Impicciato was not aware that most of his statements about Jesus Christ could be directly attributed to the *Toledot Yeshu* and to Celsus as quoted through the intermediation of Origen. We do know, however, that the cultural constructs reproduced in these texts largely drew from popular motifs that were mostly transmitted orally. Marcello Impicciato's case confirms the extent to which these themes continued to be conveyed by word of mouth in informal settings into the seventeenth century. It is likely that even in these same contexts, the contamination of this oral tradition with written culture was apparent to those who were cultivated enough to recognize it. These same people might have also contributed to reinforcing radical expressions of irreligiosity, like those of Marcello, by spreading the seeds of doubts, shaped by their readings, across class boundaries.

Was God a Sodomite?

Among the many versions of the *Toledot Yeshu,* the one by the Viennese cleric and historian Thomas Ebendorfer (1388–1464) has received particular attention from historians of sexuality because of an allusion to an act of sodomy involving Jesus and Judas. Ebendorfer included a new Latin translation of the text in his *Falsitates Judaeorum* (Lies of the Jews).[29] As Ruth Mazo Karras has pointed out, it is in this translation that we first see also the story of the inglorious conception of Jesus, which clearly echoes Celsus's account.[30]

Both Martí's and Ebendorfer's versions include the belief that, upon entering the Temple, someone could learn the *Tetragrammaton* (that is, the name of God) and thus become able to perform miracles. However, no memory of the name could be retained upon exiting. According to this tradition of the *Toledot Yeshu,* Jesus slanderously managed to take the name out by copying it on a piece of parchment that he sewed under the skin of one of his legs. He was then able to perform all sorts of supernatural deeds, including flying in the sky. The sages thus decided to instruct a man, called Judas Scarioth or Ben Asterota, to challenge Christ. Scarioth was endowed with the same powers as Jesus, and thus the two engaged in a flying battle, during which they both lost their powers and fell to the ground.[31] Unlike in Martí's version, however, in Ebendorfer's interpretation Judas sexually assaulted Jesus, causing the two of them to fall.[32]

References to Jesus as having sodomitic intercourse are also present in Impicciato's trial records. He reportedly stated that "Christ was a bugger, and he wanted to bugger, and this was the reason why he put Adam in the terrestrial paradise, and that the fruit was the ass, and Christ wanted to bugger Adam."[33] The brutality of these passages surpasses the desecrating prose of the *Toledot.* While in Ebendorfer's version the fact that Jesus suffered a sexual assault seems to be a rhetorical device used to undermine his credibility as a founder of religions, in Impicciato's interpretation Jesus is depicted as being proactive, even predatorial, in the expression of his sexual desires.

Impicciato was far from the only individual in early modern Italy to attribute sodomitic preferences to Jesus Christ. Almost fifty years before Impicciato's trial, a young priest and former Benedictine monk from Brescia, Francesco Calcagno, was sentenced to death by the Venetian Council of Ten for having stated that "Christ never was and that he who is called Christ was in his person a man in the flesh, and that he often laid with St. John and that he kept him as a catamite." He continued on saying that "a nice ass was his altar, his mass, the host, and the chalice and the paten" and that "he would rather adore a nice young boy, lying with him, than the good lord."[34] While in Impicciato's alleged statements Jesus's preference for sodomy was characterized by a rapist attitude, here it seems to reproduce the traits of the ancient Greek pederastic model involving a master and a disciple.

The opinion, held by Calcagno, that Jesus had homosexual intercourse with John also surfaced in other contexts across Europe. The English playwright Christopher Marlowe allegedly said "that the woman of Samaria and her sister were whores, and that Christ knew them dishonestly" and "that St. John the Evangelist was bedfellow to Christ and leaned alwaies in his bosome, that he used him as the sinners of Sodom."[35] In the seventeenth century, a member of the *Accademia del Cimento,* Antonio Oliva, reportedly referred to this same belief in a conversation concerning the "Most High Mystery of the Incarnation of the Son of God."[36] In this instance, the transmission of beliefs that radically challenged Christian orthodoxy seems to have occurred mostly by word of mouth, leaving only occasional traces in print and manuscript sources, which often raise more questions than historians can answer.[37]

Even those who believed that Christ engaged in anal intercourse with his apostles did not express beliefs as radical as Marcello Impicciato's. Following his line of reasoning, God himself was a sodomite, and he created human beings to abuse them anally, while prohibiting them from engaging in nonreproductive intercourse with one another. Thinking that Jesus created Adam precisely because he wanted to have sex with him places sodomy at the core of the founding myth of Christian anthropology concerning the creation and fall of humankind. In this provocative reading, the reference to sodomy does not appear to be accidental: it seems to be the purpose of the creation of human beings.

To see an explicit reference to God as a sodomite, we have to move to another case involving a Minor Observant, Giulio di Trocchia, which is preserved in the archives of the Neapolitan Inquisition. In this case, though, the documents are unfortunately not consultable because of the wear and tear of time.[38] As far as we currently know, there is no mention of the sin of Adam in this instance. However, from the correspondence between the Roman inquisitors and the local judges in Naples, we know that by 1578 Giulio di Trocchia had defended the opinion that the

Creator practiced anal intercourse, providing his audience with proof that, regrettably, now remains unknown to us.[39]

This belief emerges again later in the seventeenth century, precisely within the context of another Franciscan Minor Observant monastery. This recurring element is worth emphasizing. As far as I have been able to identify, the earliest emergence of the idea that sodomy was the original disobedience occurred in Sicily. It seems that its genesis can be traced back to religious orders, and especially to the Franciscan family. Between 1573 and 1605, nine men were denounced to the Spanish Inquisition in Sicily for this heretical statement. Among them, there was one priest, a "doctor in Natural Laws," and a theologian.[40] One of them, whose profession was not reported, stated that "there were theologians who held that opinion."[41] Another defendant confirmed that there were learned people and ecclesiastics who were spreading this prurient idea, stating, "People do not talk about anything else in these schools."[42] Octavio de Verardo was a theologian and a Minor Observant who said that he had first come across this provocative interpretation of the founding myth of Genesis as a youth, when listening to a talented Franciscan preacher.[43] In the sources, there is no further evidence that can help us identify what they were referring to when mentioning "these schools," nor have I found any hints about the identities of these theologians or preachers. Despite this gap in the evidence, it is worth noting that the richest exposition of the logic that underlaid this heretical statement is found in the trial report of another Franciscan friar, Giovan Battista d'Antrodoco. Giovan Battista's case, however, took place almost sixty years after Impicciato's, and in a completely different context.

Giovan Battista was put on trial in Rome in 1662, after he was denounced by a certain Father Cristoforo of the Convent of Saint Mary in Aracoeli. The accuser stated that he had heard Giovan Battista saying loudly to his fellow friars in the cloister that sodomy was the original sin. According to Giovan Battista, God had prevented Adam from eating the fruit because "buggery was an act of beatitude"—that is, a divine bliss whose enjoyment he "wanted to keep for himself."[44] Giovan Battista had a reputation as a sodomite, and he said that he shamelessly and publicly praised the qualities of the young boys with whom he had sex. While talking about an altar boy, he said that there was no better sacrifice (ironically referring to the sacrament of the Mass) "than being served by a nice ass."[45] Any time he saw boys wandering in the convent, he allegedly exclaimed that they were "bites of paradise" because "buggery was the real beatitude." The forbidden fruit was nothing but the "ass cheeks," and "buggery was a pasture for angels, because it had something divine in it," and it was a "bite for cardinals, angels, and prelates, that for this reason they wanted to keep it for themselves."[46] He allegedly refused to absolve ecclesiastics who confessed that they engaged in sexual intercourse with women because, according to him, the only sin that was unforgivable was to prefer women to boys. He was also accused of having kept a boy in his room for three months.[47]

Giovan Battista built his defense by accusing his detractors of defamation.[48] Yet, even among those who had been summoned to speak on his behalf, there were some who not only confirmed the suspicions but worsened his position by adding even more serious charges to those already presented by the accusers.[49] The judges decreed that Giovan Battista should suffer a "rigorous examination" (that is, a questioning under torture), but after a barber diagnosed him with a hernia, the friar was spared the torment. Despite the gravity of the charges, he was eventually condemned to the relatively light penance of five years' imprisonment.[50]

The roots of the idea that sodomy was a "bite" reserved for the upper classes were buried in a far distant past. During the Middle Ages, this idea emerged in the writings of moralists who accused the rich of indulging in sexual transgressions due to gluttonous behavior.[51] This theme was subsequently reappropriated in the repertoire of fifteenth- and sixteenth-century burlesque poetry. Antonio F. Grazzini (1503–1584), known as Il Lasca, in his *Rime Burlesche* (Burlesque rhymes), mocked "popes and emperors" because they were eager to "take such honors in their ass."[52] Anal sex was sometimes alluded to through the metaphor of the "centopelle" (omasum), a part of the ruminants' stomach that was cooked along with the "trippa" (tripe). In Tuscan vernacular, the omasum was often equated with the "budello" (intestine), a term that was commonly used as a scurrilous allusion to the anus. A carnivalesque song celebrated the omasum as a "food for Lords / which never runs the risk of being rejected / which King and Emperors have always fed on."[53] The renowned satirical poet Francesco Berni (died in 1535) directly accused ecclesiastics of preferring these kinds of "nourishment," denouncing how even the lowest ranks of the clergy were now willing to share privileges that traditionally only the higher prelates had been allowed to enjoy: "The peaches [which in Bernesque poetry were a metaphor for the buttocks and therefore for anal sex] were once a food for prelates; / but, given the fact that everyone likes the good bites, today even the friars want them."[54] Friars were indeed considered the "populace" among the clergy and were often mocked as squalid social climbers. Common people tended to view them as vulgar people who enjoyed the same privileges of the upper classes at the expense of the poor.[55]

The logic underlying Giovan Battista's subversive beliefs, however, far exceeded the satirical intent of burlesque and carnivalesque poetry. He projected the accusation leveled at the representatives of the upper classes onto God himself. The attribution of sodomitic behaviors to the saints, Jesus, and even God the Father was a recurring element in the colorful blasphemies uttered by common people and peasants during the early modern period. Giovan Battista's and Impicciato's statements, however, go beyond the coarse language registered by the judges of the faith across the Italian peninsula. In Impicciato's statements, sodomy was the purpose of the creation of Adam. In Giovan Battista's, it was the symbol of God's superiority over humankind. In both cases, it was used as a powerful tool to dismantle the foundations of Christian theology.

Vignali's *Tangle of Pricks*

This radicality emerges even more clearly when we read Impicciato's and Giovan Battista's opinions against the backdrop of disputes concerning sex, politics, and religion that were taking place in sixteenth- and seventeenth-century Italy. Sodomy was also compared to heavenly pleasures in a satiric pamphlet, *La cazzaria* (hereafter *The Tangle of Pricks*), published by the Sienese humanist Antonio Vignali. The author blatantly said:

> Paradise, Hell, and Purgatory are to be found in this world, and that Paradise is your house, where you live surrounded by servants, master of all your goods, and the angels are beautiful young men, and all the circumstances that make man content are the elements of the angelic hierarchies, and, on the other hand prison is Purgatory, poverty is Hell, and worn-out

> wretches are the devils, then I would like to believe that ambrosia and nectar are nothing but the sweet tongue of a beautiful young man and the profound secret pleasure that is to be found in his soft delicate asshole.[56]

While Giovan Battista d'Antrodoco never referred to this text during the judicial proceedings, we know that Vignali influenced Calcagno, who clearly mentioned *The Tangle of Pricks* as a source of inspiration for his beliefs during his trial. The authorship of this book was attributed to Arsiccio Introntato, which was Vignali's nickname as one of the founders of the *Accademia degli Intronati.* The *Intronati* was a literary cenacle that was created in Siena in 1525. It was one among the more than two hundred academies founded in Italy between the fifteenth and sixteenth centuries. These circles flourished in the wake of humanistic culture. They were devoted to the study of Greek and Latin classics, but they also engaged in the contemporary controversies that revolved around the formalization of the Italian language as a literary idiom. Despite these learned ambitions, the members of most of these academies also indulged in humorous, bizarre, and burlesque conversations that were often reflected in their verse and prose production. The provocativeness of these literary works was not an end in itself, for often these witty texts concealed caustic political satires and daring philosophical reflections.[57]

The Tangle of Pricks is a remarkable example of this attitude. Written around 1525–1527, the book reproduces an imaginary dialogue between two *Intronati,* the author's alter ego Arsiccio and the inveterate sodomite Sodo, who was in reality another cofounder (and the soon-to-be president) of the circle, Marcantonio Piccolomini.[58] While the starting point of the dialogue was a trivial curiosity about the reason the testicles do not enter the vagina during intercourse, the unfolding of this highly sexualized dispute surveyed the rights and duties of each anatomical part involved in the sexual act. Besides male and female genitalia, the dissertation also included the anus, which was praised for its delights.

The dispute provided Vignali with the opportunity to display an obscene repertoire of sexual debauchery, which mocked not only established religious moral values but also the pomposity of the philosophical and rhetorical disputes of the times. Notwithstanding this scornful attitude, however, some scholars have emphasized how Aristotelian naturalism (especially in its materialistic, heterodox reception) constituted one of the implicit theoretical references for this work.[59] Others have instead highlighted the predominance of political criticism in Vignali's book, the last third of which is devoted to the description of an uprising orchestrated by small penises, ugly vaginas, asses, and testicles against the tyranny exerted over society by large dicks and pretty cunts. This parody actually conveys interesting reflections on the nature of political power and the uncertain foundations of civic justice and societal harmony, and it clearly alludes to the difficult Sienese political situation of the era.[60]

These apparently conflicting interpretations can be harmonized if, along with the editor of the first modern English translation of the book, we consider the importance of bodily metaphors in past and contemporary political treatises. Vignali proposes a well-established allegory of the city as a body politic, in which every part plays its role according to its function. Usually, these representations tended to confirm the superiority of the head as the master of the body. Yet Vignali never mentions any limbs above the torso, instead making the genitals the arbiters of the commonwealth. While this satiric view certainly reflected the author's pessimism toward the capacity of human beings to control their lowest appetites (with the resulting negative impact on the civil order), it also mocked the tendency to sharply divide body and mind and assume the superiority of the intellect as a gateway to knowledge and spirituality. As Ian Moulton perceptively noted, in Vignali's narrative "there is no way to separate the intellectual from the sexual." *The Tangle of Pricks* maintains that body and mind are "in fact linked, because the mind is part of the body," and, therefore, if "scholars are serious in their desire to study the natural world," then "they should devote their attention to their genitalia."[61]

In this respect, *The Tangle of Pricks* is a compendium of sixteenth-century erotic erudition. Despite being characterized by a more elitist outlook, the book aligns with the tradition of renowned authors like Pietro Aretino, Niccolò Franco, and Ferrante Pallavicino. It extensively reviews classical sources including Horace, Martial, and the *Priapeia*; Italian authors like Boccaccio, Bembo, Burchiello, and Berni; the "low" tradition of the medieval fabliaux (along with elements of popular and vernacular oral culture); and the comedies and dialogues that came out of the same goliardic humanistic culture that characterized the *Accademia degli Intronati.*[62] Contradicting centuries of religious condemnations, *The Tangle of Pricks* praised the naturalness of sex. Philosophy, says Arsiccio to his interlocutor Sodo, "is nothing other than the knowledge of natural things. Since the cock and cunt are both natural things, and fucking is the most natural thing in the world and necessary to our existence, it seems to me a great shame that you are ignorant of these things."[63] Blowing up a well-established tradition of Christian pastoral activity—which had made sodomy not only the worst of the sexual infractions but also the greatest insult against the natural order that God had originally infused into his creation—Arsiccio claims that all sex, including anal sex, is perfectly natural. If nature, indeed, "had not wanted [human beings to bugger], she would not have made it such a pleasant thing. Besides, she would have made it so that the asshole was incapable of taking a cock, just as it is incapable of tacking a staff or whatever other thing you like, even though these things are thinner than cocks. Indeed, we see the opposite is true, for the asshole can take a cock just as comfortably as a cunt can."[64] By situating nonreproductive sex within the realm of nature, Arsiccio/Vignali appealed to a radically subversive understanding of sexual morality: pleasure was good, and it had been so since the beginning. In this view, anal sex became a radical rhetorical tool to dismantle the belief in a finalistic orientation of the realm of nature, which sacrificed pleasure in favor of reproduction and based morality on the promise of a reward in the afterlife.

Rocco's *Alcibiades the Schoolboy*

Although *The Tangle of Pricks* was rarely mentioned in literary sources, there is extensive evidence that it was well known and widely circulated, in Italy and beyond.[65] It was certainly known by the author of another text who described sodomy as a "bite" reserved for the ruling classes. We are talking about what has probably been one of the most outrageous libertine books ever written, Antonio Rocco's (1586–1653) *Alcibiade fanciullo a scola* (hereafter *Alcibiades the Schoolboy*). This book was composed around the 1630s and circulated clandestinely in manuscript form for a long time. It was eventually published anonymously with a false colophon wrongly dated 1652. This work, which was included in the Index of Forbidden Books, was first attributed to Aretino, then, in the nineteenth century, to Ferrante Pallavicino, and only eventually to its actual author, Rocco. *Alcibiades the Schoolboy* reflected the cultural climate of the Venetian Accademia degli Incogniti (Academy of the Unknowns), the intellectual sodality of which Rocco was one of the most important, and intellectually fervid, participants. The academy was active in the Republic of Venice between the 1630s and the 1660s, and it was founded by a member of the patriciate, the eclectic intellectual Giovan Francesco Loredan (1607–1661).[66] The circle reflected the cultural atmosphere of the heterodox Aristotelianism that had spread from the nearby University of Padua. It also echoed the members' commitment to the legacy of Cesare Cremonini (1550–1631), a philosopher from Ferrara who had held the chair of philosophy at Padua since 1591 and, on several occasions, had faced reprimands by the Inquisition for defending the intellectual autonomy of natural philosophers from Catholic theology.[67]

Despite its predominantly sexual content, Rocco's *Alcibiades* was more than an erotic novel. It brimmed with references to the philosophical naturalism that characterized the cultural atmosphere of Padua and of the academy. The dialogue revisited the classical theme of Platonic love in an ironic and defiling manner, by describing the interactions of two fictional characters, the tutor Filotimo and his pupil Alcibiades. Rather than praising the transcendent function of pederastic love, which, in the Platonic tradition, was grounded in the separation between carnal desire and spiritual contemplation, Filotimo used any means to convince Alcibiades to obey his sexual wishes. Despite its lighthearted tone, the text hid between the lines some of the key themes addressed in contemporary libertine debates. It contained a ferocious criticism of institutionalized religions and a proud affirmation of freedom of thought. It defended a materialistic world outlook and recognized the importance of pleasure in the frame of a eudaemonic ethic. Rocco claimed that sodomy was natural: "The works to which nature incline us are natural. . . . Do you consider nature to be so careless? Is She perhaps envious of our well-being? Is She depleted by our delights? Who can rob Her of something if She's unwilling? If She has done everything for us, it is reasonable to relish everything for Her glory."[68] These statements were clearly opposed to the Catholic principles according to which sexual pleasure was an illusion leading to the loss of the individual soul if pursued per se.

While some scholars have highlighted the paradoxical queerness of Rocco's work, others, whose interpretation I follow in this respect, have emphasized his stringent rationality and hidden philosophical meaning.[69] Filotimo referred to the trope of natural law to lay the foundation for what the historian of libertinism Jean-Pierre Cavaillé has defined as a form of "anti-Christian deism."[70] The laws of nature were depicted as those precepts "that are impressed in the intellect of any men, of any sect or origin, naturally, without artifice, and since the cradle."[71] According to Rocco/Filotimo, they would command to love both God and one's neighbor. Rocco, however, devoted almost all his attention to the second precept, stating that the former was included in the latter, thereby privileging the horizontal plane of interpersonal relationships over the vertical plane of transcendence. Surprisingly enough, anal sex was part of this dialectic of reciprocal love: "If a boy is content to grant use of himself to those who yearn for him, and he himself takes delight and advantage [from this], has anyone offended the neighbor? Who could say these insanities?"[72] These words sound shocking to a modern readership. A blatant justification of abuse in an educational relationship is a disturbing symptom of a society that was based on sexual prevarication. However, as Vignali's *Tangle of Pricks* had already done, *Alcibiades* also shows a consideration for the receptive partner that was rarely displayed at the time. Although it is hard to ignore the fact that Filotimo was trying to convince his young partner to fulfill his own desires, the passage still considered the pleasure experienced by the receptive partner in homosexual intercourse as a sine qua non for the positive moral qualification of anal intercourse. Despite being modeled on the predominant values of hegemonic early modern masculinity, *Alcibiades the Schoolboy,* even more than *The Tangle of Pricks,* constitutes an attempt to shift from a sexual morality based on the objective evaluation of the reproductive function of sexual acts to a sexual ethic that was more attentive to the relational implications of intercourse. At the time, the heterosexual rape of a child was considered less sinful than a consensual act committed "against nature" between adults. This was according to the belief that the worst sexual infractions subverted the order that God supposedly infused into the natural realm, in which sexuality was believed to be exclusively directed toward procreation. Rocco therefore attempted to find an alternative, materialistic sexual ethic based not only on the right to pleasure but also on the reciprocal enjoyment of the partners in the sexual act.[73] In this context, Rocco/Filotimo also recalled the theme of free will, which he considered a "royal gift from God," which could not have been gratuitously offered by a Creator who was "averse to our good" or "was envious of our amusement."[74]

Besides these philosophical considerations, the text also conveyed a ferocious criticism of the political and religious authorities of the time. In line with Antonio Vignali's work, the prohibition of sodomy was described as a trick devised by the members of the ruling classes to frighten the simple people and keep the most refined pleasures for their own exclusive enjoyment: "These celestial delights are hidden by the sensible [people] under a curtain of horror, in order not to give them in abundance to anyone. The precious things are highly esteemed because they are rare, and the sacred things are venerable because they are recondite: if the rivers flowed of milk and honey, milk and honey would be deemed viler than water. Politicians want to keep them as extra bites, as precious wild games, as a vital and unique fruit."[75] These analyses were accompanied by a rigorous application of critical biblical exegesis through which Rocco highlighted inconsistencies in the scriptural exegesis and theological arguments that had for centuries been used to prove sodomy's sinfulness. By closely reading the biblical text, Rocco/Filotimo attempted to prove that the condemnation of the inhabitants of Sodom was due to their violation of the laws of hospitality and their violence and that as a result it could not apply in cases of consensual homosexual intercourse.[76]

We cannot attribute to either Marcello Impicciato or Giovan Battista d'Antrodoco a similar depth of moral and philosophical reflection on the basis of the sources available. Yet it is likely that Impicciato could have known about Vignali's work, and Giovan Battista about both the latter and Rocco's. *The Tangle of Pricks* was likely known in Naples when Impicciato's trial took place. We know that Antonio Vignali's text has survived in four extant sources: two printed editions, both preserved in the section L'enfer (The Hell) of the National Library of France;[77] a manuscript from the Biblioteca Apostolica Vaticana in Rome; and a manuscript discovered only in August 1992 in Barcarrota in the Spanish region of Extremadura and currently held in the Spencer Research Library at the University of Kansas. This important discovery has allowed us to read a transcription of what is believed to be the editio princeps of Vignali's work, which, according to Pasquale Stoppelli, was the now lost print edition that was published between 1530 and 1540 by Curtio and Scipione Nanni in Naples.[78] We also know from recent research that Rocco's book circulated well beyond the elitist circle of the Academy of the Unknowns, especially in Venice, and that the reference to the "sweetest bite" was probably one of the markers of its reception. On August 7, 1654, around the time when *Alcibiades the Schoolboy* came out in print, Vincenzo Maria Nicolich, a friar from the Dalmatian island of Brazza (which at the time was under Venetian control), was anonymously denounced to the Council of Ten for his "relaxed" and "scandalous" moral conduct. He was known as a notorious blasphemer and an abuser of young novices and pupils. Several times his superiors had attempted to amend his conduct with "charitable admonitions." According to the denunciation, however, he was so deeply "sunk" and "used" to the "sin of sodomy," which he practiced "openly" and "freely" without worrying about the opinion of anyone, that he went so far as to publicly declare—probably echoing Rocco—that "buggery was a bite for princes, and not a food for pricks and persons of vile conditions."[79]

While figures like Impicciato, Giovan Battista, and Nicolich might have found in *Alcibiades the Schoolboy* or in a text like *The Tangle of Pricks* a theoretical justification for their conduct, it is equally likely that Rocco and Vignali crystallized in a piece of literature attitudes that were already present in society, especially among dissident clergymen. Contemporary inquisitorial sources have revealed how members of the academies, together with people from all sorts of social backgrounds, defended the legitimacy of nonreproductive sexual intercourse. In my research in inquisitorial archives, I have found many such examples. Don Pedro Gravino, a cleric from Catania, was denounced by four witnesses and later confessed to having suggested to a male penitent that having anal intercourse with his wife was not a sin if she was pregnant. He was also accused of declaring that "God was wicked and cruel."[80] Other defendants supported the legitimacy of anal sex among spouses under any circumstances. One was Jaime Escallon, who secretly abjured several heterodox opinions when he was examined between 1574 and 1575 by the inquisitors of Palermo. Among his charges was the belief that "God did not create the world, which existed from eternity," and that, after death, human beings would eventually "be born again along with all animals."[81] Others went so far as to claim that even homosexual anal intercourse was admissible. A singer from Toledo named Alonso de Ribera, who was jailed in Zaragoza in 1559 for sodomy, allegedly stated that two men who had sex with each other were not committing a sin against nature.[82] More examples, referring to both homo- and heterosexual sodomy, can be found in Sicily. Luca Daniel, who was born in Palermo, was forced to abjure his beliefs because he reportedly declared to a girl who refused to have anal sex with him that it was not a sin but rather an act worth performing on the altars of Rome.[83] In November 1598, a twenty-four-year-old Bourguignon named Claudio Paris said he thought that the power of absolving from sins was conferred by God to Saint Peter but not to his successors. In his opinion, John Calvin, Erasmus, and "other heretics" were incredibly learned men. He lamented the fact that they were denied access to the Council of Trent because, if they had been accepted, they would have changed the mindset of the cardinals. Finally, he stated that, in his opinion, sodomy should not be considered a sin.[84] In 1605, a ship's boy called Jacobo Philippo stated that sodomy should not be forbidden because it was allowed by nature ("la naturaleza lo permitía").[85] A Franciscan friar called Pacifico La Ficarra, who was brought before the judges in 1591, publicly asked forgiveness for having allegedly held the heretical opinions that neither sexual intercourse "against nature" nor sex with boys were sins. He reportedly suggested that these behaviors were included in the injunction to "be fruitful and multiply" that God himself addressed to Adam and Eve.[86]

While we should not overestimate the spread of these beliefs in early modern society, it is evident that it was anything but an elitist phenomenon. What is more, it seems that some of the stances taken by the defendants of these trials were even more radical, in their contents, than the contemporary elaborations of erudite libertines in Italy and beyond. The radical nature of Impicciato's and Giovan Battista's claims about God's sexual misconduct deserves to be emphasized. They allow us to appreciate the extent to which, when similar ideas circulated both orally and in print, their oral transmission gave rise to less articulated theoretical reflections but far more radical conclusions. At the same time, while it would be a stretch to superimpose Vignali's and Rocco's philosophical reflections on Impicciato's and Giovan Battista's statements, we ought not to overlook the fact that jokes and stories about sodomy as the original act of human independence from God's commands had been circulating for decades and were often associated with radically dissenting opinions that were perfectly consistent with the irreligious convictions of these libertine authors. According to these shared views, sexual deception was at the root of political and religious trickery. Our dissenters, however, went a step further: not only legislators and clergymen but God himself would forbid illicit sexual acts to keep the ignorant people under control and to enjoy, for themselves alone, the solaces of erotic pleasure. God was the father of this earthly fraud called religion.

CHAPTER TWO

Tommaso Campanella in Naples

THE BELIEFS of Marcello Impicciato and Giovan Battista d'Antrodoco were manifestations of larger cultural currents that spread across social boundaries in sixteenth- and seventeenth-century Italy. We find many parallels between Marcello Impicciato's charges and the ideas allegedly held in Naples by one of the most influent philosophers of the time, the Dominican friar Tommaso Campanella (1568–1639). Impicciato's trial occurred between 1598 and 1601, the same years that saw the incarceration of Campanella on charges of participating in an attempted coup against the Spanish monarchy in his native land of Calabria. Most of the charges against Impicciato mirrored those leveled against Campanella. While the alarm raised in the viceroyalty of Naples by Campanella's case might have influenced the attitude of the judges toward Impicciato, it is also possible that similarities in the allegations against the two rest on a common cultural background. Campanella too was accused of atheism. Given the many parallels between Campanella's and Impicciato's cases, the long-windedness of Campanella's judicial proceedings, and the fact that we can set them in the context of his theological and philosophical works, we have a unique opportunity to clarify some aspects of the context in which Impicciato's opinions took shape, deepening our understanding of the role played by sexual tropes in the radical criticism of revealed religions

Campanella and Impicciato

Campanella was accused of saying that "there was no God." There was instead "only Nature, and that it is us who named Nature 'God.'" He purportedly denied the veracity of miracles, the Trinity, hell, paradise, the immortality of the soul, and the existence of demons. Campanella also held the opinion that the solar eclipse that followed Christ's death was not a miracle but a natural phenomenon. Probably in an attempt to exaggerate Campanella's impiety, a witness accused him of hiding the consecrated particle in his intimate parts for days to see if "it was true that it could make miracles." He allegedly denied Mary's virginity and stated that "one ought not to worship the crucifix because it was a piece of wood and it was madness to worship it." He questioned the authority and infallibility of the pope and encouraged individuals to ignore the liturgical fasting and other ceremonies of the Church. He was also accused of practicing necromancy and, worst of all, of wanting to establish a new sect, which made him not just a simple heretic but a worrisome heresiarch.[1] Besides this last allegation, most of Campanella's opinions were echoed in Impicciato's trial. The simultaneity of these two judicial proceedings might explain why Impicciato was treated more harshly than the other defendants accused of believing that Adam and Eve enjoyed sodomy in the Garden of Eden. This severity was likely a consequence of the concern raised in the viceroyalty of Naples by Campanella's trial, which seemed to suggest that the spread of religious dissent had serious political consequences.

Campanella's judicial proceedings, however, did not interfere with the ordinary activity of the Neapolitan Inquisition, which kept carrying out its tasks during Impicciato's trial. The Dominican friar was judged by an ad hoc commission, nominated in Rome by Pope Clement VIII.[2] Even the physical space where the trial took place was separated from the ordinary activities of the inquisitorial tribunal. While the latter carried out its functions in the Palace of the Archbishop, Campanella's detention and trial took place in Castel Nuovo (also called Maschio Angioino). Impicciato's trial was mainly held by the then *procuratore fiscale* (public prosecutor) D. Ludovico Boido, who was nominated as a vicar by the Archbishop Alfonso Gesualdo in 1597.[3] The exceptional character of Campanella's trial necessitated the utmost independence of the court that scrutinized his conduct. It is, therefore, not surprising that the ordinary inquisitorial court that judged Impicciato had nothing to do with the extraordinary commission nominated by Rome to deal with Campanella. I have found only one reference to Boido's direct involvement in Campanella's case. However, this dates to a later time, when both trials were concluded, and therefore does not constitute evidence of communication between the two courts during the handling of the proceedings. On June 19, 1606, a congregation of the Inquisition, which also included Boido, retrospectively reconsidered the evidence collected during the Dominican friar's trial, along with a number of other cases.[4] Yet it is unlikely that the ordinary religious judges engaged in Impicciato's proceedings ignored the broader goings-on in Naples and the development of Campanella's trial. When Impicciato was sentenced to ten years in the galleys, the judges justified their unforgiving decision by stating that they wanted to turn him into an "example," so that others would "refrain from similar excesses."[5] This declaration was likely influenced by the fear—catalyzed by Campanella's sensational case—that the spread of irreligiousness in the viceroyalty had spiraled out of control, with fearsome consequences for the social and political order.

Although the similarities between the two trials may partly be attributed to judicial manipulation, we shouldn't underestimate the possibility that, albeit marginally, Campanella's and Impicciato's convictions reflect to different degrees a set of opinions that they held in common at the time of their trials. Naples was the first place where Campanella stayed when he first moved from Calabria in 1589, before going to Rome, Florence, and Padua. Campanella's stay there marked a turning point in his intellectual trajectory, representing his first release from Calabrese provincialism. In the majestic port city, he profited from the support of the influential noble family of the Del Tufos. While living in their palace, the young Campanella probably worked as a tutor to the heirs; certainly, he participated in his hosts' lively intellectual networks. He dedicated to Mario del Tufo the *Philosophia sensibus demonstrata* (hereafter *Philosophy Demonstrated through the Senses,* 1591), a work inspired by Bernardino Telesio's (1509–1588) anti-Aristotelian natural philosophy. At the Del Tufos', Campanella also met several other individuals who would have a significant impact on his life. One was Lelio Orsini, a representative of the aristocratic Roman lineage who would soon become one of his protectors. Another was the well-known writer, physician, astrologer, and magician Giovan Battista della Porta (1535–1615), who influenced Campanella's understanding of natural magic (as opposed to demonic magic) and inspired his *De senso rerum* (On the meaning of things).[6]

Campanella participated in the many philosophical disputes that frequently took place, often in churches, in sixteenth-century Naples. The erudite nineteenth-century archivist and historian Luigi Amabile found several printed and manuscript posters promoting these popular events, which are still smeared with the glue used to post them throughout the city. These advertisements included the names of the participants, the arguments to be disputed, and the times and places of the events. Some were reissued after the fact with a brief certificate giving a summary of the conclusions that were settled on in the meetings. This was a strategy to promote intellectuals specializing in almost every branch of knowledge, but especially philosophy, medicine, and law. Some of these events are documented in the Church of San Giovanni a Carbonara, in Impicciato's own neighborhood. These philosophical debates were particularly popular and often involved both ecclesiastics and university-trained doctors.[7] This may have made them even more appealing to members of the wider population, especially unquiet spirits like Impicciato, who were critical of matters that were presented as being set in stone by the post-Tridentine campaigns of popular evangelization.[8]

It was during this Neapolitan stay that Campanella underwent his first inquisitorial investigation. According to Luigi Firpo's detailed reconstruction of the elusive evidence regarding the judicial proceedings, the Dominican friar was arrested and detained in the nuncio's jails from the end of 1591 to August 1592.[9] The inquiry had been triggered by a daring joke about excommunication uttered by Campanella in the library of the local convent of the order ("What is it this excommunication? Is it something to eat?").[10] The bulk of the proceeding focused on two issues: first, an accusation that the friar communicated in private with a demon and, second, the suspicious contents of his *Philosophy Demonstrated through the Senses,* which ultimately became the most important factor in determining Campanella's final sentence.[11]

Atheism Conquered

Campanella commented on his alleged juvenile opinions in his most controversial book, the *Ateismo trionfato* (hereafter *Atheism Conquered*), which he wrote while in prison. This work was a defense against the charges of the later Neapolitan trial, after the conspiracy, but some passages can be used to shed light on these statements. The treatise's genesis leaves room for many layers of analysis, and we will quote from the first Italian manuscript, written by Campanella around 1606–1607. The book was first conceived in Italian and was then translated into Latin, the language in which it was eventually published. The first redaction in Italian was probably among the writings that Campanella sent to his friend and correspondent Kaspar Schoppe (1576–1649), who brought them to the attention of the Venetian publisher Giovan Battista Ciotti on September 26, 1607.[12] There is also a manuscript Latin translation by the author, currently preserved in the Jena University Library, which was likely drafted a few years later.[13] After it was revised by a commission of theologians between 1627 and 1628, *Atheism Conquered* obtained the imprimatur. The first Latin edition, however, which was published in Rome by Zanetti in 1630, was almost immediately blocked. A new revised version, printed by the same publisher in 1631, was again withdrawn from circulation by Pope Urban VIII. This was a direct consequence of the April 1, 1631, publication of the papal bull *Inscrutabilis,* with its prosecution of astrology and divination, both matters toward which Campanella was extremely indulgent.[14] Nevertheless, the Dominican friar managed to circulate the book clandestinely, and it was eventually republished in a 1636 Parisian edition. Campanella revised the work at every stage, attempting to respond to the censors by diversifying his strategies of intervention. By adding references to theological authorities, he changed the outlook of the text from a mainly philosophical disputation to a theological one. He attenuated the most controversial affirmations and suppressed some of the more vernacular, popular, and colorful expressions.[15]

The fact that Campanella explicitly addresses the charges levelled against him in this work makes the text a valuable resource for complementing the analysis of the judicial sources.. Using this complex work for such a purpose requires caution. We should not underestimate the extent to which the insistence on and overstatement of doctrinal infractions during the first stages of the trial was an astute maneuver concocted by Campanella and his brothers to have the trial transferred to Rome, in the hope that he would be spared the death penalty if found guilty of treason by Spanish civil justice. Campanella himself acknowledged this. Nevertheless, even the historian Germana Ernst, who has always been suspicious of the veracity of the charges, has stated that, although "it is difficult . . . to trace the continuation of such evidently heterodox affirmations in the later works, some claims turned out to be recognizable and plausible."[16]

In the first Italian manuscript version of this work, Campanella often used the first-person point of view to admit that he had indulged in beliefs that, in the treatise, he was trying to prove wrong. For the purposes of this book, on of the most important reference in the first person was Campanella's introduction to the list of errors summarized in chapter 2, titled "Arguments That Anyone Can Use to Contradict the Christian Religion in This Century, and about All the Legislators of This World: And How Reason Changed to See the Truth." The "reason" to which he refers is clearly his own reason, a fact that is confirmed in the opening statement of the inventory, which reads as follows: "I found myself in this dark time, where everyone seems of the same color, because all the people defend their own Religion, as we defend ours; and so the men of wisdom defend their doctrine with syllogisms, and the princes defend their authority with the armies. I then saw hypocrisy in the place of religiosity, and how there were many heresies, sects, and laws in the world, and I said to myself: who will make me certain among so many controversies . . . ? And if I noticed so many manifest errors in the philosophy in the bosom of which I was nourished, who then would assure me about the theology, that mine is true and that of the other nations false?"[17]

In his analysis of the Latin *vulgata* of *Atheism Conquered*, Vittorio Frajese had already hypothesized—following a longstanding historiographical interpretation—that these admissions should be taken seriously.

Campanella temporarily transfigures himself into a denier of God to confute the thesis in the following chapters, in which the "ego" ultimately shifts into the new voice of the author, reflecting his current convictions. This disconcerting strategy leads into the labyrinth of Campanella's own tormented conscience, turning *Atheism Conquered* into a book of confessions in which his path of conversion unfolds before the reader, testifying to the victory of a repentant sinner over atheism. The book constantly refers to the charges of the Neapolitan trial, which, according to Frajese, should be interpreted as a relatively faithful picture of Campanella's convictions at the time of his imprisonment.[18] Germana Ernst's research, which brought to light the earliest Italian manuscript version of *Atheism Conquered*, allows us today to partially revise the paradigm of conversion by highlighting the persistence, within the text, of deeply heterodox features inspired by a strong philosophical naturalism.[19] The question of the "truth" regarding Campanella's actual beliefs, however, lies beyond the scope of the present study. What is certain, is that both the trial he underwent and the text of *Atheism Conquered* reveal the emergence, at the time, of a well-defined cultural construct: the theory of the fraudulence of religion. The availability of such sources—by their nature far richer than the judicial records concerning the Impicciato case—offers valuable insight into the context in which his trial took place.

According to the trial records, the Dominican friar allegedly stated that "Christ was not a true God, and that he was a beggar," that he did not die on the cross, and that someone else was crucified in his place. About the resurrection, Campanella stated that "Christ [meaning Christ's body] was stolen," an opinion confirmed word for word in many depositions.[20] Impicciato too described Christ as a beggar and allegedly held the opinion that he did not die on the cross but just weakened and faked his death.[21] Another defendant accused of believing that Adam and Eve enjoyed anal sex in the Garden of Eden, however, held exactly the same belief as Campanella: that a substitute died in place of Jesus on the cross.[22] This detail deserves our attention. While these statements were only briefly mentioned in the trial reports of our dissenters, their more detailed inclusion in Campanella's judicial proceedings allows us to use this richer source to fill in some of the gaps in the evidence for our cases.

According to the summary of the allegations, Campanella associated the belief in the abduction of Christ's body and the denial of his death on the cross—which both questioned the miracle of his resurrection—with the opinion that "it was customary for legislators not to let their bodies be discovered, as Moses and Pythagoras had already done, as well as Christ." He was reported as saying that Christ "did as the other lawgivers, who do not let their bodies be discovered."[23] This reference to the founders of religions as lawgivers is reminiscent of the most important facet of the belief that religions are fraudulent, a point that is further clarified in one of the last charges against Campanella ("On the precepts of the Church"). This final charge clearly states that the philosopher was heard saying that "laws and Religions that have made their appearance in the world are nonsenses created exclusively to keep the peoples quiet."[24]

Atheism Conquered devotes many passages to dismantling this critique. The long subtitle of the first Italian manuscript draft of this work reads "Philosophical Recognition of the Universal Religion against Machiavellian Anti-Christianism." This Machiavellian characterization is crucial for understanding the roots of the opinions that Campanella took to pieces in his book, which also correspond to the main accusations leveled against him. By the mid-seventeenth century, Machiavelli's thought was increasingly identified with a theoretical and practical approach that conflated politics and religion, reducing religious credos to mere political fabrications. Although Machiavelli's thoughts about religion should not be reduced to the simplified reception of his political theory, over time the use of the term "Machiavellianism" contributed to the crystallization of this interpretation. As a corollary to the spread of this streamlined version of his thoughts, the stereotypical Machiavellian individual was eventually turned into a radical denier of God, a skeptic, and even an atheist.[25]

In the proem to the Italian manuscript of *Atheism Conquered,* Campanella highlighted this conflation of Machiavellianism and irreligiousness: "Poor Italy and Spain host the diabolic Machiavelli, who infects the noblest parts of the Republic and makes believe that Religion is craftiness on the part of priests and friars to dominate the populace with the Princes' consent, who keep it [religion] as a bawd for their frauds. Oh, Good Lord, how could you permit such a monstrosity?"[26] In a subsequent passage, where he attributed the disorders of the Reformation to the spread of skepticism and incredulity, Campanella directly connected Machiavellianism, political theory, atheism, and the genesis of the notorious book *On the Three Impostors.*[27] Campanella's zeal in condemning Machiavellianism and the theory of the fraudulence of religion was not only meant to address the charges of the Neapolitan trial. Some years before, the Dominican friar was accused of having authored this much-feared libel. In 1593, when Campanella was studying medicine in Padua, he was accused of having argued with a converted Jew with Judaizing tendencies without denouncing him to the Inquisition. This was the starting point of a trial that lasted almost two years and was closed by the humiliating ceremony of "vehement" (*de vehementi*) abjuration, a circumstance that made him vulnerable to the death penalty during the subsequent judicial proceedings in Naples.[28] Campanella was also charged with having authored an impious sonnet about Christ, possessing a manual of geomancy, disapproving the doctrine of the Church, holding Democritean (that is, materialistic) opinions, and, above all, being the author of *On the Three Impostors.*[29] Years later, in 1607, Campanella wrote to his friend and correspondent Kaspar Schoppe (1576–1649) to clear himself of this accusation.[30] Schoppe was also the dedicatee of *Atheism Conquered,* in the proem of which the Dominican friar again mentioned this juvenile incident and added that the volume was "printed thirty years before [Campanella's] birth."[31] This comment provides the first attempt to date the treatise ever found in early modern historical records. In his 1607 letter to Schoppe, Campanella attempted to locate the book's provenance, which he suggested was the Germanic territories, where he believed the rise of religious conflicts had contributed to the weakening of the faith.[32]

In chapter 13 of *Atheism Conquered,* Campanella dealt directly with the opinion that Moses, Jesus, and Muḥammad were tricksters who deceived the world. In the same chapter, he also mentioned the opinion that Christ's body had disappeared, which he directly attributed to the Machiavellianists and Peripatetics, whom he accused of comparing the account of Christ's death to those of other impostors and founders of religions who had disappeared to shroud their feigned deaths in mystery.[33] The belief of some of our dissenters that Christ did not die on the cross and that someone else's body replaced his provides the first hint that the dissenting opinions with which they were associated were not just generic expressions of popular unbelief. Rather, it seems that the defendants shared a group of ideas that were progressively becoming stable elements of the more articulated cultural construct ultimately known as the theory of the fraudulence of religions. We will further explore this connection in the chapters to come.

Figs and Apples

The summary of Campanella's trial referred to an unorthodox interpretation of Adam's sin, which contains a hidden sexual allusion that has many points in common with the specific unorthodox opinion being investigated in this book. This reference is found in the deposition of a Calabrese Dominican friar called Domenico Petrolo from Stignano. To understand the relevance of this testimony, we ought to understand who Petrolo was. Before reaching the Neapolitan inquisitorial court, both the lay and ecclesiastic investigations concerning the conspiracy had been influenced by the many civil and religious conflicts in which all of the actors were involved. In a context where everyone, including Campanella, accused one another in a desperate attempt to save their lives or deliberately damage those whom they deeply hated, Petrolo stands out as one of Campanella's most loyal friends. He declared in one of his depositions that many times he had heard Campanella talking about matters of faith with a confidence that, in Petrolo's words, he did not show with others.[34] When Campanella was caught by the armigers of the prince of La Roccella on September 6, 1599, he was attempting to escape in the company of Petrolo. According to one of Petrolo's depositions, when Campanella decided to run away, he told him, "You have been a good friend and have learned from me, it seems reasonable to me that you keep following me in these travails and that you not abandon me and be my loyal friend."[35] In one of his later poems, Campanella himself would subsequently praise Petrolo for the devotion he showed during the trial.[36] Indeed, Petrolo seriously endangered himself in the eyes of the inquisitors by initially refusing to disclose Campanella's opinions. He paid a heavy price for this. He was banned by the viceroyalty and secluded in a monastery of his order for the rest of his life, obliged to engage in rigorous penance.[37]

According to the trial records, Petrolo stated that one day, while he was in the company of Campanella at "la Roccella" (today Roccella Jonica), they were eating some figs when he asked his friend Tommaso "whether those were the fruits for which Adam sinned." Campanella replied that he did not know, although Petrolo emphasized that he said this "as though he was joking." Soon afterward, Tommaso added that "these were pranks."[38] This reference may sound rather obscure, but it was not so for many sixteenth-century listeners. The names of fruits were often used in contemporary burlesque poetry and popular jokes to designate sexual anatomy and intercourse. The fig, in Italian *fico,* unambiguously alluded to the vulva, especially in the female declension "fica" or "figa."[39] As we saw earlier, Marcello Impicciato was accused of having stated, while talking in his apothecary shop, that the apple, ostensibly the forbidden fruit, symbolized anal intercourse: "What apple? Adam and Eve fucked in the ass, and that's why they were rejected from Paradise."[40] The comparison between figs and apples was a common trope in disputes between the supporters of vaginal and anal intercourse.[41] Among the supporters of the fig was Francesco Maria Molza (1489–1544), who, in his *Capitolo de' fichi* (Chapter on the figs), accepted Apollo's invitation to save the fruit from the neglect it suffered in the literary Accademia dei Vignaioli (Academy of the Winemakers), whose members, like the well-known Francesco Berni (1497–1535), preferred the pleasures of homosexual sodomy. To prove the superiority of the figs (that is, the female genitalia), Molza attributed to them the archetypal power of having caused the Fall from Grace: "I do believe that of any other fruits / it would have been easier for Adam to beware / In the time he was seduced by the Devil."[42]

This was not an isolated dispute between Molza and Berni. This issue kept being discussed in later times by people of different social upbringings. The trial records of a notary from the Tuscan town of Poggibonsi named Giuseppe Cinatti, prosecuted in 1702, reveal that in a local tobacconist shop, people were arguing whether "the fruit that Adam ate in the terrestrial paradise" was "a fig, a pear, an apple, or another fruit." Cinatti allegedly claimed that "the transgression of Adam" was not, in his opinion, "a pear or an apple" but God's command to "use his wife by putting it [alluding to Adam's penis] into her cunt." Adam, therefore, "transgressed the precept by sticking it into her ass."[43] Other instances of these "botanic" disputes with reference to original sin will be analyzed in Chapter 6 in relation to an irreverent libel on original sin written by the Dutch humanist Hadriaan Beverland, as well as in Chapter 8, devoted to cases that occurred in female monasteries and conservatories.

The scattered references in Campanella's judicial proceedings do not allow us to understand what his opinion on the matter was, but the evidence seems to suggest that both Petrolo and Campanella were aware of the "pranks" revolving around the metaphoric interpretation of Edenic fruits. Was Petrolo simply asking whether his friend believed that sex was the original sin, or was he inviting him to take a stand in the dispute between fig and apple lovers? Given the nature of the sources, this question is destined to remain unanswered. Other evidence, however, seems to suggest that Campanella had a rather positive view on sodomy in the early stages of his life. Indeed, the accusation of sodomy had already surfaced in Campanella's entangled judicial history even before the grand Neapolitan trial. The first reference is found in what Luigi Amabile has identified as Campanella's second trial, which Luigi Firpo has characterized as nothing more than a simple inquest that apparently resulted in an absolution.[44] Campanella had just arrived in Padua when he was suspected of having been involved, with some of his fellow brothers, in an act of sodomy perpetrated against none other than the father general of the order, Ippolito Maria Beccaria.[45] We know about this episode thanks only to two letters Campanella wrote in 1607 in an attempt to wipe clean this juvenile stain: one was addressed to Pope Paul V (April 12), and the other to his friend Schoppe (June 1).[46] In the letter to the pope, he briefly mentions the episode and defends himself by noting that he did not sleep alone the night the incident allegedly took place. In the letter to his close friend, he refers to his poor eyesight as an attenuating circumstance: "It was said that it was something done at night, which for me would be impossible because I do not see very well; also, I did not have my own room and was instead billeted with others. You ought to question those who were staying with me, because if I sinned against the prelate, then they sinned too. But the aim of the injustice was not to search for the crime, but rather to find me the offending party."[47]

The episode remains unclear. Other evidence, however, appears to point to Campanella's homoerotic feelings. During the grand Neapolitan trial, the public prosecutor (*avvocato fiscale*) Juan Sánchez de Luna had two scribes hide themselves in the aisles of the jail where Campanella was guarded to eavesdrop and transcribe any conversations that might have occurred between him and other prisoners. Marcello Andreadis and Francesco Tartaglia sneaked into the prison under the supervision of two jailers, who also acted as witnesses, signing the transcripts to validate their veracity. According to these reports, during the night of April 14, 1600, the silence of the jail was broken by Fra Pietro Ponzio, a friend and accomplice of Campanella, who called his brother four times, addressing him with lovely, comforting words:

> Fra Pietro: Oh Fra Tommaso, oh Fra Tommaso! Hey, Tommaso! Oh Tommaso, don't you hear me, oh my heart?
>
> Fra Tommaso: Good evening, good evening.
>
> Fra Pietro: Oh my heart, how are you? What are you doing? Cheer yourself up, 'cause tomorrow is coming the Nuncio here, and we'll know something.
>
> Fra Tommaso: Oh Fra Pietro, why don't you do something so we can sleep together, and enjoy each other?
>
> Fra Pietro: God willing, and I would give ten ducats to the jailer; to you, my heart, I'd give twenty kisses an hour. . . . I spread your sonnets all over Naples, and I learned all them by heart, and there is nothing that I like so much as to read something from your ingenuity.
>
> Fra Tommaso: I want to write one for the Nuncio.
>
> Fra Pietro: Yes, my heart, but do me a favor: write mine first, those that I want for Ferrante, my brother, and then write the one for the Nuncio.
>
> Fra Tommaso: Go rest, good evening.[48]

Some problems of translation need to be clarified to better understand the relevance of this transcription. The term "godere"—which Campanella used when he wished to have his friend close to him in his bed ("perché non opri qualche modo et dormimo insiemi et godemo") and which I have translated here as "enjoy each other"—in Italian can also serve as an explicit synonym for "having sexual pleasure."

For our purposes, however, understanding Campanella's preferences in matters of erotism and sex is less important than determining whether sexual desire played any role in Campanella's criticism of religions, before or after the composition of *Atheism Conquered.* Chapter 14 of the trial summary, drafted by the bishop of Caserta, was entirely devoted to the many variations of Campanella's alleged belief that "venereal acts were not sins."[49] As with all the other defendants examined in this book, the Dominican friar allegedly held the widespread opinion that "the venereal act"—that is, intercourse—"was licit," arguing "that as men were free to use an arm or a foot, they were free to use their virile member." Other witnesses testified to him saying that "the coitus was licit and that the Church did wrong in prohibiting it"; still others reported that, as "fornication was not a sin," neither were masturbation, sodomy, or incest. Although these charges could be specious, they include a range of opinions that was deeply rooted among people from every social level in the early modern period. If there was a large consensus that extramarital sex between a woman and a man was, at worst, a trivial offense, we have already seen how a minority of people also defended the legitimacy of nonreproductive intercourse, as well as hetero- and homosexual anal sex. As with many other defendants, Campanella too reportedly referred to the category of "nature" and "naturalness" to praise the delightfulness of sex, including sodomy. He apparently claimed that pleasure had had a positive role in God's plan for humanity from the beginning. After stating that "they are natural things . . . why would have God created them otherwise?" he allegedly added that sodomy was not a sin. In another circumstance, he was reported as saying that "carnal acts . . . are not as sinful as men believe, and God has made the virile member for this purpose . . . and he also talked about the nefarious sin, and of other sins with women."[50]

It cannot be ruled out, therefore, that at the time of his trial Campanella shared with many women and men of the epoch a quite indulgent approach toward sex and the role that its delights played in the plans of God and the natural realm. Campanella's participation in widespread popular opinions is far from surprising. Many of his statements made throughout the Neapolitan trial reflected his modest upbringing.

Indeed, Campanella's childhood was marked by hardship and destitution. He was born in 1568, in a small house in the poverty-stricken town of Stilo, perched on Mount Consolino, facing the Stilaro creek, near the Ionian Sea. Stilo's community faced frequent troubles. It had been bled dry by the local feudatories, periodically raided by Muslim corsairs, and divided by internal conflicts and banditry. Campanella was one of many children born to his mother and his father, an illiterate shoemaker. His mother died when he was a child. Unable to pay for an education, Campanella, who even at a young age showed signs of great intelligence, eavesdropped on the lessons of the more fortunate sons of his countrymen, learning more quickly than anyone else. His thirst for knowledge, more than a religious vocation, led him to a career in the Church.[51] When his intellectual skills were being celebrated all over Europe despite his encounters with the Inquisition, Campanella never lost touch with his initial popular wit.

Unlike his statements about religious matters, however, it is almost impossible to discern his real convictions in this regard. *Atheism Conquered* does not contain any explicit praise of sexual pleasure. There might be many reasons for this. Despite *Atheism Conquered*'s audacity in interpreting the Christian faith within the framework of natural reason, the treatise was still conceived as an apology of a man who had been accused of being not just a heretic but a dangerous heresiarch. While sexual discourses were easily dealt with in print and manuscript works by daring humanists who could still use the weapon of irony to shield their conviction under the cover of witticism, integrating sexual discourses within the frame of a theological and philosophical treatise was too daring an endeavor, even for a rebellious spirit like Campanella. This was all the more the case when such a treatise was meant as a recusation of the author's past errors. Treating sex as something that had its own dignity and desirability outside the purpose of procreation was not allowed in normative discourses, and the erotic literature that we have analyzed in Chapter 1 was precisely meant to denounce this taboo and polemically correct its consequences. *Atheism Conquered* tackles the issue of sodomy in a few passages. Campanella explicitly mentioned sodomy as evidence of the inferiority of non-Christians. He criticized the "law of Muḥammad" not only because it was "founded on the glory of the army" but also because "it makes men crude and ignorant," for it allows "many vices, even sodomy with strangers."[52] Campanella also wrote that Peruvians and Mexicans deserved the servitude imposed on them by the Spaniards because of their many "nefarious vices," including anthropophagy and sodomy.[53]

Although these passages align with standard views in post-Tridentine Catholicism, if we read these polemical remarks alongside other passages in both Campanella's works and his trial concerning the relationships between Christianity and other cultures, his position turns out to be much more nuanced. Campanella's lenience toward other cultures may help provide some context for his apparently negative representation of sodomy in these passages. During the judicial proceedings, Campanella had indeed tended to open the doors to salvation to all people who embraced the principles of natural reason. Campanella allegedly cast doubt on the belief that baptism was the unique pathway to eternal salvation, a statement linked to the belief that salvation was not precluded to infant Muslims who had died innocent.[54] In regard to the "sect of the Turks"—that is, the Muslim religion—Campanella allegedly stated that "Muḥammad was a good man" and that "the law of the Turks was better than [the Christians's] law, because when the Turks go to Church [*sic*] they wash themselves and take their shoes off."[55] Campanella explicitly defended some of these claims in the first draft of *Atheism Conquered*.[56] In chapter 11, he reviewed the objections of those skeptics who polemically asked how, "if Christ was God," he "did not come before to save the world" and why he allowed for so many people to be damned, including in the "New World." To these arguments, Campanella replied that "the reason of the World has always been powerful in saving those who are willing to live according to reason; all the reasonable people are saved."[57] This reevaluation of the dignity of non-Christians seems to counterbalance the use that Campanella made of the trope of sodomy as proof of their inferiority. Although it is possible that Campanella meant to say that only those who did not indulge in nonreproductive intercourse were worthy of salvation, in light of these considerations one wonders whether he considered sodomy itself so serious an offense or if he was simply reproducing a set of well-established arguments that had been largely deployed by Christian apologists so that he could sugarcoat his fairly unorthodox conclusions about the destiny in the afterlife of people living outside the boundaries of the Church.

Bodies and Pleasure

While this issue is destined to remain unanswered, other passages of the first manuscript draft of *Atheism Conquered* are relevant to understanding Campanella's view on the body and sexual desire in light of the philosophical restatement of Christianity that he was attempting to develop. Campanella deals explicitly with issues related to sex, desire, and lust, but he avoids any moralizing and prescriptive attitude and tries to explain the advantages and disadvantages of sexual desire and pleasure in a naturalistic frame. Carnal pleasure is undeniable: "Is there a greater joy for human beings than the use of venereal pleasure?" Campanella, however, emphasizes that this pleasure is only a trick, because it causes the male animal to lose its substance and the female partner to suffer the pains of gestation, childbirth, and child-rearing.[58] Nature, which appears in this passage as a proactive cooperator with God's will, "donated this love and small joy in order to entice us into troubles, as the bait does to the fish, but God allowed this order to guarantee the succession of beings," which, in Campanella's metaphysical interpretation, are embodiments of divine ideas.[59] This analysis allows us to understand why Campanella elsewhere defined sexual intercourse as "the lash of God." When asking how Machiavellians and Epicureans could deny God's existence, he asked them, "Have you created yourself? Are you able to create human beings? Don't you see that you are drawn to coitus by violent love, and you don't know what you do, in the same way that this pen doesn't know what I am writing?"[60] Carnal desire is therefore unmistakably a part of God's plan for human beings, a fierce force that we cannot resist. As this passage seems to imply, it is also a sign of God's superiority over humans and an invitation to be humble by not presuming that we have the capacity to ignore it.

In another similar passage, Campanella confirms this call to humility by clearly stating that our reproductive power cannot be compared to that of God: "He alone is our father, because our fathers do not know how to make men, but they perform that act pulled by love, which is the lash of God, without knowing either the outcome or how it is done in the uterus."[61] The compelling force of sexual desire is therefore a sign of our creatural condition, and it serves the purpose of multiplying the images of God embodied in the natural realm. Yet it also represents a sign of our weakness, a spell that nature and the Creator have cast on us against our will.

Campanella elsewhere explains that human appetites are nothing but vanity and illusions. This theme plays a crucial role in the concluding remarks of *Atheism Conquered*, which are devoted to highlighting the ultimate differences between Christians and non-Christians. While some common people, and especially atheists and Machiavellians, pursue exclusively earthly pleasures, Christians are able to enjoy both pleasures and tribulations: "The beasts only enjoy pleasurable things," but "being able to get pleasure from unpleasurable things is great philosophy and victory against evil." In this earthly life, Christians can already appreciate the peace brought about by this approach, which experientially confirms to them the Christian belief that "death is a gateway to a better life." Those who are exclusively devoted to earthly pleasures are doomed to frustration because carnal desires are fleeting and even the enjoyment they bring about is constantly tainted by the fear of death: "Vanitas vanitatum et omnia vanitas."[62] This stance, however, does not lead Campanella to a negative attitude toward pleasure per se. As he stated previously, "Christians overcome every sect in matters of pleasure, because they enjoy both good and evil . . . therefore, pleasure for the true Christian is quadrupled." This statement implies that even pleasurable things can be appreciated in this earthly sphere, as long as their pursuit does not lead the believer to try to avoid the pain and challenges of life.[63]

This moderate attitude of the repentant Campanella as expressed in *Atheism Conquered* is further confirmed by the fact that the philosopher views God as the only source of desire, reading human beings' natural tendency toward pleasure and self-expansion as an indispensable sign of their divinely inspired nature. "Human appetite" is voracious, but this insatiability is a "most clear sign that no mortal thing is adequate enough to human desire, but only the infinite God." It is following this desire that the "wise ones, knowing that they [could not] be satisfied with fragile goods, forced themselves into investigating God, which is an infinite good, and despised wives and children, Venus and Bacchus, and every pleasure to pursue the eternal good."[64] Desire and pleasure were therefore two compelling forces that the followers of Christ, through natural reason, were required to sublimate to reach the ultimate goal of their spiritual path. This trajectory does not seem to require a radical extirpation of pleasure. Rather, it demands the reorientation of a drive that, even in its most basic manifestations, like sexual appetites, is nevertheless an expression of the dynamic procreative force that keeps things moving in the earthly realm. It is an expression of God's superiority over the Creation. If this analysis is correct, it would further prove that reflections on sex and desire played a crucial role in determining the anthropological substratum that supported views that diverged from Catholic orthodoxy. Even when Campanella abandoned the radically atheistic stances that he plausibly embraced in his youth, he still maintained an antidualistic approach toward the material world and the body. The ideas of natural reason and natural religion were powerful tools that, in *Atheism Conquered*, the Dominican friar deployed to attempt to reduce the fracture between body and spirit created by centuries of Christian theology and pastoral action. His reflections on sexual desire played a relevant role in this process.[65]

CHAPTER THREE

Sexual Morality in Post-Tridentine Catholicism

In 1686 the Holy Office in Rome investigated the prominent prelate Gregorio Corsetti, the rector of the College Ghislieri in Pavia, who had been accused of spreading the view that Adam and Eve enjoyed the pleasures of nonreproductive intercourse in the Garden of Eden. The fact that the leading authority of this prestigious institution was charged shows the extent to which this heterodox belief was circulating not only among the low-ranking clergy like the friars but also at its highest echelons. Corsetti's trial is the only one that explicitly connected this belief to an identifiable written source. Analyzing the prelate's heterodox exegesis of this idea allows us to delve deeply into the relationship that connected norm and transgression in Italian society. We can read it as a reaction to the tightening control over sexual morals exerted by the Catholic Church in the aftermath of the Council of Trent.

The Exegesis of a Sexual Heresy

The College Ghislieri in Pavia was an influential institution that embodied the values of Tridentine Catholicism in Italy. It stood in a central neighborhood of the city, close to the university headquarters. Its bulk majestically complemented an urban setting characterized by gardens, noble mansions, and religious buildings. Its architecture exemplified the representative function of the institution while providing its hosts with the peace necessary for a life of rigorous study. The institute was founded by Michele Ghislieri in 1567, just one year after his accession to the papal throne as Pius V (1566–1572). Ghislieri established his position within the papal Curia thanks to his commitment as an inquisitor during the pontificate of Pope Carafa (Paul IV, 1555–1559). The college's mission was to educate the heirs of the ruling class to comply with the religious and political values imposed by the Church after the Council of Trent.[1]

Corsetti was accused by the prefect of the college, Don Giovanni della Torre, for having publicly stated, "in the presence of several students," that, as far as the meaning of original sin was concerned, the Magisterium had not yet reached a consensus. Corsetti allegedly remarked that "some say that it consisted in eating a fruit, others however said that [Adam] sinned of the act of sodomy, and that both the Scriptures and the Most Holy Fathers explained that Adam sinned by eating the fruit so as to cover that nefarious act, and speak with more decency."[2] It seems that many of the students adhered to this interpretation for a certain time before returning to a more orthodox position. Unlike in the other cases here analyzed, it seems that there were no doubts about Corsetti's moral conduct. In fact, Corsetti made no attempt to condone sodomy. He allegedly believed that God "could not have forbidden a trivial thing such as eating a fruit," thus confirming that, from the prelate's viewpoint, sodomy was the worst of sins.[3] We cannot, however, rule out a priori the hypothesis that this effort to harmonize this heretical statement with Catholic orthodoxy represented an attempt to protect the image of an influential and powerful representative of post-Tridentine Catholicism. Indeed, the inquisitors were extremely accommodating with Corsetti. Summoned to the chancellery of the Holy Office, he was simply admonished to forever abstain from repeating his heterodox ideas, under the threat of an unspecified penalty. He got away with merely giving his word that he would obey such orders.[4]

The leniency shown by the inquisitors toward Corsetti reflects wider dynamics that characterized post-Tridentine Catholic society. Despite the commitment of the Council of Trent to reforming the moral conduct of the clergy and reinforcing the hierarchical structure of the Church, we know from the study of criminal sources that by the seventeenth century the unruliness of ecclesiastics was still far from being tamed. While the Roman Inquisition played a central role in reinforcing the grip of the Church hierarchies over society, as far as the clergy was concerned, the religious tribunal often played an intermediatory role, frequently preventing the local episcopal tribunals from acting with the rigor that the heads of the local clergy would have liked.[5]

To prove that his opinion was orthodox, Corsetti referred to the authority of "Bosio," who—himself referring to Augustine's "treatise on sodomy"—provided good reasons to support this bizarre scriptural exegesis. "Bosio" was a clear reference to Egidio Bossi (1488–1546), one of the most authoritative jurists at the time.[6] Corsetti mentioned a text titled *De criminibus,* which is in fact Bossi's most comprehensive treatise on penal law, the *Tractatus Varii* (Various treatises), which was posthumously published in Venice in 1562, in Basel in 1574, and in Lyon in 1594. The handbook was divided into more than a hundred headings, which reviewed the opinions of the most prestigious legal scholars, as well as the most significant court judgments. Paragraph four of the chapter devoted to "The Detestable Sexual Infraction Committed among Men" was titled "The Sodomitic Vice Originated from Women." To support the thesis that women were responsible for spreading the sin against nature, Bossi quoted Augustine's *Sermo ad fratres in eremo* (hereafter *Sermons*) number 47, titled "On the Vehement Detestation of the Sodomitic Sin."[7]

At that time, Augustine's *Sermons* were as influential as they were controversial.[8] Only two of the sermons collected in the book can actually be attributed to the bishop of Hippo. The others were all composed in the late Middle Ages.[9] Sermon 47 was an exhortation to repent, addressed to those hermits who were regrettably known as the "Princes of Sodomy." After listing the horrible punishments God would inflict on those stained by this sin, the homily invited them to turn their hearts back to God and cultivate that charitable and uninterested love that could only be experienced by those who had already broken the habit of overindulgence. In its conclusion, the text took a turn that distinguishes it from the clichéd rhetoric of medieval penitential literature. The author recalled the frightening end of Lot's wife, who was turned into a statue of salt because, the text reads, she was "incapable of resisting the sodomites."[10] As it is written, this passage could imply a sexual allusion, which contradicted the literal meaning of the Scriptures. The Bible referred to her failure to obey the precept not to turn, while running away, to watch the destruction of Sodom. The rendition in the *Sermons,* however, seems to allude to something much more compromising. Indeed, since the Middle Ages some iconographical representations of this biblical episode seemed to allude to connections between Lot's wife's turning backward and her inability to resist sodomy. According to the official teachings of the Church, however, this passage could only be interpreted as a symbolic representation of the resistance to change that hindered spiritual growth.[11]

The text goes on to accuse women of being particularly prone to this vice. According to this narrative, men learned the practice of sodomy from women, as explained in the passage that was literally quoted by Bossi: "O women, mothers of luxury, wasn't it enough for you to have deceived the first man?" This passage does not contain any explicit reference to sodomy as the original sin, but, as we will see, it could undoubtedly be interpreted as such.[12] A certain ambiguity was, indeed, intrinsic to the spurious *Sermons,* which had been highly criticized by Desiderius Erasmus, Cesare Baronio, and Roberto Bellarmino for the oddness of some of their passages. Indeed, in the section devoted to Augustine in his *De scriptoribus ecclesiastici* (On ecclesiastic writers), Bellarmino acknowledged that the *Sermons* were a useful source of biographical information about the illustrious Father of the Latin Church, but he also criticized them for being "trivial and full of hogwash," adding that, except for the two authentic ones, they were "odd, improper, and impure."[13] Jacques-Paul Migne, in his critical edition of the text, reports that it was also censored by the theologians of the University of Louvain. This statement, however, is not supported by Jesús Martínez De Bujanda's modern critical edition of the corresponding index.[14]

After quoting Augustine, Bossi's text goes on to cite a well-known commentary of the Pauline *Epistle to the Romans* that was attributed to Saint Ambrose but that Erasmus identified as a spurious text, renaming the author "Ambrosiaster."[15] Bossi does not quote any passage of the comment but only part of the Pauline quotation to which it refers—that is, Romans 1:25–27: "They exchanged the truth of God for a lie and revered and worshiped the creature rather than the creator, who is blessed forever. Amen. Therefore, God handed them over to degrading passions. Their females exchanged natural relations for unnatural, and the males likewise gave up natural relations with females and burned with lust for one another. Males did shameful things with males and thus received in their own persons the due penalty for their perversity."[16] As they are presented in this modern English translation, the verses seem to allude to an indisputable condemnation of both female-female and male-male homosexual intercourse.

In fact, this modern interpretation was not always taken for granted. In the seventeenth century, there were still some who read this passage as an escalation of increasingly grave sins, which led from heterosexual to homosexual anal intercourse. Ambrosiaster, who wrote around the fourth century, oscillated between the two interpretations. As shown by Theodore de Bruyn, the opinions of the author on this matter shifted in at least three successive drafts of the text. Ambrosiaster initially interpreted the passage as a progression from heterosexual anal sex to male-to-male intercourse. However, he then changed his mind and embraced the second hypothesis that women, by engaging in female-to-female intercourse, encouraged men to do the same among themselves.[17] Also included in this second version was a severe criticism of those who spread the opinion that everything started with heterosexual sodomy. It is likely that this shift reflected debates that were taking place in the Roman Christian community around the fourth century, probably in response to the practice of female homoeroticism in the late Roman Empire.[18] In Ambrosiaster's sixteenth-century print edition, there was a combination of the second and the third autographs.[19] This text is extremely complex. Men abandoned the "natural use" of women to embrace homosexual practices, while women actually "changed" the natural use of sex into a use that was against nature. The fact that the two sentences are linked by the adverb "similiter" (similarly, in the same way) seems to indicate that the text refers precisely to female homosexual intercourse.[20]

Bossi was extremely ambiguous in superimposing a passage that clearly alluded to Eve (accused of deceiving the first man) on the women blamed by Paul, mentioned through the mediation of the spurious Ambrose. He shared this ambiguity with Ambrosiaster (his source), who, in the subsequent passage, presented sexual transgressions as a consequence of pagan idolatry. There Ambrosiaster recalled the "first cause of sin" in a passage that does not clarify whether he was referring to idolatry itself or directly to the debauched sexual conduct that, in a more appropriate reading of the Pauline passage, would result from embracing idolatry.[21]

By using Bossi's passage—with its references to the pseudo-Augustinian *Sermons* and Ambrosiaster's commentaries on Paul—to justify his opinion that Adam and Eve had anal sex in the Garden of Eden, Gregorio Corsetti grasped the potential ambiguities contained in these texts and made them explicit. However, analyzing his trial in light of the other cases examined in this book, I am not inclined to believe that this specific passage can be qualified as the ultimate "source" of this heretical opinion, as Corsetti wanted it to be. It is likely that a cultivated man like Corsetti adopted this exegesis of the text because he already had in mind the belief that the fruit was a metaphor for anal intercourse, an opinion that circulated widely at the time. He probably decided to use this passage to justify his opinion because it resonated with his conviction, allowing him to connect this unorthodox interpretation to a learned reference that could increase its credibility in the eyes and ears of his listeners. When the idea that Adam and Eve enjoyed sodomy in the Garden of Eden emerged in literary sources, the authors referred to its diverse origins, which ranged from rabbinic literature to Italian humanists.[22] Similarly, in the inquisitorial proceedings the defendants referred to various roots. Some specified that they heard people discussing this unorthodox statement while commenting on theological treatises; others reported that it circulated exclusively by word of mouth. Any attempt to reduce this complexity to a single-sided explanation would constitute an unjustifiable stretch of the evidence, creating at the same time the false impression that we are dealing with a formal heresy that relied on a written text and that, therefore, could be subject to a direct, continuous transmission through some form of organized proselytism. None of the cases we have collected seem to fit that paradigm. The idea that sodomy constituted humanity's original disobedience circulated in various environments and was bent to the most diverse purposes. In most cases, as already indicated, it was clearly integrated into a radically skeptical framework that was characterized by a vitriolic criticism of Catholic sexual morality. In this context, Corsetti's approach, which conversely refers to this statement as further proof of the sinfulness of sodomy, constitutes an exception. It is possible that this reassuring interpretation of the sodomitic rereading of the myth of the Fall was the result of Corsetti's attempt to protect himself from a formal investigation for heresy and thus shield both himself and the influential institution he represented from terrible consequences.

Augustine's Influence on Sex and Original Sin

It is important to emphasize that the only source explicitly quoted in the trial records regarding the heretical claim that sodomy constituted humanity's original disobedience was the spurious Augustine mentioned through Bossi's mediation. Indeed, it is well known that Augustinian theories exerted a long-lasting influence on the Christian theology of original sin. The concept of the Fall from Grace, as it was conceived by Augustine and mocked by the dissenters investigated in this book, played a central role in the condemnation of sex and pleasure within the Christian world for centuries. Despite the variety of positions that emerged in patristic literature about the consequences of Adam and Eve's fault for humanity, it was indeed Augustine's theology that ultimately established itself as the primary point of reference for the formalization of the official doctrine of the Church on these issues.[23] Augustine was the patristic author who most profoundly influenced the history of Western thought. This is due in part to the considerable quantity of his writings, which examined almost all the doctrinal controversies that made waves in Christian communities at the time.[24] His abiding influence on the theology of original sin has contributed to the creation of a veritable black legend about his negative influence on sexual morals, which has dominated the field of gender and sexuality studies for decades.[25] Recent studies, however, challenge this view of Augustine's writings by relocating them within their context.[26] While his influence on the sexual regime imposed by Western Christianity is undeniable, it is worth noting that fourth- and fifth-century Christianity was filled with austere trends that were far more radical than what he professed.[27] Paradoxically, it was precisely Augustine's attempt to moderately reintegrate marriage as a respectable form of Christian life that contributed to making his moral theology a flexible instrument that could be adapted to the whole body of believers in Christian society. It was his moderation toward this issue that allowed his opinions about sex to spread at every level of society.[28]

Despite his positive reinterpretation of conjugal life, Augustine never stopped portraying sexual desire as a disturbing element in his writings. He condemned sexual intercourse between spouses when solely driven by lust.[29] Moreover, abstinence from sex was preferable, even among a married couple, if both spouses agreed to it.[30] As Richard Sorabji has noted, Augustine's argument on carnal lust is an exception to the principle of moderation in dealing with passions that the Father of the Church recommends in other instances of his work.[31] Augustine wrote about three types of concupiscence: *concupiscentia bona* (desire for spiritual things, which lead to God); *concupiscientia naturalis* (general inclination toward well-being and happiness, including wanting to get married and have children); and *concupiscentia carnalis* (carnal lust), which he placed outside of natural inclinations as it was a deviation from free will resulting from the Fall. While in Augustine's works original sin was not held to be a transgression of a sexual nature in and of itself, sexual desire nonetheless became its most shameful consequence, and its ability to pervade every aspect of life was proof of the corruption of humanity in its current state.[32]

Augustine's notion of original sin was still influential in the early modern period. The invention of the printing press greatly facilitated the spread of his works, collected in the first *Opera omnia* printed in Basel by Johannes Amerbach in 1506. Erasmus of Rotterdam edited for Johann Froben's Basel publishing house an edition of Augustine that appeared between 1528 and 1529. His theory of justification stood at the core of Martin Luther's reformed theology and was central to the ways in which Roman Catholicism responded to Luther's claims and redefined its own theology on original sin at the Council of Trent.[33] Analyzing this redefinition is crucial to understanding the normative framework underlying our cases. In the attempt to reframe the theology of the Fall from Grace, the council had to harmonize quite distinctive theological approaches, all claiming to represent the Catholic canon. It adopted a mediating strategy to find an internal consensus on the matter of justification. This strategy, although successful in negatively defining what was to be condemned in Protestantism, failed to establish a clear theological alternative to this controversial issue. Rather than settle the debate around justification in the Catholic world, the council helped renew it. The conciliar fathers had to navigate between the two opposing symbolic threats constituted by Lutheranism and Pelagianism.[34] In an effort to do so, they decided that it was necessary to revisit and clarify the orthodox position on original sin, as well as tackle the issue of concupiscence.[35] While the conciliar canons discussing original sin and justification left some ambiguities in the crucial issues they were trying to clarify, they were extremely clear in reaffirming the Augustinian doctrine that, after the Fall, concupiscence had become a universal force that impaired the capacity of human beings to attain salvation. When attacking the Lutheran notion of salvation *ex sola fide,* in its relations to the tenet of original sin, the prelates described concupiscence as an inborn proclivity to sin that all human beings inherited as a consequence of the Fall.[36] The cardinals finally agreed on distinguishing concupiscence and sin per se, even partially contradicting the Pauline tradition, so as to clearly distance themselves from Luther, who instead conflated the two. The distinction was subtle but crucial and allowed the conciliar fathers to save both the belief in the frailty of postlapsarian humanity and the idea that, despite its fallen nature, humanity could still "strive against" sinful attitudes with a rightful exercise of the will, provided God's merciful help.[37]

Although lust was believed to be strongly related to concupiscence, the council was extremely reticent to deal with sexual matters. So it was the 1566 *Roman Catechism*—the textbook that summarized and systematized almost every aspect of Christian theology, liturgy, and pastoral and moral teachings—that represented the keystone of the post-Tridentine ecclesiastic Magisterium. In the section devoted to the Ten Commandments, when dealing with the sixth, *Non moechaberis* (You shall not commit adultery), the text peripherally reminded the reader of the "nefarious lechery" and the fate suffered by Sodom, without ever specifying the sin its inhabitants committed.[38] This strategy was partly adopted to amend an earlier approach to sexual matters displayed by clergymen between the late Middle Ages and the early modern period. Priests, preachers, and confessors addressed sexual themes using an explicit and coarse language, often reflecting the content and style of the manuals attached to their training. After the Council of Trent, preachers and authors of devotional manuals were firmly advised not to inadvertently lure people to sin with their words. Keeping people uninformed by loosely referring to luxury was urged as a more careful way to prevent them from indulging in sexual temptations.[39]

Sexual Morality after Trent

This effort to silence Catholic sexual discourses reflects a major change brought about by the council regarding the control of sexual mores in Catholic Europe. In fact, it took place as part of a wider trend involving both Protestant and Catholic countries. Martin Luther questioned the principle of ecclesiastic celibacy, and sexual misconduct by clergy was a consistent part of the accusations Lutherans made against Roman Catholicism, with celibacy deemed to be one of its major causes. This attack against sexual abstinence represents a major shift in the history of Christianity. For centuries, celibacy had symbolized the superiority of the clergy over lay people. We ought not think, however, that Luther's stance against it was inspired by a radically innovative consideration of sexual pleasure. What changed in his view of sexual desire was not the belief that it was sinful but rather the thought that it was impossible to expect a humanity indelibly stained by original sin to rise above its decayed condition.[40] Despite reaffirming this tradition, the revolution he provoked within Christianity had some positive repercussions on the status of marital couples and on the role that sex was believed to play in reinforcing their affective bonds. Although marriage ceased to be a sacrament, Luther reevaluated the role of marriage as the foundation of civil society and as the most effective remedy for human concupiscence, which was tamed and sanctified within it. In spite of some differences, mostly related to the value that should be accorded to marital sex, this shift occurred consistently across all of the major Protestant confessions.[41]

This criticism raised many preoccupations in the Catholic world. We know that concubinage was widespread among priests, a fact that confirmed Luther's caustic comments on the Church's contradictions in matters of sexual morality until the Council of Trent intervened to regulate the issue. The conciliar fathers dealt with this matter in the fourteenth session on November 11, 1562. Canon 9 reconfirmed and definitively sanctioned ecclesiastic celibacy, a praxis that had never really taken root in Western Christianity, despite repeated attempts to enforce the injunction to chastity, which was first addressed to consecrated clergy during the Fourth Lateran Council in 1215.[42] This canon continued reconfirming the superiority of celibacy over marriage by clearly stating, "If any one saith, that the marriage state is to be placed above the state of virginity, or of celibacy, and that it is not better and more blessed to remain in virginity, or in celibacy, than to be united in matrimony; let him be anathema."[43]

Along with this declaration, the Roman Church strongly reasserted the sacramental nature of marriage as a response to the polemical stances taken by Protestants. At the same time, however, it responded to Luther's theology of marriage by devoting increasing attention to the condition of married couples, celebrating more firmly their charismatic dignity within the Christian community.[44] In this context, however, chastity and virginity continued to be assigned a major role in Christian morality, and for lay people that meant that sex was allowed only within marriage.[45] This reevaluation of marriage provoked a significant shift in the way that Christian authorities all over Europe regulated the wide range of sexual relationships and emotional bonds that took place out of wedlock. In late medieval Europe up to the mid-sixteenth century, the increased surveillance of sexual nonconformity occurred hand in hand with some forms of (conditioned) social tolerance. In fact, the intense scrutiny of sexual mores partly reflected the desire to come to terms with deeply rooted social habits, in spite of the religious interdictions. Many factors justified a tolerant approach toward sexual behaviors that were not aligned with the official teachings of the Church. Urban communities were overflowing with a male population that could not access marriage for a long period of their adult lives.[46] Many erotic and sexual tensions were therefore not able to be expressed within marriage, despite the belief that this was the only context in which such passions could legitimately be acted on. This circumstance generated tensions that religious and secular authorities were forced to handle with tact and circumspection. While control was highly recommended, repression could lead to unpredictable consequences.[47] Thus, even sodomy was among the transgressions that society was inclined to cautiously allow, at least under certain circumstances. As Michael J. Rocke has shown, what made this behavior partially acceptable was that it reinforced the hierarchical bonds that cemented male sociability. Sodomy was not to be encouraged, but when expressed in forms that did not disrupt the social order (and this was not always the case), it could at least be tolerated.[48]

The mediating approach that shaped late medieval and early modern policies concerning sexual mores disappeared in the aftermath of the Reformation. As a consequence of the reevaluation of marriage, the proscription of extra- or premarital sexual activity also became more cogent.[49] In Catholic and Protestant countries, prostitution was subjected to an increasing level of control, and an unprecedented moral stigma became paired with more coercive attitudes toward those who traversed the line dividing "prostitutes" and "honest women."[50] This emphasis on marriage also had serious repercussions for how Christian society dealt with sodomy. If in the past some room was left for negotiation, from the sixteenth century civic and religious institutions took a more radical stance against nonreproductive sexuality. These changing patterns did not always result in an increase in judiciary prosecutions.[51] Rather, those involved now tended to keep silent. In this respect, Catholic and Protestant countries adopted similar strategies. Sexual discourses in Catholic countries, however, may have been silenced in the public sphere, but they expanded in the proliferating manuals for confessors and texts of moral theology that were generated by the increasing emphasis on sacramental confession. These practices fostered a progressive internalization of Catholic moral teachings that had not been common before the Reformation.[52]

This increasing emphasis on controlling a vast range of experiences that had long been tolerated outside the prescriptive boundaries of marriage stimulated broad resistance. Although it is sometimes difficult to determine how people managed the internal conflicts between their desires and the moral codes proscribing them, many voices rose to condemn the moralizing turn that reformers imposed.[53] In the Catholic world, inquisitorial testimonies collected from the mid-seventeenth century onward demonstrate that both the clergy and laity saw the Council of Trent as a watershed moment in the regulation of sexual behaviors. An inquisitorial record from 1659 states that Francesco Pavona, "a gentleman by birth but with ill fortune," claimed that the theologians who assembled at Trent prohibited "fornication because, being old, they could not do it themselves."[54] In Venice, in 1688, Fra Illuminato Festa used similar reasoning in an attempt to seduce a woman, telling her that she shouldn't be worried because "before the Council of Trent, carnal sins were not sins, not even venial ones."[55] In 1711, a priest named Agostino Ciceri maintained that sexual activity should not be considered sinful if it was conducted to stay in good physical health. In any case, he continued, "the canon of the Council of Trent, which forbade the sin of the flesh, had not really been approved."[56] These statements show that people at every level of society were aware of the impact the council had on societal attitudes toward sexuality, although they were probably not properly informed about what the conciliar fathers actually decreed.

Resistance from Below

The prescriptive turn in matters of sex imposed by the Church over Catholic society thus generated a reactive discourse that, as the cases examined here demonstrate, could be particularly virulent. Some of the defendants analyzed here explicitly connected their claims of the legitimacy of sexual pleasure to criticisms of the intensified prescriptions on marriage in Catholic society, the reinforcement of celibacy for priests, and efforts to suppress or at least curb prostitution. These claims sometimes took the form of rational critique, but in other instances, they were simply enacted by consciously and voluntarily transgressing the norms regulating the sacrament of matrimony. Zozamo Canatta was a Sicilian surgeon who was tried several times by the Spanish Inquisition in Sicily in the second half of the sixteenth century. He was investigated for the crime of apostasy, among other charges that included the belief that Adam and Eve enjoyed anal sex in the Garden of Eden. Indeed, Canatta had been held as a slave in Muslim countries while a youth before returning to his native Sicily as an adult. After his return, he maintained some of the customs and beliefs he had acquired during his captivity, to the point that many of his neighbors thought him a bad Christian and even called him a Moor.[57] In this context, he was also accused of bigamy, a charge the inquisitors related to his suspected crypto-Islamism.[58] The issue of marriage and celibacy was also touched on by Antonio Partenio, a member of the Venetian patriciate tried by the Inquisition in 1705. Besides admitting that he believed that sodomy was what led to Adam and Eve's expulsion from the Garden of Eden, in his confession he also stated clearly that the vow of celibacy ought not be mandatory and that it had been created by the Church to maintain the wealth of princedoms, because "if any clergymen married no one would know how to maintain their families."[59] Among cases involving defendants who believed that sodomy was the first act of human disobedience, the trial of the priest Matteo da Cortona, which took place in Livorno in 1601, is particularly revealing, showing the resistance from below to the new norms about marriage, celibacy, and prostitution. Ser Matteo's case sheds ample light on how beliefs concerning Adam and Eve's sin could accompany tolerant attitudes toward both clerical celibacy and emotional and sexual bonds that occurred outside of marriage.

Called before the Inquisition of Pisa, Ser Matteo was accused both of believing that sodomy caused the Fall from Grace and of having a relationship with a prostitute to whom he had allegedly made a promise of marriage. The priest was from the outskirts of Cortona, a Tuscan town in the vicinity of Arezzo, and had spent several years as a convict in the galleys, although he often disembarked because of poor health. When the trial took place, it seems that he was employed on the shore crew because of an injury he suffered after being hit by a beam. While still on the galleys, he had scandalized another convicted clergyman, Fra Eusebio, by arguing that it was licit for a defrocked priest to have a wife.[60] The inquisitors eventually summoned Ser Matteo's supposed betrothed, Menica di Raffaelle from Monte Mozzano, the prostitute living in Livorno. She described her life experiences and her ability to construct support networks in her community of belonging, demonstrating a flexibility in negotiating between complex social and individual needs and the normative frame imposed by Church authorities. Menica declared that she first met Ser Matteo when he would greet her while she was visiting a fellow countryman of hers who was also serving a sentence in the galleys. About eighteen months before the trial, Ser Matteo sent a woman named "la Rosa" (The Rose), who Menica believed was from San Miniato, to tell Menica that he wanted to talk to her. She accepted the invitation. It was on this occasion that Ser Matteo communicated his intention to take Menica as his wife.[61] Menica accepted this betrothal, which Ser Matteo later formalized in a written marriage proposal, and made some changes in her life. She attempted to restore her reputation and leave the sex trade, but this got her into some financial trouble. To earn some money, Menica rented a room to a young Neapolitan. The lad was subsequently jailed for a crime that is not mentioned in her deposition, and, apparently, he took with him Ser Matteo's written marriage proposal, which therefore was not available among the trial evidence. In the meantime, Menica heard from many people that Ser Matteo was a priest and decided to push him away, even though he kept denying these rumors.[62]

During his questioning, Ser Matteo explained how he fell in love with Menica. When he suffered the injury to his leg, she was the only one who took care of him, and, "in order for her not to abandon [him]," he decided to write down his vow. However, he denied having publicly stated that a defrocked priest was allowed to marry. He reassured the judges that he was well aware of the fact that, despite the degradation, "[he kept] in [his] soul the indelible character" of the ordination.[63] Ser Matteo therefore showed that he was aware of the difference between transgressing norms without denying their validity and questioning their legitimacy and enforcement, an attitude that would lead to a formal accusation of heresy. Whether he told the judges that he belonged to the first category of dissenters simply to avoid a harsher conviction, we do not know. What we do know is that he managed to obtain a relatively lenient penance. The judges ruled that if Ser Matteo publicly abjured the heresies he was slightly (*de levi*) suspected of, he would be acquitted. To address the public scandal he had provoked, he was also obliged to recite seven penitential psalms every day for one year, proclaiming them out loud in the trireme to which he was confined. His abjuration was reported soon after the sentence.[64]

Instances of married priests surface in inquisitorial documents found across the Italian peninsula. Common parish and country priests, often uneducated and riotous, kept having children, getting married, and keeping concubines throughout the sixteenth and seventeenth centuries.[65] In some cases (among which we can surely count Matteo da Cortona), resistance to the decrees of Trent was accompanied by a critical approach to the theological foundations of post-Tridentine reformism. In 1600, a friar of French origin living in Sicily, known as Marco Andrea, was accused before the Spanish Inquisition in Palermo of having spoken favorably of some Dutch men who were detained in the viceregal jails. He also questioned the validity of sacramental confession, saying that the

Confiteor had been the proper form for confessing sins since the times of the primitive Church, thus denying the necessity of the intermediation of an ordained priest to receive absolution. While talking about the French clergy, he said that if the Church had not allowed priests to marry, it would have lost France within ten years. His scandalized listeners reminded him that he was just a lay brother and that therefore he did not have the authority to talk about these matters. He provocatively replied that there was not just one Holy Mother Church. He was also accused of being a radical iconoclast. He allegedly refused to honor holy images, adoring natural elements like "the east, the west, and the south." He allegedly committed several acts of blasphemy against sacred effigies. He declared that he had been granted a license from his order to go back to his hometown and that, from then on, he had started going on pilgrimages, wandering about different parts of France, Spain, and Italy. Although eventually deemed mentally unstable, he was nevertheless condemned to serve three years in the galleys of the viceroy.[66]

Juan "the Bell Ringer" (Campanaro) was a Carmelite friar and prior of the Convent of Saint Catherine in Espacafurno, a small town that was also homeland to Zozamo Canatta, whom we encountered earlier. The common features between the charges against this prominent member of the local clergy and those against Canatta are striking. Friar Juan's judicial proceedings took place in 1603, when Canatta's court case was about to come to an end after almost half a century of intermittent prosecution.[67] The Carmelite friar was accused by seven witnesses of keeping dirty animals inside the Church, even letting them on the main altar where the Blessed Sacrament was kept. He also allegedly let in his young child, putting him on the altar, holding him when he was in the choir reciting the office and even when he was administering the sacrament of confession. He purportedly bragged about having many female lovers, some of whom he had allegedly solicited during confession, while others he had carnally known inside the church, right in front of the Sacrament. Other witnesses reported that he customarily sang dirty songs that mocked the saints, while still others remarked that he "had held that he valued more knowing carnally a woman (saying this with dishonest words) than the whole paradise together, and that he would have liked that there hadn't been death so as to enjoy this world, and that when one died, everything ended, and both the body and the soul died."

As with some of the other dissenters we have encountered, he said that he would have liked to be abducted by the Turks so he could abandon the Christian religion. Like Marcello Impicciato, he swore when he lost at cards. He hated religious hierarchies and all the founders of religions across the world: "All those general bishops and religious leaders that are in the world, all those who invented the religions and made me friar." He allegedly said that all the things that had been done by pontiffs and generals of religious orders were "asininities" and that "[religious authorities] should let everyone live life in their own ways." He was eventually condemned to vehemently abjure, banned for life from the territories of Espacafurno, and, finally, condemned to serve for ten years in the galleys.[68]

These cases show that our dissenters participated in a larger social context that questioned the turn imposed on sexual morals by the Council of Trent. This chapter, however, has shown that the belief in Adam and Eve's sodomy was a flexible instrument that could find its ways within both normative and nonnormative discourses. This flexibility was made possible by the fact that norms and transgressions both relied on a common anthropology, which was deeply shaped by the Christian notion of original sin. By mocking this fundamental tenet, those who held the belief that anal sex represented the first infraction of God's commands hit the nail on the head. More or less consciously, they subverted the theoretical foundation that justified a century-long condemnation of sexual pleasure. As we will see in Chapter 4, however, this creative readaptation of the myth of the Fall went beyond the reevaluation of bodily jouissance, allowing one to question also the boundaries dividing Christianity from other world religions.

CHAPTER FOUR

Sex and Cross-Cultural Interactions

We will now investigate the relationship between the belief that Adam and Eve enjoyed anal sex in the Garden of Eden and the idea that "all can be saved in their own law"—that is, that eternal salvation is possible outside the boundaries of Catholicism. This opinion was widespread among people coming from the most disparate social, economic, and cultural backgrounds in the European world, especially in the Mediterranean area and the Atlantic colonies.[1] In some instances, our dissenters paired these two apparently distinct assumptions. For this group of radicals, criticism of Catholic sexual morality was the key not only to dismantling the control exerted by the Church over Catholic society but also to softening the boundaries dividing faiths.

Let's return to the case of Ser Matteo da Cortona, analyzed in Chapter 3. It was his beliefs, not his behaviors, that caught the attention of the judges. Indeed, his actions fell outside the competence of the inquisitorial tribunal. During the proceedings, he was questioned about his conviction that Catholicism was not superior to other faiths. The Carmelite friar Fra Eusebio Consoli testified that he was convinced that Ser Matteo would have moved to Calvinist Geneva, where ecclesiastic marriage was allowed, if he had had the chance to flee from the galley. He once heard him saying, indeed, that "the Supreme Pontiff does not have more authority than theirs," alluding to Calvin as the supposed pontiff of the Calvinists. Fra Eusebio also accused Ser Matteo of believing that the religious leader of Geneva should be preferred over the pope "because he lived in poverty following the life of Saint Peter, while our Roman [Pontiff] maintained dogs . . . and the Cardinals too maintained whores, horses and dogs, and they did not spend well the wealth of the Church . . . and those Lutherans who come to Rome are right to be scandalized because they see these things, and they see that [the Pontiff and the Cardinals] make their relatives rich with the Church properties." Ser Matteo allegedly also sympathized with the Queen of England Elizabeth I, who was known for turning the tables on her predecessor Mary Tudor's Catholic restoration and reestablishing the independence of the Church of England from Rome. And he was pegged as a blasphemer, although no one in the galley really paid attention to this aspect of his conduct because, admittedly, in those places it was "customary to swear."[2]

Ser Matteo's latitudinarian attitudes demonstrate the sympathy that our dissenters had for people belonging to non-Catholic Christian confessions and to other world religions. Some of them paired their radical reinterpretation of the myth of the Fall with the idea that "all can be saved in their own law." This belief emerged in judicial trials but was largely covered in the theological disputes that took place in those times of religious turmoil. This was one of the beliefs attributed to the young Campanella during his grand Neapolitan trial, and, unlike the accusation of atheism, he did not recant it in the first drafts of *Atheism Conquered.* Indeed, his conviction that natural reason was present in all human beings preoccupied the censors who examined the manuscript. In 1626, when he was transferred from Naples to Rome in the custody of the Holy Office, Pope Urban VIII (Maffeo Barberini, 1623–1644) declared that he wanted to know more about the errors found in Campanella's writing. He asked Cardinal Desiderio Scaglia to open an inquiry into the manuscript and decreed on January 7, 1627, an ad hoc commission to evaluate its contents. Thanks to the work of historian Germana Ernst, we can now read the minutes of the eleven-member commission, composed between November 1627 and February 1628. The main accusation against Campanella's work was, indeed, that of Pelagianism—that is, the belief that salvation was possible for human beings through their natural virtue. In *Atheism Conquered,* Campanella saw Christ as a manifestation of the pristine rationality infused by God in human beings. Every religion, inasmuch as it manifested the prime reason, was an embodiment of the same natural law, with varying degrees of fidelity to the original. Therefore, all human beings, as long as they participated in this natural rationality, were to be considered, at least implicitly and to some degree, Christians. The censors were aware of the dangers of such a viewpoint: by making salvation accessible to anyone who lived according to the inherent precepts of natural reason, the exclusive mediating role of the Church and clergy in accessing the divine would be called into question. As one of the members of the commission pointed out, by following Campanella's line of reasoning, one would open the gates of salvation to "infidels" and "heretics."[3]

The Council of Trent tackled this idea of universal salvation in the decree on justification, which was discussed in conjunction with that on original sin, and clearly condemned Pelagianism.[4] The synod established that, "for the correct and sound understanding of the doctrine of Justification," it was necessary for everyone to recognize and confess that, since "all men had lost their innocence in the prevarication of Adam . . . not the Gentiles only by the force of nature, but not even the Jews by the very letter itself of the law of Moses, were able to be liberated, or to arise, therefrom." This statement was immediately counterbalanced by a closing sentence that clarified that "although free will, attenuated as it was in its powers, and bent down, was by no means extinguished in them." This decree was ultimately stating that, notwithstanding the fact that human beings maintained some of their original goodness, this natural proclivity could not prevail against the omnipresent force of concupiscence without the help of the Catholic Church and its sacramental economy. Pelagianism and universal salvation constituted a threat to their authority.[5] Reading these cases in the light of this normative frame helps make explicit connections that would otherwise remain implicit if one referred only to the evidence contained in the judicial sources. I would argue that the connection between the quest for a looser sexual morality and a less rigid understanding of interfaith relations was not accidental. By explicitly addressing the issue of original sin, these dissenters, at some level, grasped the centrality of this tenet in reinforcing both the belief that the ubiquity of sexual desire was a consequence of the Fall and the idea that original sin could be removed only by the Catholic Church through its sacraments. Polemically reinstating sexual pleasure within the realm of nature coincided with claiming that natural reason was accessible to all human beings, notwithstanding their cultural or religious background.

The case of the Venetian patrician Antonio Partenio, put on trial in 1701, adds further layers of complexity to this analysis. Besides the belief that Adam and Eve enjoyed anal sex in the Garden of Eden, among his many charges was the idea that "all can be saved in their own law." According to his voluntary deposition, Partenio discussed this belief along with his opinion "about Predestination." He believed that it was not possible to predict the outcome of individual merits, either before or after their achievement, precisely because, in his opinion, "all can be saved in their own law."[6] This affirmation suggests that he thought that doing good deeds was not enough to ensure individual salvation because the ways of God were wider and less predictable than any certainties imposed by religious credos. This connection was common among reform-minded individuals across the Italian peninsula.[7] The propensity to pair the belief in predestination with a firm confidence in God's mercy was influenced by both Huldrych Zwingli's theology and the belief in the "boundless mercy of God," as formulated by Desiderius Erasmus in his *De immensa Dei misericordia* (On the boundless mercy of God), published in Basel in 1524.[8] Among Italian reformers, faith in predestination worked as a tool to question the stifling burden of ritual obligations and "the works of the Law" imposed on the believers by the Catholic Church, without preventing a limitless hope in the goodness of God, who conquered human beings through the sacrifice of his son. This in a nutshell was the content of the *Il Beneficio di Cristo* (The benefits of Christ), a spiritual treatise written by the Benedictine monk Benedetto Fontanini of Mantua and revised by the Italian humanist Marcantonio Flaminio that largely circulated in unorthodox circles across the Italian peninsula. The book bridged Calvinist themes and the wisdom of the Spanish spiritual teacher Juan de Valdés, whose teachings helped shape the character of the fluid movement known as Italian evangelism.[9]

Historians have long investigated how the debates on universal salvation, which stemmed from sixteenth-century confessional clashes, played a crucial role in affirming the ideal of religious toleration in early modern Europe.[10] Beyond the history of ideas, concrete practices of coexistence created a foundation for a de facto toleration from below, well before the idea of tolerance broke into seventeenth-century political debates.[11] Recent historiography has emphasized that both experiences of coexistence and theoretical reflections repurposed and reworked everyday habits and beliefs long shaped by the history of conflicts and interactions between the three Abrahamic faiths.[12] The rest of this chapter is devoted to a case that shows not only how cross-cultural interactions contributed to softening the boundaries between the faiths but also how much of a role sexual transgrèssions played in questioning religious fundamentalism. Its protagonist is a Sicilian "renegade": a former Christian who apostatized in favor of Islam during a period of captivity in Muslim lands and then converted back to Christianity after returning to his native land.

A Troubled Life Journey

Zozamo Canatta was a surgeon born in Espacafurno (present-day Ispica), a small town in the far south of Sicily. From the late sixteenth century, he was accused several times of apostasy by the Spanish Inquisition. He had first rejected the Christian faith in 1560, when he was twenty-six years old.[13] His trial, and those of eight other Sicilian men, included the charge that humanity's first rebellion was committing sodomy. Unlike other cases we have analyzed so far, for these first Sicilian occurrences the full trial records were unfortunately lost when the archives of the Sicilian Inquisition were destroyed in the eighteenth century.[14] Yet since Sicily was under the control of the Spanish crown when Canatta's trial took place, we do have available the dense correspondence between local judges and the Consejo de la Suprema y General Inquisición (Council of the Supreme and General Inquisition) in Madrid, which includes the many *Relaciones de causas,* brief reports that summarized the judicial activity undertaken by the judges of the faith on the island. The fragmented nature of these sources makes it extremely difficult to appreciate the nuances of this case. The idea that Adam and Eve savored anal sex in the Garden of Eden is only mentioned in passing, as one of a cluster of beliefs registered by the notaries. The witnesses first referred to this in 1582, when they reported him saying that "the prohibition of the fruit in the Earthly Paradise meant that Adam should not have used Eve against nature" and adding that "preachers did not say this from the pulpit out of decency."[15]

Zozamo Canatta was enslaved by Muslim corsairs when he was only fifteen, and he lived like a "Turk" for six years (literally "en habito de turco," or "wearing Turkish garments"), during which he eventually embraced the Islamic religion. Like many other "renegades"—Christians who had converted to Islam—he stated that, in the depths of his heart, he had never rejected the Christian faith and that he spent his time in Muslim lands waiting for the opportune moment to return to Christianity.[16] This defense was quite common among those who attempted to free themselves of the accusation of apostasy. At the time, inquisitors commonly accepted this stereotypical justification as a practical way to address a widespread phenomenon that could hardly have been solved with a repressive policy. The phenomenon of apostasy to Islam was indeed so frequent that, after much discussion, the inquisitors decided to punish those who accused themselves before the court with only a light spiritual penance. This decision was aimed explicitly at encouraging the return and reintegration to the faith of Christians from Muslim-majority countries.[17]

Notwithstanding this first voluntary abjuration, in 1564 the inquisitors collected new information concerning Zozamo Canatta. He was accused of being a bigamist and a blasphemer. He had reportedly said that sodomy and other sins of the flesh were not to be considered sins. He was absolved *en la ynstancia* (suspending judgment) in 1574 and then faced inquisitorial justice again in 1582.[18] Despite his spontaneous confession, seven witnesses testified that he said that, like Christians, "Turks and Moors" too could find eternal salvation, even while remaining "in their sect."[19] Zozamo confirmed all the charges, receiving a conviction of seven years' imprisonment in a local hospital. They specified that the "lightness" of the penalty was due to his mature age and emphasized the ways in which his forced service in the hospital could be beneficial to the community. As his previous conviction had not rested on clear judicial evidence, he was not considered a relapsed heretic, and so he escaped the death penalty.[20]

Nevertheless, it seems that seven years of imprisonment were still not enough to discipline his unruliness. He was listed yet again in the 1600 *Auto da Fé* in Palermo, accused of having mocked the sacraments by making fun of Christians, "who believe in a host, which they eat through the mouth and expel through the arse," and of consuming meat on Fridays. It was also said that he had vehemently defended the benefits of religious indifference. For unknown reasons, he was again reconciled without being considered a *relapso*.[21]

Nevertheless, by the late winter of 1605 he had apparently still not amended his conduct. His name appeared again in the inquisitorial reports of March 13, 1605, the final act of this tangled court case. The synthetic report sent by the Sicilian inquisitors to the central council of the Spanish Inquisition in Madrid reads as if the judges were taking stock of Zozamo's entire existence. They recalled all the previous proceedings, revealing that in 1593 he had also been accused of carrying weapons illegally and of practicing the art of surgery. He managed to get away with nothing more than a simple reprimand, which was nevertheless followed by an overt threat: if he did not change his behavior, he would incur a grave penalty. Between 1599 and 1603, the Inquisition continued to collect information on him, and it seems that Zozamo had not changed his mind. Some witnesses testified to hearing him say that "Turkish Moors and Jews are saved thanks to the foreskin"—that is, that their circumcision was equal to the baptism of a Christian. In this report, we also find again Zozamo's curious interpretation of the Fall from Grace: when God forbade the eating of the fruit in the Earthly Paradise, he was referring to the "nefarious sin." Zozamo then died, and his nephew took up his case, suggesting the possibility of a conspiracy against his uncle organized by one of his bitter hometown enemies. This time, the defendant found no mercy, and Zozamo Canatta was finally burned, although in effigy.[22]

All Can Be Saved

Zozamo Canatta was accused also of believing that "all can be saved in their own law"—that is, that Jews, Muslims, and Christians could attain eternal salvation if they behaved well. This idea appears twice in his trial records. In its first occurrence, the witnesses reported that Canatta, in one of his daring public performances, said:

> The world is divided into three parts, Asia, Africa, and Europe. I have walked all around the world. In Africa there are Jews, Turks, and Moors; in Asia too there are Jews, Turks, and Moors; and in Europe as well, where we live, there are Turks, Moors, Christians, and infidels, so that only a few Christians are left. Do you wish, or do you think, that all these people will go to Hell, and the few Christians will go to Paradise? That is why I do not want to believe in anything.[23]

This picturesque depiction of Canatta's wanderings probably exaggerated the scope of his travels around the world, but it surely reflected an animated life journey that traversed the borders dividing Christianity and Islam. It is likely that his attitude reflected his multiple experiences of conversion. Cultural crossings like those undertaken by Canatta had a significant impact on the construction of early modern religious identities.[24] Historical studies on conversions have revealed that crossing boundaries that divided faiths often led to the development of a complex religious and cultural identity, in which individuals maintained aspects of their native religion as well as the one (or ones) to which they converted.[25]

The idea itself that salvation was not the prerogative of a specific religious affiliation often recurred in cases of multiple conversions. It could also be traced back to the direct influence of Islamic beliefs, to which Canatta was exposed for a significant part of his juvenile life. Mercedes García-Arenal has pointed out that anti-Muslim polemicists attributed the idea that "all can be saved" to Islam.[26] In his *Antialcoran* (1535), the preacher Bernardo Peréz de Chinchón (1488/93–1556?) stated that "some of the learned men among the Muslims say that each can be saved in his own law." In his history of Valencia, Gaspar de Escolano (1560–1619) placed this belief in the list of errors he attributed to Muslims. The opinion was not unfounded. At least two passages of the Qur'ān clearly refer to the universal salvation of the good. There is evidence that these Qur'ānic passages were discussed both by Christian philosophers who, from the fifteenth century on, were willing to reconsider the official position of the Church regarding the relations between historical religions and by orthodox preachers and theologians who wanted to halt the spread of this opinion in Italy. In the thirteenth century, William of Auvergne (1190–1249) had quoted the Latin translation of the Qur'ān in his *De legibus* (On the laws) as one of the channels through which the idea that "all can be saved" circulated in the Christian West.[27]

The second time that Canatta mentioned this irenic belief, he allegedly tried to explain it to his acquaintances by referring to a parable. He reportedly said that we are all like a man who "enters a dark cave, where there are three columns, the first made of gold, the second of silver, and the third of metal, and does not know which is the best."[28] This imaginative tale clearly echoes the popular novella of the three rings. Much has been written in an attempt to identify the tale's origins and multiple offshoots across the Mediterranean world, which go beyond Christianity to include the Jewish, Arabic, and Persian traditions.[29] Muslim Spain (Al-Andalus) was probably the crossing point through which this tale was transmitted to European Christianity.[30] Once it was incorporated into Christian European culture, however, "the Parable took on a life of its own, as a literary motif."[31] In less than fifty years, the parable emerged and circulated throughout the Italian peninsula in three different but closely related versions—including the famous one by Giovanni Boccaccio—which makes this region one of the most important centers for the reception and circulation of this theme.[32] In the *Decameron*'s third story of the first day, it is told that Saladin (representing the Muslim world) asked the Jew Melchisedech which one of the three monotheistic religions, Judaism, Christianity, or Islam he believed to be the true one. Melchisedech replied by telling a parable about a father and his three sons. The father declared that the one to whom he had passed a precious ring, which had been passed down from father to son for generations in his household, would inherit the family possessions. However, loving his three sons equally, he made copies of the ring and gave one to each of them. Therefore, none of them could know who possessed the true ring and who the false ones. Melchisedech explained that the religious meaning of the parable is that "the same applies to the three laws which God the Father granted to His three people, and which formed the subject of our inquiry. Each of them considers itself the legitimate heirs to His estates, each believes it possesses His own true law and observes His commandments. But as with the rings, the question as to which of them is right remains in abeyance."[33]

The result of the popularization of this tale, however, was not just the formulation of an ideal of religious tolerance but also the adoption of a skeptical approach toward religions generally, symbolized by the fact that the siblings were ultimately deprived of the possibility to discern the truth in this world.[34] The skeptical implications of the parable made historians reflect on its relationship with the idea of the fraudulence of religion as it was taking shape between the late Middle Ages and the early modern period. In a book devoted to Gotthold Ephraim Lessing, Friedrich Niewöhner emphasized the interconnections between the traditions of the three rings and the three impostors.[35] More recently, Guy G. Stroumsa explicitly mentioned these two cultural constructs in the title of an influential essay on the comparative study of Abrahamic religions, where he emphasized the "thematic affinity" between these two myths, which in his opinion constituted the backbone of a long-term history of philosophical and theological reflections on the contradictory relationships between Judaism, Christianity, and Islam.[36] In the most recent and updated history of the origins and circulation of the tale of the three rings, Iris Shagrir devotes an entire chapter to the legend of the three impostors, which she describes as a "mirror image" of the parable, whose message it "sharpens by inversion." Shagrir points out that, "rather than arguing that the three religions are equally valid, it denies the validity of all three in equal measure." Or, to put it in other terms, it assesses that "true religion cannot be determined, because there is no true religion."[37]

The connection between these two cultural constructs has emerged not only in the present-day reflections of historians of religion but also in a vast array of early modern literary and judicial sources.[38] As Stefania Pastore has pointed out, the Iberian Peninsula—with its multicultural character and the interplay of coexistence and conflict among different faiths—was an ideal setting for cultural translation and adaptation, which in turn nurtured a spectrum of doubts, occasionally culminating in open dissent. In this context, while some arrived at beliefs that were close to "certain deistic standpoints," which would later emerge in France and Holland, others adopted forms of "radical skepticism, which resulted in the denial of the immortality of the soul and of the validity of all religious precepts," echoing "the centuries-old theories on the three rings, or the three impostors."[39] The tale of the three rings was also part of the cultural universe of the Friulian miller Menocchio, whose case, immortalized by Carlo Ginzburg, has been crucial to our understanding of the phenomenon of religious doubt and skepticism in early modern Italy.[40]

This skeptical interpretation of the parable seems the most consonant with Zozamo Canatta's attitude as it has emerged from the sources. His life journey and his contacts with Muslim countries in North Africa may have made him particularly receptive to this story, which was also well known in Christian Europe at the time. Some elements in Canatta's account, however, point to a specific version of this literary construct that was dependent on a refined and rare learned source. His reference to the dark cave and the columns is reminiscent of a passage from a work by Emperor Manuel II Palaiologos, the *Dialogues with a Persian.* Manuel II was the last great ruler to lead the Byzantine Empire during the epoch of decadence, before the fall of Constantinople to the Ottomans in 1453. In his *Dialogues,* the emperor reported a legend he had heard from a Muslim scholar (a "müderris"), where the theme of the three rings is reinterpreted through the image of the three columns. The king was reported as ordering the construction of a "very large and utterly dark lodge . . . with no lighting . . . , and to place a number of pillars within it, each made of some kind of material, and to place one golden column somewhere in the middle." He then summoned to his court "one person from each religious faith," whom he ordered "to enter the guest rooms and to search for the golden column. The rule was that each person must strongly grip the [first] column he encountered (the number of columns matched the number of people); the column would earn him the greatest honor and largest gifts if it turned out to be the golden column." In the tale, the king is depicted as "extremely wise," since "nothing was dearer" to him "than general concord." For these reasons, he "could not bear the division into different sects due to divergent faiths, nor the quarrels and the killing due to conflict and confrontations."[41]

In this version of the parable, the golden column is only one, a detail that emphasizes the existence of one exclusive truth. The skeptical implications of this account, however, are undeniable. The story seems to invite a modest and non-dogmatic adherence to one's own beliefs, while the ultimate truth remains shrouded in darkness in our present age. This conclusion was made explicit by the Muslim sage who, after Manuel II

Palaiologos's narrative, clearly stated that the moral of the story was that "there is no person who knows for certain that the tenets of his religion are the most correct and superior to those of the other religions. Each person thinks he is the only one to hold the 'golden pillar,' but in fact, only God alone knows the truth, while we humans rely on mere opinions that are cast in doubt."[42]

The origins of this version of the legend are unknown, as are the pathways through which it reached our Sicilian surgeon. He might have learned it through the mediation of the written page. Given his profession, it is likely that Canatta possessed some reading skills, although they could vary substantially according to his degree of specialization, which we do not know.[43] It is highly unlikely that he was able to read Greek, the language in which the only three known extant manuscript versions of the work were written. The oldest was probably written by an Italian scribe in the sixteenth century and was likely produced in the Italian peninsula.[44] This makes it more likely that Canatta was in touch with someone who, even indirectly, had knowledge of its contents. The presence of this reference among his allegations could therefore suggest that, besides his continued allegiance to some Muslim habits and beliefs, after his return to Sicily he also sought to establish relationships with members of other religious minorities living in his native country. Greek Orthodox Christians were conspicuously present in Sicily and the rest of southern Italy. Even though they were considered schismatics rather than heretics *strictu sensu,* the Spanish inquisitorial tribunals kept these Orthodox communities under strict control. The Greek rite was practiced in Sicily and Calabria by Albanian communities that had migrated there during the fifteenth century and continued to preserve their own structure, language, discipline, tradition, and liturgies. In 1564, after the turn of the screw against Orthodox Christians imposed by Pius IV's apostolic letter *Sane nonnulli,* Archbishop Ludovico I Torres of Monreale ordered a visit to the Sicilian Greek communities in his dioceses. These were entrusted to the Augustinian friar from Trapani, Antonio Castronuovo, who eventually composed a *Trattato contra li Greci* (hereafter *Treatise against the Greeks*). The *Treatise* denounced what the author believed were the many superstitions of the Orthodox Christians. It also criticized them for their loose sexual morality, which went so far, from a Catholic perspective, as allowing priests to marry.[45] Given Canatta's profile, it is possible that he might have been attracted to these aspects of the Greek communities' sociability in his homeland. His unquiet spirit may have inspired him to meet with members of this religious minority, some of whose most learned members might have known, directly or indirectly, the contents of the dialogue, which was authored by an iconic historical figure of the Byzantine tradition.

Sex and Cross-Cultural Interactions

Zozamo Canatta's multiple conversions and his curiosity about other confessions were crucial to the genesis of his positions in matters of faith. When reading his case alongside similar instances of religious dissent in inquisitorial sources, we might hypothesize that his attitudes toward sexual morality were also influenced by his experiences of cultural crossings. Another early instance that testifies to the circulation of the belief that Adam and Eve engaged in anal sex in the Garden of Eden suggests that this idea merged with themes that originated at the intersection of the three main Mediterranean monotheistic faiths. In 1600, while Canatta's tangled court case was still awaiting resolution, a thirty-two-year-old priest and theologian from the city of Messina in Sicily, named Octavio de Verardo, was brought before the Spanish Inquisition. According to the trial reports, he allegedly said that "the Scripture, in so far as it forbade Adam to eat the fruit of the forbidden tree, meant sodomy, that is, it forbade Adam to use Eve against nature, saying that the woman is the man's garden."[46] The metaphor of the woman as a garden, or else a tilth to be cultivated (or, more explicitly, "plowed") by her husband as he wishes, is not a random sexual allusion. Across Europe, it was associated with the Islamic religion in late medieval and early modern anti-Muslim literature. This idea was based on a passage from the Second Sura of the Qur'ān (The Cow, 2.223): "Your women are a tillage for you; so come unto your tillage as you wish, and forward for your souls; and fear God, and know that you shall meet Him. Give thou good tidings to the believers."[47]

From the first attempts to translate the Qur'ān into Latin, this passage had been interpreted by individuals in the Christian West as a justification for sodomy. In the twelfth century, Peter the Venerable, abbot of Cluny, gathered a team of scholars in Toledo to work on a ponderous translation of Islamic texts that were collected under the title *Corpus Toletanum* and included a Latin rendition of the Qur'ān by Robert of Ketton. Peter of Poitiers, who was Peter the Venerable's notary, helped the abbot draw up a first draft of the list of contents for the work that was meant to refute what he thought were the most pernicious errors of Muḥammad's followers. Peter of Poitiers included sodomy in the index, stating in a letter that "all Saracens perform this act licentiously, as if it were a precept of Muḥammad." The index, in fact, included a paragraph (the sixth of the second book) devoted to rebutting "what [Muḥammad] taught on the very foul act of sodomy in his Qur'ān, as if speaking on behalf of God: 'Men, plow your women from whatever side you like.'" Although there was ultimately no mention of this passage in the final version of Peter the Venerable's *Liber contra sectam sive haeresim Saracenorum* (Book against the sect or heresy of the Saracens), the sodomitic interpretation of this Qur'ānic passage became commonplace in fourteenth-century anti-Muslim polemics. Moreover, as Vincenzo Lavenia has pointed out, "from a vice practiced with their brides it became one performed between men, and even with animals."[48]

Despite this distorted cross-cultural mirroring, we ought not assume that the sexual content of verse 223 from the second Qur'ānic Sura was exclusively the result of anti-Islamic Christian polemicists projecting their prejudices onto Muslim texts. Without referring to male-male sodomy, this passage was discussed in sexual terms in Islamic exegesis as well, especially in the context of intense religious dialogue with the Judaic rabbinic tradition. The professor of Arabic and Islamic history Ze'ev Maghen has highlighted the points of contact between Jewish rabbinic exegesis and the Muslim commentaries on this specific verse of the Qur'ān, which he has attributed to documented episodes of cross-readings of fundamental Jewish exegetic texts by Muslim scholars.[49] This theme was therefore debated at the intersection of Jewish and Islamic cultures and subsequently made its way into the anti-Islamic propaganda in European Christianity, ultimately becoming a recurring theme among Christian polemicists beginning in the late Middle Ages and lasting throughout the early modern period.

In Western Christianity, the sexual stereotypes built by anti-Muslim polemicists sometimes had an opposite effect to what was intended, attracting those who rejected the restrictions on sexual behaviors imposed by the Church. People searching for a less narrow-minded sexual morality often idealized the Islamic world as a land of freedom. Zozamo Canatta was prosecuted for bigamy, which was considered a crime for Christians, who supported the view that Muslims, who allowed this practice, were carnal and lascivious beings. It was not unusual for defendants investigated by the inquisitions throughout Italy to express their interest in Muslim polygamy. It was often paired with a fascination with the Islamic alimentary precepts, which were perceived as less restrictive than the Christian ones.[50] The myth of the seraglio also titillated the fantasies of men, but in some instances, it was precisely the allusion to sodomy that aroused the interests of early modern Christian "maurophiles."[51]

Canatta allegedly maintained that sodomy and other forbidden sexual acts were not sinful. Others in Sicily associated this belief with their fascination with Muslim culture. Vincenzo lo Restivo, a native of Camarata in the diocese of "Girgento," was a twenty-two-year-old saddler who abjured *de vehementi*[52] in the *Auto da Fé* that took place in Palermo on February 25, 1600. He was given a tremendously harsh punishment, being condemned to life imprisonment for stating that Christians should not confess their sins. He allegedly said that he had been sodomized by many Muslims when he was kept as a captive in the crown's galleys. He added that he had confessed this sin directly to God in the same way that the Muslims did—that is, by purifying his body with water and by pronouncing ritual prayers. A witness said that Vincenzo wanted to encourage his wife to prostitute herself. Facing the reprimand of an acquaintance, Vincenzo replied that no woman—including Mary, who in his opinion was not a virgin—had ever lived without being carnally known by someone. When asked about his refusal to attend Mass, he provocatively replied that "[he] always listen[ed] to it in the tavern." Even though he had already confessed to all the charges, during his incarceration many of his fellow prisoners referred to him having said that the soul dies with the body. He also reportedly declared that he would refuse to fast, even if God himself and all the apostles commanded it. Finally, he was accused of invoking the devil. When he was again put on trial, he confessed that he believed "in the—supposed—opinion of the Turks" that, in fact, the soul was not immortal.[53]

This case reveals the ways in which marginalized environments, such as galleys and jails, could act as a backdrop against which social actors elaborated radically heterodox opinions. It seems that the hatred of Christian religious authorities and dissatisfaction with contemporary moral standards sometimes triggered the idealization of those–in this case, Muslims–who were more regularly perceived as the most dangerous enemies of Christian society. Other dynamics, however, might also have been at play in this case. On the one hand, the inquisitors may have reflected the attitude of Christian heresiographers who interpreted Muslim beliefs as having many aspects in common with radical Christian heresies characterized by strong skeptical, and even atheistic, leanings.[54] On the other hand, however, Lo Restivo might have interpreted (even if unconsciously) his experiences of contact with Muslims through the lens of these polemical interpretations of the Islamic faith, turning their negative evaluation into a matter of fascination and attraction.[55]

Cases like those of Canatta and Lo Restivo, therefore, testify to the relevance of the cross-cultural interactions between Muslims and Christians in the development of both radically skeptical positions in matters of faith and the diverging understandings of sexual morality that foregrounded pleasure. They found in the Islamic faith an object of attraction and a possible, alternative way to salvation, as well as a perspective from which to criticize a status quo that they perceived as profoundly distorted and unjust.

The Substitution Legend

At first glance, Canatta's proximity to the Muslim faith seems to be an exception among the cases analyzed here. Yet it is not. Zozamo Canatta declared that he believed only in the first part of the Christian credo and not in the verses referring to Jesus Christ.[56] The Neapolitan apothecary Marcello Impicciato assumed that Jesus did not die but only weakened on the cross. This charge appears in almost all the witnesses' accounts collected against him. Moreover, he allegedly denied the resurrection, claiming, "It is not true that Christ died on the cross: he just pretended to be dead. If he had died, he wouldn't have come back to life. . . . When have you ever seen someone resurrect from the dead?"[57] The Palermo jurisconsult Ludovico Garrano also repeatedly stated this opinion, arguing that Simon of Cyrene had been sacrificed in place of Jesus.[58] We have already seen the idea of the crucifixion of a Christ look-alike emerging in Campanella's trial transcriptions. Garrano's very specific identification of Christ's substitute as Simon of Cyrene, however, can also be found in the trial of the Friulian miller Domenico Scandella (1532–1599), known as Menocchio, made famous by Carlo Ginzburg's *The Cheese and the Worms.* Many of Menocchio's beliefs resonate with those of Canatta, Impicciato, and Garrano: the resistance against the doctrinal rigidity of the Catholic Church; the possibility of salvation in every religion; the notion that religious hierarchies served the interests of the ruling classes. Along with these similarities, however, there were also important differences. The core theme of this book, the sodomitic reinterpretation of original sin, has no parallel in Menocchio's trial. There are only a few brief mentions of the sin of Adam and Eve in his judicial proceedings. In the first trial in 1584, witness Tita, the son of Domenico Corradina, said to the judges, "It may be about four months ago that Domenego Scandella loaned a book called *Il fioretto della Bibbia* in the vernacular and I read only one page, I read about when Adam and Eve ate the apple."[59] Tita was referring to *El fiore della bibbia hystoriato* (The illustrated flower of the Bible), and in the versions of this work that I have consulted, there is no hint of the possible imputation of the crime of sodomy to Adam and Eve.[60] Conversely, in our cases there is no mention of the complex cosmology that constituted the most interesting part of Menocchio's system of beliefs. Ginzburg placed Menocchio's original "peasant cosmology" at the center of his analysis. The miller, however, was also accused of having claimed that "it is not true that Christ was crucified, but rather it was Simon of Cyrene," though it is worth noting that in both Garrano's and Menocchio's cases, these beliefs were reported not directly in their testimonies but in allegations made by other witnesses.[61] In Menocchio's case, they also appear in the abjuration and final sentence of the first trial (May 1584) and in the sentence of the second trial (August 1599).[62]

This circuitous circulation of themes between different regional areas in the Italian peninsula is not surprising. From the reports of Garrano's trial, we know that some of his acolytes lived between Naples and Palermo and that the Sicilian necromancers smuggled books from Venice, which they received unbound and then bound on arrival.[63] Venice was one of the places where some of Scandella's opinions originated, so it is likely that people like Canatta, Garrano, and Impicciato shared readings or opinions in common with the Friulian miller or those in a similar cultural milieu. Both Menocchio and the defendants under examination referred to friars as sources of their heretical opinions. The dissenters under examination may have learned of the substitution legend through contacts with intermediaries that connected Naples and Palermo to Venice.

The Italian historian Andrea del Col has hypothesized that some of the Friulian miller's unorthodox beliefs may have had Gnostic roots. That Jesus only seemingly underwent the Passion and crucifixion was in fact an opinion that was widely reported in the early anti-Gnostic heresiographies.[64] Irenaeus of Lyon explicitly attributed to Basilides the idea that Simon of Cyrene was transformed and crucified in place of Jesus.[65] Furthermore, it should not be forgotten that the miller was also explicitly accused of bringing back to light "the Manichean belief in the double principle, namely of the good and the bad."[66] This Gnostic belief also circulated in Muslim countries. The denial of the crucifixion and the "substitution legend" that someone else was crucified in Jesus's place were widely discussed within the Islamic faith. There is only one passage in the Qur'ān that directly refers to Jesus' crucifixion, when the Jews are quoted as saying, "Surely we have killed the Messiah, Isa son of Marium, the apostle of Allah; and they did not kill him nor did they crucify him, but it appeared to them so . . . and most surely those who differ therein are only in a doubt about it; they have no knowledge respecting it, but only follow a conjecture, and they killed him not for sure."[67] While there is no explicit reference to the so-called substitution theory in the Qur'ānic passage, the ephemeral nature of Christ's death as described leaves the doors open for this interpretation. The substitution theory was largely accepted in Qur'ānic *tafsīr* (exegesis), although this opinion first occurs not in Islamic exegetic literature but in the final chapter of the treatise *De haeresibus* (On heresies) by the Arabic Christian theologian John of Damascus (died 749), which was dedicated to the followers of Islam.[68] It is not by chance that this association appears for the first time in the writing of an Arabic-speaking Christian. Anti-Islamic Christian writers devoted considerable effort to portraying Islam as being opposed to Christian "truth." Emphasizing the incompatibility of Islam with the core of Christian revelation—the universal salvation through the incarnation and sacrifice of God's son—was an efficient strategy to reach that goal.[69]

Regarding the Islamic exegetical tradition, there was no consensus among scholars as to the veracity of the "substitution legend." Some versions of this story have been criticized as *Isrāʿiliyyat*—that is, as being allegedly dependent on the authority of Christian and Jewish traditions rather than Islamic sources.[70] It has been suggested that the traditional account of "the crucifixion of a look-alike substitute" might have originated in "circles in contact with Gnostic Christians."[71] Yet the consolidation of this belief in different religious traditions was clearly a response to the ongoing conflicts between Christianity and Islam. For Christian polemicists, the substitution legend proved the errors of the Islamic faith and its dependence on heretical Christian sources. For Muslims, it served to undermine the theological foundations of Christian soteriology.

The substitution legend also appears several times in the first Italian translation of the Qur'ān, though with no reference to Simon of Cyrene. The translation by Giovanni Battista da Castrodardo had great success in the sixteenth and seventeenth centuries. Despite the claims on the title page, this text was based not on the Arabic original but on a number of European sources, including chronological rearrangements of medieval Arabic-Latin texts and an abridged version of Robert of Ketton's Latin translation (1143) in Theodor Bibliander's edition (1543).[72] Pier Mattia Tommasino's research on this work, titled *The Venetian Qur'an,* suggests that Menocchio read Giovanni Battista Castrodardo's adaptation of the foundational text of the Islamic religion. Tommasino drew his conclusion by analyzing Menocchio's comments on the biblical episode of Abraham destroying the idols. Tommasino identified in the Friulian miller's wording a "concrete foothold to demonstrate the reading of the Qur'ān and, therefore, the anti-Catholic use of Islam and the Qur'ān on the part of Ginzburg's microhero."[73]

Although it is not possible to determine with the same certainty where the reference to Simon of Cyrene as a substitute at Christ's crucifixion came from, either in our cases or in Menocchio's, some of the cultural tropes that nourished the speculations of these restless spirits clearly originated in debates that took place at the intersections of different religious traditions. These cases show that, even beyond the conscious claims of the actors involved, the lived experiences of people from every level of society were shaped against the backdrop of a shared Mediterranean cultural background and conflicts between the faiths. This context fostered critical approaches toward religion that ultimately weakened the belief in religious revelations across social ranks.

CHAPTER FIVE

Esoteric Private Libraries

The cultural identity of some of our dissenters was deeply shaped by the forbidden books they consumed. The books mentioned in some of these trials clearly represent an identifiable cultural milieu, showing the defendants' interest in ceremonial and demonic magic. Some of these same readings emphasized that religions in general, and Catholic Christianity in particular, were frauds invented by the ruling classes to maintain their privileges. Our dissenters' interests were not particularly theoretical, and they probably approached these texts exclusively as manuals of magic. Yet the trial transcripts show that those interests sometimes went beyond mere practical purposes. The investigation of the powers of natural and demonic forces led them to draw conclusions about the world, its origins, and the place human beings occupied in it that were clearly at odds with Christian and Catholic views.

This chapter will describe first how the defendants applied the knowledge contained in these books to the practice of magic and then how these readings might have influenced their system of beliefs. In doing so, it will emphasize the extent to which these literary works were also read in the libertine circles of that time, constituting a source of inspiration for the opinion that religious revelations were frauds. Although it seems that the dissenters analyzed here were not aware of the contemporary reception of these texts in elitist circles in Italy and beyond, they reached very similar conclusions thanks to their reading.

In Marcello Impicciato's case, he repeatedly claimed that he was ignorant and illiterate. There probably was a dose of dissimulation behind this claim. Feigning ignorance was certainly a good strategy to alleviate the burden of a "vehement suspicion" of heresy. Other defendants accused of believing in Adam and Eve's sodomy blatantly bragged about their literary cultivation, discussing their readings with their friends and acolytes. Matteo da Cortona, the defrocked priest in the port of Livorno, often flaunted his culture, insulting his fellow galley oarsmen for being ignorant illiterates. One of the witnesses reported that when he was alone with Ser Matteo they used to talk about religion as well as other intellectual interests, which ranged from Plutarch's *Lives* to the works of Jacopo Sannazaro and Torquato Tasso's *Jerusalem Delivered.*[1] Ludovico Garrano was reported by a witness as having often argued with his friends about belles lettres, as they called the forbidden books in their jargon.[2] The Venetian patrician Antonio Partenio believed that the religious and political authorities censored books to subjugate people and keep them ignorant: "And for this reason," he claimed, "I tried to read as many books as I could"—especially all the prohibited ones.[3]

Matteo da Cortona, Ludovico Garrano, and Antonio Partenio are the only defendants accused of believing in Adam and Eve's sodomy in the Garden of Eden whose readings were listed in the judicial sources. While in Matteo da Cortona's case there seems to be no direct connection between his intellectual interests and his heterodox positions, Garrano's and Partenio's reading lists consist of extremely refined collections of esoteric texts, whose contents can be straightforwardly associated with their convictions in matters of faith. Their cases took place in different times and places. While Garrano was brought before the judges of the Spanish Inquisition in Sicily in the 1630s, Partenio was convicted of his crimes in Venice in the early eighteenth century. Despite these temporal and geographical differences, the books that both possessed and read reflect the same cultural interests. Partenio's private library had many titles in common with Garrano's. This suggests that the opinion that sodomy represented the first rebellion against God's commands circulated in circles that shared intellectual concerns and that these concerns remained consistent across time. In these two cases, the belief that sodomy was the original rebellion against God's commands remains a side accusation that, although listed in the final summary of the charges, was only mentioned in passing in the trial records as if it did not attract the attention of the judges. Nevertheless, the reports of their judicial proceedings are archival gold when it comes to reconstructing the wider cluster of opinions that consistently surrounded the emergence of this belief throughout the centuries.

Garrano, the Necromancer

Ludovico Garrano was a jurisconsult and a prominent figure in an extensive network in Palermo characterized by a common interest in esotericism and magical arts. Involved in a tangled judicial case, he was forced to abjure *de vehementi* in 1633 and was sentenced to five years of imprisonment in solitary confinement, a verdict that was eventually commuted to house arrest.[4] The inquisitorial reports listing the texts allegedly read by Garrano and his group of friends reveal his interests in natural philosophy and magic. These texts included the *Clavicula Salomonis*;[5] works by Virgil,[6] Girolamo Cardano,[7] Julius Caesar Scaliger,[8] Johannes Trithemius,[9] Pietro d'Abano,[10] and Artemidorus of Daldis;[11] and the *Liber de Syndicatu.*[12]

According to the charges leveled against him, Garrano attempted to put into practice the knowledge he acquired from his books. Along with seeking treasures, he was accused of casting a spell on the archbishop of Montereale, Don Geronimo de Veniero, and the inquisitor Juan de la Cueva. He allegedly wanted to provoke their deaths because of the enmity some in his sodality held toward these eminent religious authorities. This extremely serious episode was at the root of Garrano's conviction. His main accuser was Iacopo Cerasa, a twenty-six-year-old priest who named Garrano as his accomplice in the plot against the two prominent ecclesiastics. When Cerasa appeared before the judges in 1626, there were already many suspicions surrounding him. Knowing that the judges were about to summon him, he played the card of confession in the hope of easing the burden of his charges. Unfortunately for him, the political situation did not play out in his favor. Born in Bisacquino, a fief in the diocese of Montereale, Cerasa was at that time a vicar forane of Chiusa Sclafani, a town in the Agrigento diocese. When the scandal exploded, the bishop of Agrigento, Francesco Traina, was in open conflict with the inquisitors in Palermo. The friction between the two was so high that Pope Urban VIII himself felt compelled to intervene, recommending levelheadedness to both parties. It seems that this resolution had an immediate impact on Cerasa's trial, since the local inquisitors reported to the Council of the Supreme Inquisition in Madrid that Traina had finally become cooperative and agreed to work toward a prompt solution of the case. Cerasa's prosecution was only the tip of the iceberg in a much larger and more worrying affair. The investigations revealed that the conventicle of necromancers included nearly eighty participants. Given the scope of the scandal, the inquisitors eventually decided to proceed exclusively against the master magicians within the circle, along with their main accomplices. Among them, the reports list Don Geronimo Reitano, a twenty-eight-year-old physician born and living in Palermo; Vincenzo Bova, age thirty-one, who was also from Palermo and worked as a silversmith; and the twenty-nine-year-old jurisconsult Ludovico Garrano. Garrano was accused by Cerasa of materially contributing to the execution of the spell against La Cueva and Veniero. In a 1626 letter, the inquisitor La Cueva himself described his shock when, during a terrible hailstorm, he saw a thunderbolt suddenly strike the place that he usually occupied in his private library, which he "miraculously" had left shortly before. La Cueva believed what was reported by many witnesses: in that instant, the followers of the necromantic sect were operating a spell against him. Cerasa subsequently accused Garrano of having been with him when they modeled two virgin-wax figures representing their targets, which they then pierced with two nails, one made of cypress wood and the other of laurel, on which they had engraved the sigils of Lucifer and the Archangel Michael. According to Cerasa's deposition, while they were hammering the nails, the two recited some psalms. They then put the two figures close to the fire and watched them melt, until the rite was brutally interrupted by the same thunderstorm that hit La Cueva's house. Cerasa also revealed that someone paid them 250 scudi to orchestrate the spell. The instigator, however, remains unknown.[13]

Forbidden Books

What was the relationship between Garrano's practices, his beliefs in matters of faith, and his readings? Garrano's interest in applying the magical arts is attested to by the presence among his readings of the *Clavicula Salomonis,* the most popular handbook of magic that circulated in early modern Italy. Despite the fame of this work, historians have amply demonstrated that this title did not designate a single, coherent piece of work. A variety of versions of the *Clavicula* were reproduced, copied, readapted, and forged, mostly for moneymaking purposes. They all contained concrete descriptions of how to operate spells and charms. Their pages were filled with graphic representations of circles and other symbols to be used in different ritual contexts. If correctly performed, these charms were thought to have the power to modify the surrounding environment and produce all sorts of desired effects.[14]

Much more relevant, from a theoretical perspective, is the presence among Garrano's readings of a work by the abbot of Sponheim, Johannes Trithemius (1462–1516). Trithemius supported the use of ceremonial and demonic magic in a time when these subjects were increasingly coming under the control of the Inquisition. He defended the esoteric nature of magical practices and clandestinely circulated his books in manuscript form within his close circle of initiates. When his work the *Steganographia* was discovered, the scandal was so great that Trithemius lost his title as abbot along with his vast and precious library.[15] The book mentioned in Garrano's trial records was the *Polygraphia* (1518), which Trithemius most likely wrote to clear the negative reputation that surrounded his previous work. Both were manuals of cryptography, but, unlike its predecessor, the *Polygraphia* did not conceal secret magical formulas. Despite its apologetic intent, however, even this later work was believed by Trithemius' contemporaries to hide secret instructions and spells. It is probably due to this obscure fame that it aroused the curiosity of Garrano and his acolytes.[16]

The scope of Garrano's interests went far beyond the practice of necromancy. Besides practical magic, all the major adepts of the sect were also charged with formal heresies, likely drawn from their readings. When discussing the idea that sodomy led to the Fall of our ancestors, Garrano reportedly quoted "the doctrine of a Doctor whose name he did not remember." He was also accused of denying the immortality of the soul, of believing in God's impassibility, and of negating the divine nature of Jesus Christ, who he claimed was composed of both an earthly and a celestial nature. In a passage that contains many ambiguities, it seems that he had intimated that, as a consequence of Christ's descent into the underworld, hell was completely emptied.[17] As we have seen, he was also the one who stated that Simon of Cyrene died on the cross in place of Jesus.[18]

Garrano also did not believe in the authority of the pope, denying his power to free souls from purgatory.[19] A witness reported him as saying that, if he were to reveal all his secrets, he would ruin many people in Palermo. This threat apparently alluded to a strange rite that Garrano allegedly celebrated, which he called the "crescite et multiplicamini" (increase and multiply). According to the reports, this ceremony involved many men and women who purportedly gathered in a dark chamber lit by candles. As the candles were blown out, they would start engaging in every sort of sexual sin, including sodomy. The *Relación de causa* of his trial does not provide us with further details about this mysterious service, which recalls a long-standing tradition within western European Christianity of ritual initiation, historically attributed to groups of sorcerers and necromancers beginning in the late Middle Ages.[20]

Some of these beliefs were clearly consistent with the contents of the prohibited works read by the members of the conventicle. Garrano's reading choices were indeed characterized by a high degree of internal coherence. Trithemius was a great admirer of Pietro d'Abano (died 1316), who in turn influenced Girolamo Cardano's thought. We do not know which of Pietro d'Abano's works Garrano read and possessed. In the absence of a clear textual reference, we cannot even assume that what was referred to as a work by this author was actually one of his writings. Federico Barbierato notes that in circles that practiced magic, a "text may have been sold, lent, or presented under the title of *Clavicula Salomonis* or as a work by Pietro d'Abano" despite the fact that "it was something completely different, often an imperfect fragment whose image was enhanced by a high-sounding and eloquent title."[21] Trithemius himself criticized the proliferation of superstitious books attributed to Abano, denying that they could be ascribed to him.[22]

What is relevant here is that both Pietro d'Abano and Cardano have been recognized by historians of skepticism and unbelief as relevant links in the genesis of the opinion that revealed religions were frauds created to maintain the existing social order to the advantage of the privileged. This fact further reinforces the hypothesis that the belief in sodomy as the original sin was integrated during the sixteenth century into this wider cultural construct and that it circulated in dissenting circles for almost two centuries. Indeed, Pietro d'Abano overtly advocated for the astrological theory of the cyclical nature of religions, which itself represented an important thread within the development of the theory of the fraudulence of religion.[23] In his *Conciliator differentiarum* (The mediator between the differences, written around the beginning of the fourteenth century), Abano argued that the birth of each religion, as well as other relevant events like Noah's flood and the birth of Muḥammad, were related to favorable astral conjunctions. He also suggested a relatively rational approach to miracles, trying to reduce them to natural explanations. In his opinion, the prophets' supernatural powers could also be explained by the influences of the stars and notions of "complexions."[24]

Girolamo Cardano (1501–1576), who was also among the authors that Garrano read, was probably one of the major contributors to the transmission of this astrological theory. Cardano was a renowned mathematician whose eclectic interests embraced a wide range of disciplines. As an authoritative early modern champion of astrology, he made it his lifelong goal to restore the tradition of Ptolemaic classical astrology, which he wanted to purify from the subsequent influences of Arabic authors, who had "encrusted" its pristine body during translation in the Middle Ages. Paradoxically though, the aspect of his thought that left the most lasting legacy was precisely the only part he decided to save from this tradition: the theory of the great astrological conjunctions, which rendered all religions equal insofar as they were subject to natural cycles.[25] Along with other charges, Cardano was prosecuted by the Inquisition for having analyzed the figure of Jesus Christ through his horoscope.[26] Moreover, we know that Cardano was deeply interested in the interpretation of dreams and that he knew very well the dream interpretation by Artemidorus of Daldis (second century BCE), which was also mentioned in Garrano's list of readings.[27]

Cardano's transmission of the theory of the cyclical nature of religions was undoubtedly a source of inspiration for many radical thinkers. Campanella knew Cardano's astrology and especially his commentary on Ptolemy's *Quadripartitum.*[28] A witness in Campanella's trial reported that the Calabrese Dominican friar taught that "there were several epochs, which renewed themselves every four hundred years, making a new conjunction, and that in December 1603 the great conjunction was similar to that which took place four years after Christ's birth," and, therefore, "there [would] be great wars on earth." In this respect, Campanella was reported as recommending the study of "Cardano and other similar authors."[29] Giulio Cesare Vanini (1585–1619), too, incorporated into his *Amphitheatrum aeternae providentiae* (Amphitheater of eternal Providence, 1615) the theory of the astral conjunctions,[30] which was also evoked in one of the most notorious compendiums of atheism, the *Revived Theophrastus.* Both works recalled Cardano's horoscope of Christ and helped to situate religious astrology even more firmly in a strictly naturalistic and overtly irreligious intellectual frame.[31]

Among Cardano's works, the book that Garrano and his companions allegedly read was *De Subtilitate* (hereafter *On Subtlety*). This text was published in three main editions during Cardano's life, but we do not know which of these versions Garrano possessed.[32] The importance of this work in Renaissance culture cannot be overstated. *On Subtlety* plays a central role in the development of natural philosophy as a distinct field of analysis. Cardano's work represents an attempt to draw the foundations of natural philosophy by investigating the innermost causes of natural phenomena. The "subtleties" to which the title refers are "the feature by which things that can be sensed are grasped with difficulty by the senses, and things that can be understood are grasped with difficulty by the intellect."[33] In this definition there is an obvious allusion to a form of obscure knowledge that lies beneath the appearances of the material world, as well as to the subtleties and conundrums of the human intellect. This ambiguity in the definition raised Scaliger's severest criticism, which culminated in an accusation of esotericism and magic.[34] Despite his notoriety as an occultist, Cardano rejected the esoteric aspect of the magical tradition. Instead, he should be considered as one of the first authors who broke the silence concerning speculation regarding the hidden forces that regulated natural phenomena. In so doing, he made available to a wide audience forms of knowledge that, until then, had been considered part of an esoteric heritage meant for only a small circle of adepts.[35] For this reason, Cardano's book piqued the interest of many readers, being reprinted several times and sold in numerous copies across Europe after its first appearance.[36] The fact that Cardano used secretive magical knowledge to explain a "reformed, post-Aristotelian natural philosophy" was central to the work's success. Its popularization of seemingly esoteric wisdom attracted a wide readership among the curious, and even Cardano himself acknowledged in his autobiography that *On Subtlety* was more famous among the "multitude" than it was among the learned.[37]

As John M. Forrester has perceptively pointed out, this "multitude" can be most likely identified with "those who, in the disciplinary hierarchies of the day, were below the status of natural philosophers and theologians: mathematical practitioners, alchemists, elite craftsmen, and others who made a living from trying to understand, and exploit, natural phenomena."[38] Ludovico Garrano clearly fits this profile. He and his acolytes were probably interested in Cardano's investigation of the hidden powers of minerals, as well as the many references to demonology included in the volume.[39] However, given the allegations made against Garrano in matters of faith, it seems that the sect of necromancers from Palermo also retained some aspects of the most audacious speculations regarding religion contained in Cardano's *On Subtlety.*

Two passages in this book are particularly relevant to the crystallization of the theory of the fraudulence of religion. One is contained in book 9 ("On the Necessity and Form of Man"), which includes a lengthy reflection on the genesis of humanity. By evaluating contrasting opinions, Cardano managed to introduce a set of philosophical ideas stretching all the way back to Epicurus and Lucretius that were profoundly subversive of Christian (and Catholic) tenets. Born naked, human beings started using their reason "to find essentials: home, clothing, weapons, food." Then, "to measure out land and seas; and not satisfied with these, by planispheres, gnomons, and armillary sphere," they "summoned down to earth the wide mass of heaven, barely conceivable by the mind." To this purpose, they "established natural philosophy, and the other sciences." Then, and only then, human beings turned their minds to religion, qualified as mere "laws with which the multitude could live." Science therefore preceded religion, and it clearly occupied a higher position in the hierarchies of knowledge, leaving to religion a subsidiary role as the cement for societal values that had no relation to any genuine understanding of divine "revelation." This disconcerting passage was followed by a comparison of the "four laws"—"those of the Idols, the Jews, the Christians, and the Mohammedans"—all of which were evaluated by taking into account their pros and cons in a dispassionate way. This led Cardano to admit that even "the Mohammedans themselves have strong points." Although Christianity is finally judged as the noblest faith, it is not because of the supernatural qualities of its founder but because it is the tradition that most resonates with the basic principles of "natural law," which appear to be the ultimate yardstick for evaluating the reasonability of any religious tradition.[40]

The qualification of religions in book 9 as "laws with which the multitude could live" echoed Machiavelli's political theory of religion. In this case, it is reasonable to assume that the reference was not coincidental. Despite the fact that Cardano publicly condemned Machiavelli's work, we know that he heavily drew from the writings of the Florentine secretary.[41] The relationship between Cardano and Machiavelli did not go unnoticed at the time, as it was emphasized by the subsequent European libertine tradition. When dealing with the necessity of dissimulation in politics in his *Considérations politiques sur les coups d'Estat* (Political consideration on the coup d'état, 1639), French scholar Gabriel Naudé equated Cardano, Machiavelli, and Pierre Charron.[42] Naudé used Cardano to introduce the archetypical Machiavellian theme of the ultimately political nature of religion, thus emphasizing the political consequences of Cardano's thought by underscoring the influence of Machiavelli—and a particularly radicalized reading of Machiavelli—on the works of the eclectic mathematician and astrologer.[43] The equivalence of religion and political laws, as portrayed in *On Subtlety,* reveals Cardano's reception of a stereotyped Machiavellian idea—that religions were founded and maintained for so-called "Reasons of State." This opinion was also echoed in Garrano's trial records. According to the sources, Ludovico Garrano reportedly claimed that "the Holy Office forbade the books for reasons of State."[44] Another defendant in the same trial, Carlo di Alcamo, who came from the viceroyalty of Naples and was a Franciscan Third Order, explicitly stated that the belief in the immortality of the soul was inculcated in the populace for reasons of state, for only the threat of eternal punishment was an effective deterrent against sedition.[45] While this reference does not constitute evidence of an actual circulation of Machiavelli's works within the sect of necromancers, it is undeniable that the term "reasons of state" was often associated with a vehement suspicion of Machiavellian leanings. Although this definition does not appear in the writings of Machiavelli himself, at the time of Garrano's judicial proceeding, Clement VIII's *Index of Forbidden Books* (1596) had already conflated the vulgarization of Machiavellian thought (infamously known as "Machiavellianism") with this simplified and partially improper definition of his political theory.[46] The Italian libertine Antonio Rocco would soon associate the notion of reasons of state with his vitriolic criticism of the clerical prohibition of sodomy. In a passage of *Alcibiades the Schoolboy*, this member of the Academy of the Unknowns commented on the ban of nonreproductive intercourse by clearly stating that "many human and religious laws are founded upon this damned reason of State, so that some of them, which are execrable, are considered venerable and sacrosanct by the foolish people."[47]

The second passage of *On Subtlety* that reveals Cardano's acquaintance with the opinion that revealed religions were deceptions created to defend the social order is contained in the notorious chapter "On Demons." Here, Cardano reported a curious family memory according to which his father was able to communicate with demonic entities. As Anthony Grafton has pointed out, Cardano—despite seemingly denying the possibility of such communication—"left the reader with the clear suggestion that his father had conversed directly with spirits."[48] Apparently transcribing his father's first-person memories, Cardano described him as questioning seven demons about the immortality of the soul, to which they responded "that nothing survived of each person's own." Pressured by the queries of his human interlocutor, one of them "denied that God had created the world from eternity." In the three hours that the demons allegedly spent talking with the old Cardano, they discussed "the disputations of Averroes, although that book had not yet been found." It is not clear to which of Averroes's works this passage referred. However, the demon continued by mentioning again "the names of certain books, of which a part had been found, but a part is still undiscovered. Yet all these were works of Averroes"; indeed, the leading demon "used to call himself an Averroist openly."[49]

Cardano's reference to the Andalusian philosopher Ibn Rushd (520–594 AH/1126–1198 CE), more commonly known in Christian Europe as Averroes, is of utmost importance for the purpose of this book, as it supports the hypothesis that our dissenters' readings were linked to the development of the theory of the fraudulence of religions. The many translations of his works helped make Aristotle available, and his commentaries on the Greek philosopher were subject to materialistic interpretations that tended to emphasize the eternity of the world and the immortality of the soul. This radically skeptical interpretation of Averroes was the result of an instrumentalization and misinterpretation of his work, which was further emphasized by the guardians of orthodoxy, who had coined the pejorative term "Averroistic" to condemn a set of overtly atheistic positions that were making waves in the thirteenth century. Averroistic philosophers were associated with an ambiguously Aristotelian tendency that was characterized by an eminently rationalistic approach.[50] Nevertheless, only some of these doctrines—for instance, that of the unity of the intellect—can be attributed to Averroes. Others were eminently Aristotelian, like the belief in the eternity of the world. Still others reflected radically skeptical positions that soon became a stable element in the stereotype of the premodern radical unbeliever. They included denying life after death, hell and paradise, the incarnation and resurrection of Christ, and the virginal birth of the Messiah by Mary.[51] In the light of this stereotyped representation of his work, Averroes was interpreted by some radical early modern thinkers across Europe as an incarnation of Machiavellian dissimulation *ante-literam*, a precursor of materialism, a pantheist, and even an atheist. Despite the fact that the Latin translations of his works were widely read in the sixteenth century, these polemical stereotypes persisted and contributed to reinforcing this myth, making him the hero of some manifestations of *libertinage érudite*, especially in Italy.[52]

This materialistic interpretation of Averroes demonized by the censors and praised by radical religious dissenters in the Christian West was paired with the belief that he was the father of the legend of the three impostors, which was thought to have reached Christian Europe through the intermediation of Frederick II's court.[53] These ideas were first ascribed to him in Benvenuto da Imola's *Commentary* on Dante's *Paradise* (1379), where the author accused the Arabic philosopher of having "impudently and impiously" said that "three were the tricksters of the world, that is,

Christ, Moses, and Muḥammad, of whom Christ, for being young and unaware, was crucified."[54] This attribution, however—despite becoming a commonplace in religious disputes—was first proved incorrect by scholars in the late nineteenth century.[55] Cardano himself, like Pietro d'Abano before him, was accused of authoring a *Treatise on the Three Impostors* and of holding Averroistic leanings. Pietro d'Abano underwent two inquisitorial investigations during which his beliefs in matters of natural philosophy were strongly suspected of Averroism, as Abano narrates in his *Conciliator.* While he successfully defended himself in Paris, he did not manage to satisfy the Paduan Inquisition, in whose jails he died while waiting for his sentence—death by fire—to be fulfilled.[56]

Cardano, for his part, cannot be considered an Averroistic philosopher tout court and, despite his training at the University of Padua, was not even a typical representative of Paduan Aristotelianism. Nevertheless, in his book *De immortalitate animarum* (On the immortality of the souls, 1545), which was a response to the mortalist thesis worked out by Pietro Pomponazzi's *De immortalitate animae* (On the immortality of the soul, 1516), he largely drew on Latin translations of Averroes, who, in the treatise, was the most extensively quoted author after Aristotle himself.[57] While the book clearly advocated for Christian orthodoxy by overtly defending the immortality of the soul, its inclusion of Averroistic themes was one of the main issues that concerned the Congregation of the Index when they considered Cardano's writings. Indeed, no one kept the censors busier than Cardano. In examining the documents from the Congregation, we can see that it was precisely the implications of Cardano's natural philosophy, in its understanding of both human psychology and political-religious theories, that raised suspicions of Averroism.[58]

Antonio Partenio, the Swindler

Antonio Partenio was a citizen of the Most Serene Republic of Venice. When tried by the Venetian Inquisition in 1705, he was accused of the belief that Adam and Eve enjoyed nonreproductive intercourse in the Garden of Eden. Among the defendants investigated in this book, Partenio was the one who claimed most overtly that religions were impostures fabricated by the ruling classes to keep the people under control. In his final confession, he stated, "Religion it is nothing but the cover of political power, so as to conceal its tyranny." This pointed clarity ("cover," "conceal," "tyranny") reflects a full and mature interiorization of the libertine notion of the fraudulence of religions.[59]

Partenio, who at the time of the trial was thirty-seven years old, offered his spontaneous confession on April 8. He was in custody as part of a larger judicial proceeding that involved many Venetian citizens accused of religious nonconformity and necromancy. Once summoned before the judges, he confessed his crimes in a long and detailed deposition. He opened his statement by declaring that, about ten years earlier, he had fallen in love with a girl he was unable to marry despite having already contracted a formal betrothal. To soothe the pain provoked by this disappointment, he admitted to seeking the devil's assistance. From then on, he had constantly tried to strike a deal with the Lord of Darkness to regain the girl he loved. He specified that he had never resorted to spells or magic formulas but had limited himself to persistently invoking the devil's name. We do not know whether he added this detail to clear himself from the accusation of practicing black magic. The suspicion that he was trying to deceive the judges seems to be confirmed by his subsequent statement. He declared that, deep in his heart, he had always been willing to cheat the devil and abolish the pact if he obtained what he was yearning for.[60]

From what we can tell from his deposition, eventually he did fulfill his desires. He married the girl, but the longed-for marriage proved less blissful than expected, plagued as it was by frequent financial struggles. Finding himself unable to support his family, in despair Partenio turned again to the supernatural aid of the underworld. This time, however, he decided to shift from occasional and spontaneous prayers to a formal, ceremonial invocation. He turned to the help of a bookseller in Campo San Rocco who provided him with a copy of the *Clavicula Salomonis* and a "small book" (*un picciolo libro*) that he had heard called the *Clavis Secretorum Tritemij*, which could have been a misinterpretation of the title of Trithemius's *Clavis Steganographiae*. It could also have been a readaptation of the title of this notorious book of magic, which for profit-making purposes was transferred to a spurious or completely forged edition that was loosely related to the contents of the original. Whatever the case may be, we know from the deposition that these texts did not meet Partenio's needs. He kept looking for answers to his pressing demands by turning his attention to other volumes authored by Pietro Bailardo, Cecco d'Ascoli, and Pietro d'Abano. He eventually burned them all, probably afraid that he would attract the attention of the Inquisition.[61]

Despite the seventy years that separated their trials, the consonance between Partenio's and Ludovico Garrano's reading choices is striking. Besides the titles and authors that the two had in common—including the *Clavicula,* Pietro d'Abano, and Trithemius—Partenio mentioned other writers who, however, are perfectly aligned with the others in terms of contents. Among them, Pietro Bailardo was an important representative of magical secret knowledge.[62] Bailardo, who specialized in astrology, medicine, and alchemy, was born and lived in Salerno between the second half of the eleventh century and the first half of the twelfth. During the late Middle Ages, he was mythologized in the southern Italian regions of Campania and Abruzzi, in whose popular culture he was remembered as a magician and a necromancer endowed with extraordinary powers. Beyond this myth, scholars now generally believe that Bailardo (also known as Barliario) was also a real historical figure. Whether he joined the medical school in Salerno or not is still disputed, but it is almost certain that he favored the study of the Arabo-Islamic medical and scientific tradition.[63] We do not know which book in Partenio's possession was attributed to him.

Other authors were more strictly involved with the elaboration of the theory that institutionalized religions were frauds. Like Pietro d'Abano, Cecco d'Ascoli (Francesco degli Stabili, 1269–1327) was one of the figures historically associated with the circulation throughout medieval Europe of the theory of the great astral conjunctions. As we have already emphasized in our analysis of the works by Pietro d'Abano and Cardano, this theory was intimately connected with the development of the idea that revealed religions were not based on eternal truths, which further supported the supposition that they were ultimately nothing but well-conceived frauds. Cecco d'Ascoli was an astrologer and a mathematician active in Bologna and the first university scholar to be burned by the Inquisition during the late Middle Ages. Accused of heresy, he ran away and sought shelter in Florence, where he served Charles, duke of Calabria, and the son of the king of Naples, Robert of Anjou. Known today for his harsh polemics with Dante, during his lifetime he had a reputation as an eccentric intellectual and a magician.[64] According to the brief account of his trial and death in Giovanni Villani's (d. 1348)

Istorie Fiorentine, his alleged nonconforming ideas are consistent with most of the core themes we have already widely discussed. He allegedly thought that Christ lived with the apostles "as a loafer" and that he did not die on the cross for the redemption of humankind but died because of astral conjunctions.[65]

Partenio also eventually listed among his readings "the occult philosophy of Cornelius Agrippa, and his letters." This was a clear reference to Heinrich Cornelius Agrippa von Nettesheim's (1486–1535) *De occulta philosophia* (hereafter *On the Occult Philosophy*).[66] First drafted in 1510, this book was the most important work by Agrippa. The fact that this seminal book was dedicated to Agrippa's mentor Trithemius—who was also among Cardano's inspirations—is revealing of the internal coherence of the corpus of texts that attracted the interest of our dissenters. Given the brevity of Partenio's deposition on this matter, it remains unclear what he actually retained from this reading. It is well established, however, that the reflections on the secret powers of the natural realm developed in *On the Occult Philosophy* ultimately led to a spiritualized understanding of religious phenomena—one that clearly questioned the role of institutional churches as intermediaries between the earthly and the celestial spheres.[67] The radical nature of these ideas helps explain the fierce opposition Agrippa encountered during his life. All of Agrippa's works were highly controversial and ultimately brought him to a bad end. He died in 1535 while he was trying to dodge condemnations of his writings and while he was in prison, probably at the order of Francis I of France. Twenty years later, his works would formally be condemned by Paul IV, being placed on the *Index of Forbidden Books* (1559). Long before his death, however, Agrippa had already raised suspicions. After studying the humanities, theology, law, and medicine, and while working as a university professor, he was accused of Judaizing by the inquisitor of Dôle (and prior of the Franciscan order) Jean Catilinet for having taught texts by the Christian cabalist Johannes Reuchlin (1455–1522). Besides his interest in magic, it is clear that other aspects of Agrippa's work align him with the cultural climate in which the idea of sodomy as the first act of disobedience against God began to circulate: themes of sexuality and gender, together with a radical critique of Church fundamentalism, emerge prominently from his writings. Agrippa's engagement with these issues is exemplified by his writings in support of female dignity

(*Declamatio de nobilitate et praecellentia foeminei sexus* [Declamation on the nobility and preeminence of the female sex]) and by a now lost treatise against the workings of the Inquisition.[68] We also may wonder whether Partenio was aware that Agrippa was known for authoring an influential treatise on original sin that long before had contributed to establishing a sexualized interpretation of the biblical narrative of the Fall. When he was around thirty-two years old, Agrippa wrote his *De originali peccato declamatio* (Declamation on the original sin), which was published in 1529 and 1532. The treatise's provocative sexual contents made the historian of ideas Antonello Gerbi list Agrippa's work as one of the more explicit early modern testimonies of the belief that the first lapse of our ancestors consisted of carnal knowledge.[69] The *Declamation*'s sexual bluntness is undeniably provocative. The author's dependence on Hermetic sources is equally explicit.[70] The *Declamation* was published when Agrippa was in Antwerp as Emperor Charles V's historiographer and archivist, but he had worked on it between 1518 and 1519, when he was staying in Metz, the then-imperial city that is today in northern France. While serving as a lawyer and a diplomat for the city government, he lectured on theology at the local Celestine monastery, where he discussed with his friend Claude Dieudonné the biblical exegesis of the Fall. Dieudonné, who later became Protestant, was also the *trait d'union* between Agrippa and Jacques Lefèvre d'Étaples, the famous French humanist and theologian who published an influential edition of the 1505 *Corpus Hermeticum,* which had a lasting impact on Agrippa's work. As he declared in a note to the text, it was precisely this work that provided the philosophical substratum of his sexual interpretation of original sin.[71]

Whether or not Partenio was aware that Agrippa had authored a treatise on original sin filled with sexual allusions remains uncertain. What is clear, however, is that none of Partenio's readings served his original purpose of finding a way to invoke the devil to deal with his financial setbacks. When he realized that these works did not meet his expectations, Partenio decided to turn from books to the help of experienced advisers. The events he described in his testimony occurred about six years before his trial, and the story is a complex account of entangled vicissitudes of magical practice and trickery, circles, magic operations, treasure seeking, and demonic invocations.[72] These were all undertakings that, at the time of his deposition, he rejected (in his formulaic wording, he "anathematized, detested, and abominated" them).[73] While this could have been a strategy to deceive the judges, he declared that he regretted involving and tricking gullible people, admitting that he had claimed to be invested with supernatural powers, which he knew he did not possess.[74]

The final part of Partenio's deposition shifts from his morally questionable career as a swindler to a list of errors in matters of faith. Once again, we note how these views were consistent with those attributed to the other dissenters examined in this book, just as they aligned with the broader themes that might be inferred from the books Partenio had consulted throughout his tortuous career as a necromancer. He introduced this section by claiming that he often spoke out against Catholic orthodoxy. Partenio stated that he had frequently denied the existence of hell and purgatory and also the immortality of the rational soul. As previously noted in Chapter 4, he discussed predestination in connection with the belief that "all can be saved in their own law." With regard to this aspect, the persistence in Venice of themes that had been widely debated since the first wave of Italian evangelism is worth noting.[75] When Partenio was put on trial, the activity of the inquisitors was directed mostly toward containing the spread of a generalized unorthodoxy whose outlines were rather undefined but could loosely be characterized as irreligiousness, unbelief, and even atheism. The inquisitors were also engaged in containing the spread of magic and necromancy and monitoring the discipline of the clergy, especially in sexual matters. The control of Lutheranism, Calvinism, and other doctrinally structured, formalized heresies had already waned by the late sixteenth century. Partenio's reference to predestination and salvation, however, shows that, even in this new early eighteenth-century scenario, themes that were relevant to sixteenth-century Italian reformers continued to be discussed and merged with the manifestations of radical unbelief that appeared later in the Venetian public arena. Later discussions of these themes can be read as a sign of the failure of the Inquisition to eradicate the seeds of religious dissent, due in part to the difficulties that it encountered in establishing firm control in the city.[76]

Partenio's confession seems to be in line with this climate of relative freedom. He admitted that privately and publicly he "eerily interpreted many passages of the Scriptures." To exonerate himself, he emphasized that he did so "out of a passing fancy," as if he was denouncing the "excessive" freedom he enjoyed while, at the same time, inviting the inquisitors not to take his pronouncements too seriously. Partenio confessed that he had asserted many times that he had cursed "the devotions practiced in churches," adding that fasting was not commanded by God but by men who wanted "to profit from fishing." He also denied the efficacy of sacramental confession. The Mass, in his opinion, was just a ruse to fill up priests' purses. He also advocated against the pope's temporal power, wishing that the head of the Catholic Church would be degraded to the status of a bishop, instead of having that of a monarch. He publicly stated that he had envied the heretics, but only for their wealth. Here, he was probably referring to the prosperity of the merchants coming from northern Europe, who were allowed to engage in commerce rather freely in Venice. He denied the value of indulgences and harshly criticized the workings of the Holy Office for using torture to uncover the intentions of the defendants and interfere in matters that had nothing to do with heresy. He wanted to see the religious tribunal's authority diminished not only in words but in actual practice. In one instance, he actively pursued this goal by paying a lawyer to assist a man who was in the Inquisition's custody, eventually ensuring that the trial never took place.[77]

Moreover, during the vacancy of the Holy See, the period between the death of one pope and the election of another, he wrote many satires addressed to dead pontiffs and the conclave, taking particular aim at the cardinals. We do not know which one of the conclaves that took place during his life was subject to Partenio's gibes. However, we have firm evidence that his verses were not the result of an individualistic whim. He stated that he "composed the satires for a young man who paid for them." While Partenio claimed that he did not know the name of the purchaser, he identified another partner in crime, a priest whom he gave a copy of the manuscripts, which ended up burned and destroyed (apparently to try to cover up judicial evidence after suspicions had already been aroused). The original was given to another priest, a certain Father Alzenago.[78] This underscores how widely radically dissenting ideas circulated in Venice. The Most Serene Republic offered an environment where publicly criticizing religious tenets and the authority of the Church was a way not only to assert one's discontent with the status quo and surround oneself with an air of wit and provocative respectability but also to make occasional profits.

Partenio further stated that he had "maintained with some firmness of opinion the motion of the earth."[79] This reference to the heliocentric theory shows how different cultural currents could converge in the intellectual trajectories of individuals who felt uncomfortable with the Catholic Church's traditional responses to the most puzzling questions about the world and human beings' place in that world. The association between writings on magic like the *Clavicula Salomonis,* the works of Trithemius, and the writings of Agrippa and the opinions inspired by experimental methods like the heliocentric theory reveals the eclectic approach to knowledge that many seventeenth- and eighteenth-century dissenters embraced. Such a realization invites us to rethink excessively compartmentalized interpretations of early modern cultural and intellectual phenomena that are often interpreted as being opposed to each other, such as magic and libertinism, on the one hand, and the modern experimental sciences, on the other.[80]

Partenio's stance that religions were the "cover" of political power was immediately followed by the admission that "[he] believed with [his] intellect that Adam committed the sin of sodomy with Eve."[81] He was hardly unique among Venetians, as we can see from other inquisitorial cases. In 1679, Marco Visonio, who was a *sollecitatore di palazzo* (a kind of legal procurator); the violinist Carlo Plati; and an unidentified German priest were described in a judicial proceeding as often frequenting the house of the prostitute Zanetta Burchiereta. One day the three allegedly engaged in a discussion during which Marco interrogated the priest about "what it was that had been forbidden to Adam in the beginning of the world." While the priest confirmed the orthodox view that God forbade an apple, Marco urged him to reconsider his position because, he stated, "it wasn't true that God had forbidden the apple, but that he had forbidden sins against nature, and that this is the reason why he [Adam] sinned."[82] Partenio's mention of the belief that sodomy was the first act of human disobedience in his confession is limited to the pointy assertion reported above. Yet in the same line of his confession, he associated this with the notion that religion was a fraud. Although the connection between the two statements is not made explicit in his confession, the cumulative evidence gathered thus far strongly suggests that this association was far from coincidental. Given his list of readings and his bluntness in denouncing the fraudulence of religion, it is reasonable to hypothesize that he was aware of the libertine interpretation of the prohibition of sodomy and that it was at least in part through his reading that he came to interpret the belief that the Fall from Grace was caused by Adam and Eve's anal intercourse through these lenses.

CHAPTER SIX

Hadriaan Beverland's *On Original Sin*

THE BELIEF that Adam and Eve had anal sex in the Garden of Eden also emerged in seventeenth-century written culture, where it was linked in different degrees to the theory of the fraudulence of religions as that was taking shape in libertine circles across Europe. This chapter and Chapter 7 will explore the continuity between the written and oral circulation of this belief. When transmitted orally, these opinions could be sharply framed; when put into print, they gained theoretical sophistication but lost some of their unapologetic radicality. Manuscript and print works provided rational arguments that were incomparably more refined and cogent in their deconstruction of traditional views than the piquant opinions our dissenters shared in taverns and on street corners. None of these texts, however, went so far as to attribute sodomitic preferences to God himself.

The belief that sodomy was the first act of rebellion against God's commands is discussed in one of the most scandalous books of the seventeenth century, Hadriaan Beverland's *De Peccato Originali* (hereafter *On Original Sin*; two editions, 1678 and 1679). In this work, Beverland reviewed a vast repertoire of texts intending to prove his deepest conviction concerning the fate of postlapsarian humanity: that the Fall was caused by a sexual infraction and that, ever since, humankind had been irredeemably stained by lust. Beverland placed a particularly explicit account of Adam and Eve's sodomy among a jumble of erudite references on sexual themes drawn from classical and contemporary literature, Christian theology, rabbinic traditions, and philosophical reflections. Reference to Renaissance Italian erotica is crucial to this narrative. When dealing with Adam and Eve's anal intercourse, Beverland quoted the Italian humanist and bishop Giovanni Della Casa. We also know from extraliterary sources that this idea reached Beverland's circle of friends through the intermediation of a German humanist residing in Italy, who was linked to ecclesiastic circles in Rome. This reference is consistent with the evidence collected so far and therefore allows us to establish a direct link between the circulation of this idea in the Italian peninsula and its reception in Dutch academic environments.

Beverland and his circle discussed the most innovative contributions of contemporary philosophers like Thomas Hobbes and Baruch Spinoza, and, although Beverland himself cannot be considered a Spinozist tout court, his approach to the Scriptures was strongly indebted to the method of biblical criticism developed by the philosopher. In *On Original Sin,* Beverland established a direct connection between Spinoza's divinization of nature and the tradition of Italian Renaissance naturalism and drew both Spinoza and the Italian libertine author Giulio Cesare Vanini into the genesis of the theory of the fraudulence of religions.

Sex in the Garden

Beverland was obsessed with proving that sex was the original sin. Although he was smart enough to introduce a brief passage where he commented, in line with the Reformed and Catholic interpretation of the Scriptures, that "transgression, disobedience, and ambition, as well as self-love and depraved calculation have preceded intercourse," he framed this brief, "orthodox" passage within a number of quotations derived from refined literary material that supported the belief that the first transgression consisted of sexual intercourse.[1] Despite his tendency to overquote, the first account of the Fall reported in his text is

Beverland's original creation. It brims with sexual innuendos and baroque literary inventiveness, in a kaleidoscopic rendition of the whirls of sensations and urges that struck Adam and Eve once they surrendered to temptation. His fervid description of Eve's reaction after hearing the mellifluous voice of the snake gives a sense of this:

> She gets carried away by a frenzy and rising heat, she growls, loses control over her bladder and her stomach disobeys, she is wet. The sounds and sights make the pent-up urine flow. She is in heat, desirous, obtrusive, and promiscuous like young cattle in a stable. She rushes bereft of her mind and rages, inflamed, through the whole city. Until the little virgin, in whose body the fatal arrow sticks fast, contemplates the very desirable extended tree stem, apt and pleasing to her sex, goes to her husband with a wanton face and embraces his neck. She kisses him and he does not resist, lavishes his leg and arms with serrated mouth, and rouses his very innocent member with her wanton hand and flattering words that have fingers. . . . In this way, she gave her body to her man through the accursed appetite for his hard member.[2]

This inventive sexual interpretation of original sin echoes, and magnifies, Agrippa's previously mentioned work on original sin. Beverland acknowledged authoritativeness of the German humanist and philosopher, while simultaneously (and awkwardly) trying to minimize his own dependence on him. He opens his praise of Agrippa by stating, quite improbably, that only "about two days ago" he "learned that Cornelius Agrippa . . . agree[d] with the opinion" that the original sin consisted in the discovery of sex. Besides this forgivable affectation, Beverland celebrated Agrippa's merits with admirable courage—and probably some lightheartedness—given the *damnatio memoriae* that burdened his work: "Cornelius Agrippa, a man who has been praised and must now be praised above others here, a man of marvelous intellect."[3]

In several passages of *On Original Sin,* Beverland mentioned many different opinions about the botanical symbolization of sexual pleasure and genital anatomy, taken from both the Christian and classical traditions. The encyclopedic style of these passages celebrates both the author's erudition and the immense variety of human creativity when it comes to honoring or despising the pleasures of love.[4] Beverland strategically used the longest list of plant metaphors in the text, reported in chapter 7, to contrast this diversity with his conviction that the biblical Tree of Knowledge was to be interpreted as a metaphor for the erect penis: "Therefore the tree forbidden by the Supreme Legislator to the first mortals, was not a bush or branch, nor its fruit, wild strawberries, red fruits with a more wine-like juice, or in another species the very abundant Figtree," nor was it "a peach tree" or "a grapevine or grape, or quince" or "wheat or nuts or cherrytrees" or "Pomegranates or a peartree or appletree, very pleasing for its fruit." Instead, Beverland claims that it was the "male bird, with which the gladiator shines, the young man beams, the man exists, the paterfamilias is celebrated. Placing a crown on this scepter, the wife becomes one with her man, so that the two remain one in the act, while they are joined together, sticking closely to each other with the glue of Venus, so that you would dare to swear the two are becoming one in their bond."[5] By following this stream of associations, Beverland not only stressed the ubiquity of sexual desire but also reaffirmed the patriarchal centrality of the male member, the subordination of the female sex to the penis, and the superiority of vaginal intercourse to other forms of pleasure seeking.

How, then, does the belief that Adam and Eve enjoyed the pleasures of sodomy in the Garden of Eden fit with all of this? The idea that they indulged in anal sex is reported by Beverland in chapter 11: "Hence it has been brought about that the Church Fathers and the most learned priests in the church's eminent hierarchy have affirmed that the first transgression of those first created was simply that Eve, turned around and on hands and knees, had awkwardly presented her narrow asshole (which Casa, that porcupine suffering from piles, proclaimed as the *Fornellino* [the Little Oven]), to Adam and he, still unwell from the dinner of the previous night, approached it."[6] Beverland then indulged in a tirade against the decadence of the present state of humanity by emphasizing the number of Eve's "granddaughters, who one moment enjoy being taken looking at their man and the next from behind and gratify in this way their ill-advised longing for a scandalous love affair."[7] This last passage clearly picks up the idea that women were the originators of sodomitic proclivity.

With his characteristic dissembling approach, Beverland immediately distanced himself from this interpretation of the Fall: "However, because there is not a single syllable of this slippery attitude in the text [i.e., the Scriptures], I hardly had the courage to approve this view based on conjectures with my vote." He added soon after that his "conscience" and the "light" of his "heart" had already demonstrated that his view—that the original sin was vaginal intercourse—"[was] more in line with the utterances of God." Here he quite blatantly contradicts what he has stated just a few lines earlier, where he claimed that Adam and Eve's sodomy was not "impossible or unspeakable" or "so far from the truth" and that those who had not "feared to support it with both thumbs" were "the more judicious interpreters."[8]

Beverland references Giovanni Della Casa's (1503–1556) *Capitolo del Forno* (hereafter *Chapter on the Oven*), revealing his dependence on Italian Renaissance erotic literature when it comes to dealing with the most irreverent subjects. Della Casa's composition was renowned as an irreverent poetic dissertation on sodomy. A prominent ecclesiastic, who was made archbishop of Benevento and papal nuncio in Venice by his protector Pope Paul III, he is better known for the famous dialogue *Il Galateo* (posthumously published in 1581). In his youth, he authored verses of Bernesque poetry, including the notorious *Chapter on the Oven.* This poem, modeled on the burlesque rhetoric of Berni's poetry, supported different layers of interpretation. While the manifest meaning was a praise of the bread and the oven, between the lines was hidden an exaltation of sexual pleasure. Despite mostly praising heterosexual intercourse, some passages of Della Casa's poem clearly alluded to homosexual sodomy. These suggestions haunted Della Casa's reputation in his later years, fueling the black legend of the poem *In laudem pederastiae seu sodomiae* (In praise of pederasty or sodomy), or *De laudibus sodomiae* (On the praises of sodomy), which was falsely attributed to him. He was gained notoriety among anti-Catholic propagandists for having become an inquisitor later in life.[9] Della Casa's notoriety had repercussions for Beverland during the latter's 1679 trial after the publication of *On Original Sin,* when the Synod of Gouda and the States of Holland accused him of reprinting Della Casa's *Chapter on the Oven,* among other charges. The judges referred to a 1678 printed text probably published anonymously, without indication of place and titled *Rime di autori diversi* (Rhymes of different authors). The text included four Italian poems accompanied by Latin translations. The compositions were Della Casa's *Chapter on the Oven*, Giovanni Mauro's *In lode di Priapo* (In praise of Priapus), Giovanni Francesco Bini's *Del mal Francese* (On the French disease), and Francesco Maria Molza's *Capitolo in lode dei fichi* (Chapter in praise of the figs). One of the accusers believed that Beverland was responsible for the Latin translations and was involved in the publication of the work.[10]

Beverland characterized the allusion to Adam and Eve's sodomy as one of the most scandalous opinions reported in his treatise. In the context of the chapter in which this opinion was mentioned, it occupied an important place in the author's reflections on the state of humanity after the Fall. Chapter 11 begins with a series of allusive references to procreativity and fertility on one side and infertility and death on the other. Here, original sin was depicted as a malign form of fecundation, which planted the seeds of a monstruous breed in the bosom of humanity:

> Humankind, therefore, allured and made pregnant by his own lust, has conceived and given birth to sin, which brought forth complete death. This lethal arrow, which the demon planted, remains stuck in our body. This wound cannot be healed with any dittany, as it has formed into an intricate crust deep inside our marrow. In fact, the ubiquitous adultery of humankind is evident, as they are bound by every type and kind of wickedness and having sex with prostitutes and turning away from God.

From then on, "Corrupted Adam begets corrupted offspring, not in the image of God, which he had wasted, but in his own image."[11] This reflection introduced a long digression on nonreproductive sexual intercourse, which was sealed by the sodomitic account of the Fall, placed at the end of the chapter. Between the introduction and the conclusion, Beverland provided the reader with a list of sexual practices worthy of the Marquis de Sade: "It is not one type of spittle that torments the minds of people: there are masturbators, lesbians, men who jerk off, women who jerk off, poo-eaters, practitioners of cunnilingus" and also "pederasts, sodomites, catamites," along with "those who submit to anal sex and men or boys who offer sex for money, masculine lesbians," and, likewise, "those who either mount or submit to animals, and drinkers of menstrual blood." The list goes on, including "bearded men who cheat on their wives with other men," who "are known everywhere, as are castrated male prostitutes, sissies, chick-squeezers [pedophiles], and other grandsons of Romulus who wiggle their arses, have polluted a pond or waters, have stained mother earth."[12]

This long list is connected to the opinion that Adam and Eve had anal intercourse in the Garden of Eden by a concise quotation from Catullus: "All things licit and wicked mingled together in mad fury."[13] Given the structure of the chapter, therefore, it seems that Beverland used the sodomitic account of the Fall as an explanation for the widespread desire to seek sexual gratification outside the boundaries of heterosexual, vaginal intercourse. But if Beverland rejected as foolishness the sodomitic interpretation of the Fall, how then do we take seriously his distancing, given that he acknowledged as fact the ubiquity of what someone might now call "sexual perversions"? Where do these yearnings come from?

To answer these questions, we need to go back to Beverland's first, dramatic depiction of the Fall. There the author connected the instant when Adam became suddenly aware of his mistake—uttering the desperate exclamation "Oh shameful deed!"—and those moments when "one tends to be disgusted with the fulfilled sexual act following the wickedness of *certain ways*" (emphasis added). But what were the "certain ways" Beverland was alluding to? In the immediately preceding passages, the author described Adam and Eve's enjoyment by stating, "Finding fulfillment in the mutual staining of lust and wickedness, the two perfidious creatures ate the mellow *apples* and ripe *grapes*, plucking *from both sides.*"[14] Here, Beverland used the same botanical metaphors that he would soon dismiss in the patriarchal celebration of vaginal intercourse that we quoted earlier. The reference to the act of "plucking from both sides," however, is a clear sexual innuendo that might contain an allusion to either vaginal sex from behind or anal intercourse. Which of the two options he was winking at, however, is an issue that is probably destined to remain buried underneath the surface of his convoluted and baroque Latin prose. Many hints, however, seem to suggest that, despite condemning it, Beverland took the hypothesis that sodomy was the first lapse quite seriously. Why would he otherwise refer to two distinct fruits when alluding to intercourse occurring in "both sides"?

Beverland, Libertinism, and Social Reform

Indeed, Beverland concealed his genuine convictions with a complex writing strategy that makes it particularly difficult to interpret the real meaning of his text. He acknowledged this approach in the introductory remarks to his work. *On Original Sin* began with a dedication to his stepfather Bernard de Gomme,[15] followed by an open epistle addressed to his close friend Jacob de Goyer, a Dutch lawyer, whom he referred to as an "initiate of more elegant learning" (Elegantioris Sophiae Initiato). De Goyer (1651–1689) was among the inner circle of Beverland's friends, a group of scholars whom he met while he moved through many Dutch universities as a student in training. Beverland enrolled in the Latin School of Middelburg in 1663, starting a brilliant career as a scholar of Latin and the humanities. He earned a degree at the University of Franeker in 1669, after which, in 1672, he spent a year at the University of Oxford, where he researched and studied at the Bodleian Library. When he returned to the Netherlands, he completed his studies in Leiden, Franeker, and Utrecht, receiving his doctorate in 1677. It was during these formative years that he established the relationships that would leave an indelible mark on his life. Beverland's close circle, which he called the *Initiati* (the initiated ones), was made up of scholars who were (or would soon become) professors of theology, law, and the classics. Along with de Goyer, this inner group also included Nicolaas Heinsius (1621–1681), Isaac Vossius (1618–1689), and Johann Georg Graevius (1632–1703).[16]

As he stated in the preface to *On Original Sin,* Beverland published the three books of his former work *De Prostibulis veterum* (On the prostitution of the ancients) with the intention of sharing their contents with the *Initiati* only. *On Original Sin* winked at this restricted circle of perceptive readers; indeed, several passages were directly addressed to an "initiate man." In the preface, Beverland emphasized how long the real meaning of the Fall had been kept secret before he eventually attempted to unveil the truth. He remarked, "Among the leaders of the early church some bishops and elders seem to favour my opinion, yet I do not know whether they explained it correctly and thoroughly. *You,* meanwhile, *sharp-sighted* man, will be able to see and judge it with the *trustworthiness of sight.*"[17] Beverland, thus, attributed prophetic qualities to those who he wished to be able to decipher his hidden message. This reference to the shrewd ones clearly recalls libertine, elitist strategies of concealment.

As Karen E. Hollewand has noted, whether Beverland can be considered a libertine tout court is a highly controversial matter. Certainly, he was fundamentally an elitist who did not want his message to reach the fringes of society and the uncultivated "populace." *On Original Sin* was hard to read even for the most educated seventeenth-century bibliophiles.[18] Yet, unlike many libertine authors, Beverland did not exclusively address his work to a narrow circle of intimate friends. While the *Initiati* were clearly the ideal recipients of the hidden meaning of *On Original Sin,* the text also contained a more overt and explicit political agenda. Beverland openly fought for a concrete reform of sexual morals. With his words, he was advocating for the entire learned community in Dutch society to tear off the veil that concealed the truth about sex. This engagement with contemporary societal attitudes toward sex, and his willingness to subvert them, distinguished Beverland's actions from the traditional strategies of concealment adopted by libertines and was the main cause of Beverland's isolation during his prosecution. Once his closest friends understood the scope of his ambitions, they betrayed him. His audacity had gone too far. In the last chapter of the book, Beverland denounced the hypocrisy of contemporary Dutch society. He shamed his learned peers, who publicly condemned sex while privately indulging in the most refined sexual mischief. After exposing their shortcomings, Beverland pointed the finger at the representatives of the Dutch Reformed Church ("These are the men who attack me with their forked tongue").[19] By emphasizing the ubiquity of sexual desire, Beverland was advocating for a more humane approach to sexual morality. He was not calling for an unrestrained free-for-all. What he had in mind was a more realistic, sympathetic understanding of the role sex played in orienting human behaviors, in spite of the hypocritical facade erected by conformists.

The final pages of *On Original Sin* sound like a humble confession, a call for honesty, a cry of despair against the cruelty of moralists, which broke the injunction to secrecy and concealment among contemporary libertine writers. While publicly depicting himself as a humble penitent, conscious of his weakness, Beverland asked others to follow his example: "Let us not like Cain flee from sight of God, but filled with shame like Mary

Magdalen behind Jesus Christ—in memory of whose very noble person we must bow our head—invoke Him as our judge, but also as our protector. Finally, like the tax-collector Zachaeus and Prudentius let us be ashamed of and repent for the past impudence and wanton playfulness."[20]

This desire to break the veil of hypocrisy that covered sexual matters cost Beverland his career and, eventually, his mental stability. The publication of *On Original Sin* led to his arrest, trial, and banishment from the republic. The Dutch Reformed Church, toward which he was so harsh, played a crucial role in his ostracization. The States of Holland pressured the University of Leiden to solve this thorny issue. The university handled the trial, as was customary, within its own special court. University courts tended to settle issues involving scholars and students with moderation and tact, so as to primarily preserve the honor of the institution. Beverland, however, faced an exceptionally harsh treatment. In 1669, he surrendered to all the conditions imposed on him by the court. He promised not to deal with scandalous matters any longer, to hand over the manuscript of *On the Prostitution of the Ancients,* and to accept his banishment from the provinces of Holland and Zeeland, temporarily establishing himself in Utrecht. The situation, however, grew worse for him when the theologian Leonard van Rijssen (1631–1716) published in Gorinchem the *Justa detestatio sceleratissimi libelli Adriani Beverlandi, "De Peccato originali"* (On the just abhorrence of Hadriaan Beverland's most wicked book, *On Original Sin,* 1680), a long text that was entirely devoted to dismantling Beverland's work. His life and moral conduct, as well as his ideas, were again under the spotlight, and Beverland chose to cross the Channel and start a new life in England.[21] There, Beverland felt increasingly isolated. He developed anxiety and paranoia that, from his epistles, appear to have verged on madness. Poor and rejected, he died in London on December 14, 1716. He had had two daughters by a woman named Rebecca Tibbith, whom he never married. In his altered state of mind, he was convinced that she had not been faithful and that their last daughter, Anna, was not his. He left them almost nothing in his testament. The epitaph on his headstone in the yard of Saint Paul's Church in Covent Garden, however, mentions Isaac Voissus and Nicolaas Heinsius, his fellow scholars and juvenile friends, by whom he felt abandoned and betrayed.[22]

Atheism

Beverland was also accused of atheism. He believed that this allegation was used by those who had no better response to his thesis, but his work certainly contains many example of what others took as irreligiousness.[23] When writing the entry on the *Book of the Three Impostors* in his *Dictionnaire historique* (hereafter Dictionary), Prosper Marchand listed Beverland among the links in the chain of transmission that spread the belief that Moses, Jesus, and Muḥammad tricked humanity with their lies. Marchand mentions two titles attributed to Beverland, the *Epistolium ad Batavum, in Britannia hospitem, De tribus impostoribus* (Short letter on the Three Impostors to the Dutch hosted in Britain), and *A Discovery of the Three Impostors, Turd Sellers, Slanderers, and Piss-Sellers by Seignor Perin del Vago.*[24] These little pamphlets report episodes of a feigned epistolary exchange between Beverland and the fictional character Perini del Vago, which was published approximately between 1702 and 1710 in London.[25] The letters brimmed with paranoia and conspiracy theories, and they give one of the most vivid indications of the inexorable decline of the author's mental health during his English exile.[26] In spite of their titles, however, the *Little Epistle* and the *Discovery of the Three Impostors* are not significant in the history of the transmission of the legend of the three impostors. They were written in an attempt to counter three English bishops who he believed were intent on restraining the licentiousness of his writings.[27] It is hard to believe that a knowledgeable man like Beverland, so deeply involved in the intellectual disputes of his day, was unaware of the implications of including a reference to the three impostors in two of his published works. One wonders whether he wanted to draw attention to himself at a moment when, perhaps as a consequence of his weakening mental stability, he thought he was falling into oblivion. Whether or not this was his intent, these texts attracted the interest of his contemporaries. Besides Marchand, we know that the German bibliophile Peter Friedrich Arpe (1682–1740), long associated with the circulation of the legend of the three impostors, acquired a copy of Beverland's epistles, possibly when he was drafting his *Apologia pro Vanino* (1712), dedicated to the Italian humanist and philosopher Giulio Cesare Vanini.[28]

Vanini was one of the most radical representatives of Italian libertinism, a daring intellectual who paid the price for his intellectual audacity by being burned at the stake as a heretic in Toulouse in 1619.[29] Arpe probably thought that Beverland's epistles might have contained some elements of interest regarding his research on the Italian dissenter; in his *Dictionary*, Marchand noted that Beverland had included Vanini in his genealogy of the theory that organized religions were frauds.[30] Beverland included this attribution in the first section of *On Original Sin*. In chapter 5, Beverland alludes to his need to cleanse his work from the accusation of atheism.[31] To distance himself from irreligiousness, Beverland condemned Giulio Cesare Vanini, Virgil, and Girolamo Cardano as the founders of the astrological theories of religion, which held that historical faiths were subject to a cyclical rhythm that included their origin, development, and decadence. As with other natural phenomena, these cycles were regulated by astral influences. In Beverland's words, Vanini "teaches that with the finger of that God, enclosed within the eighth celestial sphere, everything is brought to perfection through the influence of the heavenly bodies." Beverland conflated this with the belief that "Moses, Christ, and Mohammed were therefore lawgivers from the stars and through the destiny of the stars Judaism yielded to Christianity and Christianity yielded to Islam." He closed this passage by stating, "The impious man wickedly raves that, like Ninus by the sorcerer Zoroaster and Apollonius by astrology, many other lawgivers have deceived the world in the same way and with the same guilefulness." He then closes with a trenchant quote from Horace's *Carmina*: "Nothing is difficult for mortals, even heaven itself is reached through stupidity." This passage also needs to be read within the wider context of *On Original Sin*. In the following lines, Beverland associates Vanini with Spinoza: "O crooked minds, empty of heavenly things! My age has also seen a true descendant of Lucian, namely Spinoza, who based on Hobbes's hypothesis, honours no God apart from that fixed order of nature or destined sequence of natural phenomena."[32]

Did the condemnatory tones with which Beverland depicts the genealogy of atheism reflect his real convictions, or were they part of a concealment strategy? To attempt an answer, we need to shift our attention to the second part of *On Original Sin*, which, in the 1679 edition, is mainly focused on a biblical exegesis that is reminiscent of Spinoza's scriptural criticism. Beverland here explicitly criticizes Spinoza as "a Jew turned sceptic and a disciple of Celsus."[33] However, he devotes chapters 18–19—the longest of the entire book, numbering sixty pages out of a total of 167—to dismantling the inconsistences of the biblical text. He emphasizes the problems connected to its multiple redactions, the accumulation of different, contradicting versions, and the crystallization of different canons (with the arbitrary dynamic of inclusions and exclusions that that implies). Beverland meticulously accomplishes this task before erupting in a cry of despair: "For how many errors have the notaries, scribes, assistants, booksellers, and printers committed, through whose negligence and weakness many things have been put into disarray! It is like the rules of the kitchen have been turned into a mess by a naughty child with various fluids. A perspicacious man will also see many matters have become disfigured."[34] He exclaimed all this despite later claiming, "These subtleties do not at all shake our faith," distancing himself from Spinoza and Hobbes, who were portrayed as epitomes of wantonness.[35] Despite this brief apology, Beverland dismissed blind faith in the Scriptures when he mocked "the phalanxes of the Council of Trent," which "threaten with a shirt of flame: 'The Vulgate must be considered as the original text in public lectures, disputations, expositions, and sermons.'" This he immediately and bluntly dismissed as "Nonsense."[36] He criticized the Protestants, and especially the Dutch Reformed Church, as equally nonsensical, for their reverence of the vernacular Bible, which they worshipped without taking into account the many problems raised by translating the Hebrew and Greek originals into modern languages.[37]

Isn't this a tribute to Spinoza's biblical criticism? The relationship between Beverland and Spinoza has already been explored meticulously. Jonathan Israel considered Beverland a representative of late seventeenth-century Spinozism in the Dutch Republic, and the Dutch historian of philosophy Wiep van Bunge emphasizes Beverland's contributions to the early Enlightenment and the spread of Cartesianism.[38] Jetze Touber's sees Beverland's criticism of the Scriptures as providing hints into the conflation of biblical antiquarianism and Spinozian textual criticism in seventeenth-century Dutch intellectual circles.[39] While biblical history and antiquarianism were tools theologians often used to deepen the knowledge of sacred texts, the conclusions Dutch intellectuals reached from their rigorous analysis sometimes led to disconcerting results. The proliferation of critical approaches to the Scriptures facilitated the assimilation of Spinozian criticism into the erudite speculations of learned bibliophiles and literary antiquarians.[40]

At the core of Beverland's works was an effort to prove the ubiquity of sexual desire, and he used whatever textual material he could to make his point. By attacking the credibility of the Bible, Beverland claimed his right to restore what he believed to be the proper meaning of the foundational myth of the Fall: that Adam and Eve had committed a sexual infraction and that humanity had been governed by lust ever since. What mattered was proving that lust had been the force driving the whole world since the Fall.[41]

The Gifts of Nature

Beverland concluded his tirade against Vanini, Spinoza, and Hobbes by claiming, "These are speculating impostors under the feigned and concealed appearance of an atheist." He quickly added, "Please forgive my abuse of the term [atheist] for the latter considered nature and the other the sun to be God." In Beverland's opinion, the fact that Spinoza conflated God and nature does not imply that he denied the existence of God. But then what did he mean when writing that they "feigned" and "concealed" the appearance of an atheist? By stating that they believed in a divinized Nature, was Beverland trying to subtly defend them from the accusation of atheism? Was he distinguishing atheism and pantheism? Was he suggesting that his Dutch contemporaries were actually projecting onto Vanini and Spinoza an atheism that did not correspond with their true convictions? Or was he embracing this radicalized framing of their thoughts while making it clear that he was cultivated enough to notice that it stretched their real message? There is no simple answer. Beverland accompanied his ambiguous condemnation of atheism with a statement that aimed to prove the indubitable existence of God. Yet he did so not on the authority of the Scriptures or of any religious institution but solely by celebrating the wonders of nature, through which the Creator shines in the eyes of the openhearted beholder. Among the many available proofs of the existence of God, this was certainly more compatible with the naturalism of Vanini and Spinoza: "On the basis of the bubbling spring of living waters," Beverland writes, "we know that the Almighty had existed in eternity. Raise your face upwards and turn your raised faces and eyes to the stars and see who created those and via His creations you will ascend the stairs to God."[42]

Nature is therefore the key to understanding the mysteries of God. Read in this light, Beverland's attitudes toward nature sound dangerously heterodox, particularly when extended to the important role played by nature in his speculations on human sexuality. His approach was twofold. He did not attempt to diminish the sinfulness of sex and pleasure, interpreting the unbearable and omnipresent cravings of sexual desire as the punishment we all have to pay for the fault of our ancestors. Yet the assumption that original sin was sex was essentially heterodox. This duplicity left him oscillating between obsessive rumination on the pain inflicted by sex on human beings to an overt and glamorous celebration of sexual debauchery. Beverland's apparently negative anthropology—we are hopelessly lost in sex—also implies a more benevolent, embracing perspective. Since lust transcends our control, there is no point in attempting to resist its urge. Since nature is irredeemably stained by the consequences of the Fall, Beverland alludes to the possibility of enjoying its "dirty" pleasures with no guilt. We are all "by nature" prone to sin, which is "a guide and companion that cannot be absent."[43] At the same time, nature is the origin of the feelings of shame that have accompanied sexual desire since the Fall: "Adam and Eve were nude and blushed, says the text. This inborn shame originates only in this shamefulness of pleasure and this shame and pleasure overwhelmed us first after the sin. . . . Hence nature has taught us to always cover with clothing these parts of nature, which shame covers with a garment."[44] In passages that reveal Beverland's deep compassion for the human condition after the Fall, nature is depicted as the cause of our deepest fragilities. Quoting Cicero through Augustine, he states, "Humans are placed by nature in the world with a naked, fragile, and weak body, a mind distressed by troubles, humble with fears, weak for labours, prone to lust, in whom the divine fire has been covered, as well as his character and habits."[45] This understanding of human fragility led Beverland to provide a psychological interpretation of the frailties of individual natures and call for an ever greater moderation in judging the incapacity of many to resist the tyranny of lust: "Everyone follows the seeds of his own nature. But if our nature has been imbued in this nettle and eruca and begins to be stirred, then it may be eradicated with a shovel, yet it would grow back, even if you cut off your testicles or penis with a knife as Origen hastened to do."[46] Repression only increases the pressure of desire, while, conversely, "whoever is allowed to sin, sins less."[47]

In the most heated passages of *On Original Sin,* Beverland praises nature in a way that recalls radical libertine writers like Vignali and Rocco. Eve is initially depicted as candidly replying to the serpent: "The fruit of the tree of life and any plant has been permitted to us to enjoy, but God has forbidden us to pluck the fruit of the tree, of the wood and most beautiful flower, which the *maker of nature* has planted in the middle of Adam's body, lest we might die."[48] After she surrenders to the tempter, dizzy with desire, Eve "laugh[s] and, taking" Adam's "manhood in her wicked hand, she [says]: 'Your penis clearly enjoys the stolen love, husband. *Make use of the gifts that nature has given.* I am not so strict that I would condemn the fires I have felt.'"[49] After the Fall, nature teaches us how to have sex: "Although a virgin may not be a good teacher, we nevertheless know this practice so well through nature that we do not need to seek lessons in sexual intercourse from a mistress in the Suburra." Yet Beverland then soberly observes that, "as the first knowledge, this knowledge of the flesh is death and hostility towards God."[50]

Beverland's position on the relationships between God and nature is rather ambiguous. He clearly defends the almightiness of the Creator to clear the suspicion of atheism that weighed on him and his work. He does so, however, by reflecting a posteriori on the goodness of his creation, an argument that could be harmonized with the revaluation of nature (and its gifts) brought about by most of the libertine authors he was trying to distance himself from. At the same time, his polemical scriptural exegesis was indebted to the biblical criticism of Spinoza, which was providing new theoretical substance to the critique of revealed religions as it was taking hold in the seventeenth century. It seems that, in Beverland's view, only the spike of carnal desire, to which he was particularly sensitive, called for an explanation that was not accessible to the natural reason alone. The scriptural myth of the Fall, originally interpreted by Beverland, provided a rationale that helped him understand, and accept, why human beings were enslaved by lust and desire. Beverland, however, also depicted these same cravings as enticing, desirable, and ultimately natural. This swinging was probably the result of the interplay of two different attitudes. On one hand, we can read them as a typical manifestation of the libertine strategy of concealment, which winked at an inner circle of initiates. On the other, it probably reflected the meanderings of Beverland's own tormented conscience, divided between desire and shame, blame and pleasure, the quest for forgiveness and unrepentant pride.

Beyond the Printed Word

Several sources that testify to Beverland's sociability while he was still a renowned academic celebrity in the Dutch Republic provide us with an indispensable tool to clarify the ambiguities of his thought, making more explicit the issues that can be read only between the lines in his works. Between 1677 and 1680, Beverland was under the scrutiny of the authorities of Utrecht, a city that he often frequented and where he was well known for the impression he made on young scholars who were fascinated by his provocative manners and ideas. Beverland's letters hint at the atmosphere that surrounded these informal gatherings of young intellectuals, who confidentially met their masters in taverns and inns, some of which were known for being nests for suspected atheists. We know that once the scandal caused by the publication of *On Original Sin* had broken, Beverland declined an invitation to one of these meetings, for he was afraid that it might be an ambush orchestrated by his enemies.[51]

What did Beverland, his friends, his colleagues, and his students discuss in these gatherings then? An anonymous private notebook containing entries ranging from learned disputes to contemporary news and gossip has been attributed to a student belonging to Beverland's entourage.[52] The author's proximity to Beverland is clear from a number of entries, some of which prove that he even had direct access to the manuscripts of the yet unpublished, and extremely secretive, *On the Prostitution of the Ancients.* It shows the overwhelming presence of Spinozian themes in the discussions of Beverland's acolytes, although the anonymous author did not always understand and probably never read Spinoza's works.[53] In his scattered entries, the writer of the notebook mentions Vanini and demonstrates an insider's knowledge of the contemporary editorial vicissitudes involving the works of other deeply suspected authors: "Through an edict here in Utrecht the books of Spinoza, the *Leviathan* of Hobbes, the writings of Socinus have been prohibited, and a fine of 3,000 florins is imposed on the bookseller if he sells such books or if they are found at his place."[54] The notebook transcribes several statements that are directly attributed to Beverland, one of them explicitly depicting the Dutch humanist as endorsing Spinoza's biblical criticism: "From Beverland: The Bible we read is not the true Bible, as can be shown from the Hebrew language, and as Spinoza also states. True is only that which secures the covenant made by the Israelites with God. The rest, which was added by Joshua and others, was written and invented by the Jews."[55] Many of the entries also contain direct quotations or paraphrases of Beverland's works.

The anonymous author cites Beverland's opinion on the real nature of the Fall into sin: "There were two trees in paradise. Eve ate from one, i.e., was fucked by it, i.e., by Adam's dick, which was the forbidden fruit; when they approached the other tree Adam and Eve were chased off by angels," as well as "That Eve had touched Adam's dick instead of apples is apparent from the words of the text, for the snake said to Eve: 'If you taste this apple, your eyes will be opened and you will be able to procreate human beings just like God himself.' That tree, then, is a dick and the fruit of that tree is sexual love."[56] These passages include direct quotations from *On the Prostitution of the Ancients,* from a chapter where Beverland presents the arguments that he subsequently reworked and published in his most famous work. One of these entries reveals that the anonymous author had access to the manuscript of the unfinished work, and this renders his testimony on the discussions of Beverland's treatise particularly interesting. He includes a sketchy entry giving a competing interpretation of the nature of the Fall, attributed to one of Beverland's closest friends: "According to the opinion of Heinsius, Eve was buggered by Adam and taken from behind, and hence arose this sin and all evils. Many learned men assert the same, and Heinsius has various letters of learned cardinals about this matter."[57] Nicholaas Heinsius was one of the *Initiati* and maintained an extensive intellectual network composed of various scholars based in the Italian peninsula. One of them was Lucas Holste or Holstenius (1596–1661), who was a coordinator of the Vatican Library appointed by Pope Innocent X.[58] The notebook reference directly connects the belief that Adam and Eve enjoyed the pleasures of nonreproductive intercourse in the Garden of Eden to intellectual and ecclesiastic circles in Italy, aligning with the testimony that we have seen in several Italian trial cases. And here too, the most daring opinions took shape and were transmitted more often in informal discussions on the benches of taverns and inns than in the formal setting of a university. Only afterward were they committed to writing, in either manuscript or printed form, by some of the more audacious and scornful writers. It's striking that in both Italy and the Netherlands the belief in sodomy as humanity's first act of disobedience emerged largely as a scurrilous joke and that only as we have looked more closely into its contexts and meanings have we come to recognize its philosophical and theological implications and associations with early modern European atheism and unbelief.

CHAPTER SEVEN

French Translations

THE FRENCH libertine and skeptic François de La Mothe Le Vayer (1588–1672) is another influential author who, in his writings, considered the belief that sodomy was the act marking Adam and Eve's rejection of God's commands. Le Vayer was a respected seventeenth-century French humanist and philosopher. Elected to the *Académie Française,* he was a protégé of Cardinal Richelieu, to whom he dedicated one of his works, *De la vertu des payens* (hereafter *On the Virtue of the Pagans*). Anne of Austria chose him to be a tutor for her son, the future King Louis XIV. Yet in one of his early poems, he expressed his ideas about sodomy and original sin. Compared to the other authors we have analyzed so far, he was even more explicitly linked to the theory of the fraudulence of religions. Large excerpts of *On the Virtue of the Pagans* would be included after his death in the first print edition of the notorious *Treatise of the Three Impostors,* which was printed in The Hague in 1719. Here, they contributed substantially to the layout of the chapters devoted to Jesus Christ.

Cave of the Nymphs

In a juvenile manuscript titled *Explication de l'antre des nymphes descript par Homere au tresieme livre de son Odyssée* (Explication of the cave of the nymphs described by Homer in the thirteenth book of his Odyssey), Le Vayer wrote that Adam and Eve savored anal sex in the Garden of Eden.[1] He then incorporated an abridged and reworked version of this text into a later poem titled the *Hexaméron Rustique.* The *Cave of the Nymphs* was a burlesque allegorical interpretation of verses 95–112 of chapter 13 of the Odyssey, where Ulysses, who had just landed in Ithaca, hid the gifts that the Phaeacians left him while he was asleep, before they set sail again and left him alone on the island.[2]

Le Vayer named this jocular composition after *The Cave of the Nymphs,* a treatise by the Phoenician philosopher Porphyry of Tyre (ca. 234–ca. 305 CE). The choice was not accidental. By proposing a witty reinvention of Porphyry's allegorical style, Le Vayer was caustically critiquing the hermeneutic tradition of interpretating ancient Greek literature. Le Vayer was not questioning the poetic value of Homer's work but criticizing the common tendency to attribute to the poet a perfect mastery of all sciences and explain his verses allegorically as a repository of all sorts of secret knowledge. Stoics, Epicureans, and Academics had long tried to pull Homer—the textual authority par excellence—to their side. Le Vayer skeptically challenged this approach and comically subverted the use of allegoresis to parody Homeric poetry.[3]

In Le Vayer's poem the image of the lair clearly functions as a sexual innuendo. The *Cave of the Nymphs* is a symbolic representation of sexual organs, with references to both the front and back door as a clear allusion to vaginal and anal sex. The back door is reserved for the deities, making this humorous allegory yet another example of the literary trope that depicted sodomy as a delight reserved for the most refined palates. "Venus postica" (literally "the Venus from behind") guards this door, which is reserved for the "immortal Gods, who glorify their Ganymedes." Le Vayer explained this passage by referring to a popular French proverb that states that only the great, "who are the Gods of this earth, dare take this path," along with an analogous Italian mot according to which "this Gomorrhean path" is neither made for the simple folk nor is it "'a business for porters.'" Le Vayer likely regarded Italian popular culture as a source of sexual knowledge and recognized a certain affinity between his interpretation of the Homeric verses and the theme of homoerotic love ("the masculine love") dear to Greek and Latin authors as well. This was their supposed "vicious liberty." Yet Le Vayer focused mainly on heterosexual sodomy and mentioned the Athenian tyrant Peisistratos, described by Herodotus as preferring anal sex to avoid impregnating his partners. He quoted the letters of Augier Ghislain de Busbecq on Turkish women who denounced their husbands to the qadis (Islamic judges) for taking this "irregular path" during sexual intercourse. While Le Vayer assembled a host of erudite and exotic curiosities, he also shrewdly feigned his disapproval of the practice with an almost untranslatable pun. A "cul pro con" in marriage was no less dangerous than a "qui pro quo" in the pharmaceutical arts. In French, "cul" means "ass," while "con" can be translated into English as "cunt." Playing on the assonance between "cul pro con" and "qui pro quo," the pun means that "to mistake an ass for a cunt" is as risky as using the wrong ingredient in a pharmaceutical recipe.[4]

Le Vayer further developed his argument on sodomy by quoting a passage of the *Controversies* by Seneca the Elder (ca. 54 BCE–ca. 39 CE) that referred to the "wrong place" in intercourse as "inepta loci," a passage Seneca had incorrectly attributed to Ovid. Le Vayer imaginatively suggested that Seneca the Elder had been deceived by "the interpretation of some Rabbis," who believed that "the apple which tempted our first father was the symbol of the rear parts of her woman, which very well represents an apple split in half." In this way Le Vayer could repeat the belief that the apple was a symbol of the buttocks, which the sacred texts had concealed for the sake of decency, while dissimulating by claiming that "to interpret the Scriptures in a sense which is reproved is equivalent to desecrating them." He claimed disingenuously that, despite some regret, he had been pushed by the nature of the subject to report this opinion.[5]

The maneuver allows Le Vayer to mock an established tradition of allegorical interpretations of Greek cultural heritage while also challenging the Judeo-Christian tradition. This ironic approach to sacred matters is consistent with his philosophical outlook, although a full understanding of his message still proves elusive to historians of thought. Commonly regarded as a prominent representative of the so-called *libertinage érudit*, Le Vayer has been interpreted by some scholars as belonging to the tradition of Christian skepticism. He asserted the radical inconclusiveness of human reason professing a Christian fideism. For some historians, there is no conclusive evidence to claim that this was mere dissimulation.[6] Others, however, tend to emphasize the *pars destruens* of his work. Some underline how his methodic doubt led him to agnostic conclusions, precluding any certainty across all domains of knowledge[7] while still others believe his arguments against fundamentalism so strong that they can be brought to their extreme conclusions and challenge the foundations of revealed religion per se.[8] Among them, Jean-Pierre Cavaillé has also emphasized the extent to which Le Vayer's positions on love and desire were consistent with some of our dissenters' most radical claims. Indeed, his skepticism coexisted with a radical naturalism that recalls Antonio Vignali's and Antonio Rocco's stances toward sex. In *Le Banquet sceptique* (The skeptical banquet), he mentioned bestiality along with "man to man love" (l'amour d'homme à homme) with the unambiguous purpose of highlighting the immeasurable variety of human customs, which he attributed to the immense creative power of nature. He then listed a wide array of literary sources to prove that sodomy had always been present in human societies, and especially in Ancient Greece.[9]

Despite this consonance, what is more striking for the purposes of this book is that Le Vayer's works were extensively quoted in the first printed edition of *The Three Impostors*. The selective use of his work by the editors of this scandalous handbook for atheists substantially distorted the interpretation of Le Vayer's original thought, turning his radical skepticism into a form of explicit and militant atheism. This operation is not unlike others we have encountered in various contexts throughout this book. However, despite these distortions, this case study too seems to confirm that the idea of sodomy as the first act of disobedience against God tended to emerge in contexts marked by a notable coherence in their internal logic and underlying vision, both of which revolved around the theory od the fraudulence of religion.

Le Vayer and the Three Impostors

The notorious legend of the three impostors finally came to light in an edition published in The Hague in 1719 and presented as a transcription of the supposed medieval original attributed to Frederick II's chancellor Pier della Vigna. It was obviously a forgery. The book was a patchwork of passages from the most radical writers of the seventeenth century, and the philosophical pastiche helped spread the message of Baruch Spinoza and Thomas Hobbes. The editors substantially trivialized Hobbes's and Spinoza's philosophies by juxtaposing them with excerpts from libertine authors like Gabriel Naudé and Giulio Cesare Vanini, and they subtly bent toward an overtly irreligious interpretation, which contributed to making their publication the most overt and philosophically grounded defense of atheism yet written.[10]

The genesis of this first print edition of *On the Three Impostors* is extremely intricate,[11] and hypotheses of its authorship emerged almost immediately.[12] The one advanced by the French bibliographer Prosper Marchand (1678–1756) in his *Dictionary* still appears the most plausible. Marchand attributed the volume to Mr. Jan Vroese, or Vroesen, a councillor of the court of Brabant at The Hague, and a document found by Silvia Berti seems to confirm this, although Berti herself thought more proof would be necessary to confirm it.[13] Regardless of the problem of authorship, we know that *The Three Impostors* was published anonymously by Charles Levier in collaboration with Thomas Johnson, who substantially reworked the original text with the aid of two friends and collaborators, Jean Rousset de Missy and Jean Aymon.[14] For a long time the book was difficult to find. Given its notoriety, Prosper Marchand burned more than three hundred copies of the first edition after the death of his friend Levier in 1734, at the request of his heirs. This edition then remained lost until 1985.[15]

The 1719 Hague edition, lacking either place or date of publication, was originally titled *La Vie et l'Esprit de Mr Benoît de Spinosa* (The life and spirit of Mr. Baruch Spinoza). This title referred to a biography of Spinoza, written around 1678, almost certainly by Jean-Maximilien Lucas, a French "*gazetier*" who migrated to The Hague after launching a staunch campaign against Louis XIV's absolutism.[16] The biography of Spinoza constituted the first part of this first edition. The second part was subsequently republished again anonymously and without the biography as the *Treatise of the Three Impostors* (since it circulated along with a different Latin version of the legend, I will refer to this particular edition by its French title, *Traité des trois imposteurs*).[17] The decision was obviously deliberate. Spinoza and Hobbes contributed the theoretical substrate of the treatise, and this edition was important for popularizing their philosophical systems.[18]

The fact that Le Vayer was also widely used in this work testifies to the enduring legacy of his thought. The four chapters of the *Esprit de*

Spinoza on Jesus Christ (chapters 7–10, "De Jésus-Christ," "De la Politique de Jesus Christ," "De la Morale de Jesus Christ," and "De la Divinité de Jesus-Christ") contain extensive extracts from Le Vayer's *On the Virtue of the Pagans* and quotations from Giulio Cesare Vanini's *De arcanis,* Jean Bodin's *Colloquium Heptaplomeres,* and Celsus's notorious biography of Christ.[19] In some passages of the *Traité,* Celsus was quoted not directly but by way of excerpts of his work found in Le Vayer's *On the Virtue of the Pagans.*[20] The chapter devoted to Christ's morals was indeed almost entirely drawn from the latter, with extensive quotations substantiating the thesis that Christians were not morally superior to the pagans. In Le Vayer's dialogues, Socrates, Confucius, Pyrrho, Plato, Aristotle, Pythagoras, Epicurus, and Diogenes were all worthy of salvation, apart from Christ and Christian revelation. The passage of the *Traité* that privileges Plato's explanation of the creation of the world in the *Timaeus* over the biblical account of Genesis is almost entirely based on a paragraph by Le Vayer. The *Traité* also drew from *On the Virtue of the Pagans* regarding the origins of humankind: "The description made by Socrates to Simmia in the Phaedo, is infinitely more gracious than the Terrestrial Paradise, and the androgynous is incomparably better crafted than anything that Genesis tells about the extraction of Eve from one of Adam's ribs."[21] Although it is not characterized by the radicalism of the notion of sodomy as the original sin—as found in our case studies and mentioned by Le Vayer in his youth—this passage nevertheless reveals that the interest in alternative readings of the creation myth was widespread in skeptical and erudite circles, which drew on it to ground alternative views of sex and gender in the early modern period.

The reception of Le Vayer's work in the first print edition of the *Traité* has partially distorted and radicalized the skeptical stances of the French philosopher. This radicalization, however, provides yet another indication that the belief in anal sex as the first violation of God's commands surfaced in contexts that were linked, in varied degrees, with the larger theory of the fraudulence of religion. This connection is further confirmed if we take a deeper look at the cultural milieu that gave rise to the first print edition of the *Traité.* The renowned French publisher Jean-Frédéric Bernard (1683–1744), who was close to some of the intellectuals involved in the redaction of the treatise, also translated Hadriaan Beverland's *On Original Sin* into French, turning its sexual interpretation of the Fall into a Trojan horse that aimed to destroy revealed religion from inside.

Jean-Frédéric Bernard's *State of Man*

Jean-Frédéric Bernard has long been overlooked, but he was a key figure in the early Enlightenment. His bustling life, his movements across Europe, his intellectual curiosity and refined literary works, the talent he displayed in cultural business, and his audacity in challenging religious hegemony over European culture are all emblematic of the character of this era of transition. In 1711, he wrote and published under a false imprint a work titled *Reflexions morales satiriques & comiques, sur le Moeurs de nôtre siècle* (Moral satirical and comic reflections on the mores of our century), an imaginative account of the reflections of a fictional Persian philosopher who observed, with a critical eye, religious intolerance in Europe. This work was among the sources that inspired Montesquieu's better-known *Persian Letters,* published ten years later.[22] As one of the financiers of the weekly journal *Nouvelles Litéraires* (Literary news), Bernard put pressure on Henri du Sauzet, a Huguenot refugee in the Dutch Republic, to convince him to publish Jean-Maximilien Lucas's (died 1697) biography of Spinoza, which was eventually integrated into the first edition of the *Traité.* While his philosophical outlook is deistic, Bernard echoed the theme of the fraudulence of religions in his writings. This is particularly the case in the 1735 edition of his *Dialogues critiques et philosophiques* (Critical and philosophical dialogues), where he envisioned Jupiter and Muḥammad discussing how to attract followers before making a secret alliance to gain mastery over the whole world.[23]

Together with the engraver Bernard Picart (1673–1733), Bernard produced the *Cérémonies et coutumes religieuses de tous les peuples du monde* (Religious ceremonies and customs of all the people of the world), a groundbreaking illustrated multivolume work that set a new standard in the development of a protoanthropological approach to world religions. Picart too was part of the same environment, joining a sodality called the Knights of Jubilation, which celebrated a lifelong commitment to merriness and enjoyment with wine, laughter, and fun. Other members included John Toland; Charles Levier, the publisher and editor of the *Traité*; and Prosper Marchand, whose *Dictionary* gives us the most complete surviving information about the vicissitudes that led to the publication of the *Traité* and who later sought to destroy most of its copies at the request of Levier's family. Marchand was originally a French Huguenot and a lifelong friend of Picart. The two decided to leave France together, seeking religious freedom and better opportunities in the Dutch Republic.[24]

Religious Ceremonies was published between 1723 and 1737 in seven volumes.[25] The book became a bestseller, contributing to the development of a radically new approach to religious studies. Relying on a wealth of sources—but predominantly travelogues—Bernard described the religions of the world, including Christian confessions and radical sects within Christianity, with a nonjudgmental and comparative approach. Picart's graphics contributed to magnifying the dignity of people from across the globe. His work was especially remarkable because it purposely avoided the visual stereotypes that for centuries had characterized the negative depictions of Jews and Muslims in Christian iconography. Bernard's text was essentially based on the idea that religiosity was an inborn tendency shared by all human beings, which simply took different forms in different times and places.

Bernard developed the core theoretical frame of this groundbreaking work by starting from a point that he had already introduced in the French adaptation of Beverland's *On Original Sin.* Bernard first outlined his assumption that a pervasive and universal sense of guilt was at the root of all world religions, a psychological interpretation of religions that would soon influence wide sectors of the European elite and public opinion.[26] Beverland's notion of the omnipresence of sexual desire after the Fall played a crucial role in this psychologization of religious beliefs and makes Bernard's *État de l'homme dans le péché originel* (State of man in the original sin) a powerful example of how seventeenth-century religious criticism, irreligiousness, and doubt were merging with the pragmatic approach to knowledge of a new generation of engaged scholars. While some aspects of Bernard's work as both author and publisher align with this new tendency, others show significant continuity with the tradition of libertine irreligiousness.

The elusive, anonymous frontispiece to Bernard's *State of Man* (1714) gave as its place of publication "in the World" (dans le Monde). It was reprinted six times during the author's lifetime.[27] The *State of Man* recalled Beverland's core thesis: original sin was nothing but the discovery of sex, and the sexual drive was a ubiquitous force whose devastating consequences no one could avoid. However, Beverland's arguments were heavily reworked, to the extent that the *State of Man* stands as a completely original work that fits into Bernard's broader intellectual, political, and religious outlook. Bernard clearly targeted the arrogance of the "pretended masters, the directors of our consciences, and of our faith; those who fiercely place themselves in the tribune of our Supreme Legislator, and who would like us to blindly follow their opinions and works." Unlike Beverland, who tried to qualify his endeavors as an attempt to restore the original meaning of the Scriptures, relying heavily on the dignity of Christian and classical traditions, Bernard claimed his freedom from the influence of both these legacies: "Thank God we are born free, and we do not want to side with either Paul or Apollo." "We," Bernard went on, "will use our reason, if you don't mind, and we will investigate, far from the theological thorns and cardoons, the woeful sources of all men's iniquities."[28]

At the same time, Bernard was much more explicit than Beverland in denouncing the iniquities of institutional religions, condemning the sophistry of theologians and moralists who transformed religion into superstition, while reproaching the corrupt morals of contemporary society.[29] Bernard suggested a subtle psychological interpretation of the hardships of Christian religion that proposed "an impracticable ethic." He praised this arduousness, which allowed the Christian credo to be coherent while keeping human pride under control, yet his line of thought became increasingly subtle as he proceeded. He did not deny that Christian radicalism was capable of producing an inner circle of select and extraordinary saints. Yet by being preached to the masses, it created a multitude of hypocrites who were persuaded that they were "immensely superior to the rest of humanity" and that "Pagans and Turks are nothing but wicked masqueraders."[30]

In his free rendition of Beverland's work, Bernard maintained a double standard, radically critiquing religion while distancing himself from the most subversive libertine positions. Yet he left so much space to these positions that his critique appears to be more an attempt to circulate libertine themes than a sincere effort to dismantle their theoretical foundations. While criticizing the libertines' tendency to conflate religion with political interest at the expense of the uneducated masses, he defined original sin as an "inexhaustible source of evil and errors." The belief in the ubiquitous consequences of the Fall was the "veritable treasure of our Masters," who used it to instill fear in the populace.[31] The sense of guilt we feel as a consequence of the Fall is the source of all sorts of superstitions and, at the same time, of the control exerted on us by religious hierarchies.[32] In Bernard's opinion, this was still part of God's original plan. God allowed our reason to be corrupted to let his virtue shine through the salvific gift of grace through the "Divine Savior."[33] Thus, while not abandoning a fundamentally Christian outlook, Bernard inverted it by depicting the Magisterium of the Church not as a remedy to humanity's present state of ignorance but as the epitome of it.

While Bernard's *State of Man* is not exclusively devoted to sex, sexual themes nevertheless play a crucial role in the construction of its main argument. When dealing with the omnipresence of sexual desire as a consequence of our ancestors' fault, Bernard aligns with Beverland's strategy of balancing condemnatory rhetoric and ambiguous complacency. The latter mainly manifested itself through the author's allusive and titillating prose: "This is the era of Original Sin, and this is how the unfortunate Human Genre learned how to put into practice kisses, whispers, fondling, sweet murmurings, tender attacks, charming returns, delightful emotions, delicious agitations."[34]

The expression "eating from the Tree of the Knowledge of Good and Evil" was interpreted by Bernard as a synonym of the "commerce of love" because, as Bernard suggests, the verb "to know" and its derivates were often used by sacred authors to refer to sexual intercourse.[35] Although the "Knowledge of Good and Evil"—that is, sex—had negative consequences on the rational faculties of our species, it was nevertheless "closely allied to the Generative faculty," which was "absolutely necessary to the conservation of Humankind."[36] Bernard seals this timid revaluation of sexual desire by stating that because of this generative power, "we can even say about voluptuousness, that it is the visible Divinity of Humankind."[37] These statements are clearly reminiscent of Campanella's treatment of sexual desire in his *Atheism Conquered,* reinstating sex into the natural realm to challenge the foundations of Christian ethics. Bernard went so far as to cast doubt on the utility of a restrictive sexual ethic to contain the grip of sexual desire, daring to say that "the corruption of the flesh and the sensitivity of original sin assault the believers more strongly."[38] Although he did not overtly ridicule the heroic struggle between the flesh and the spirit, his text masterfully shifts from paying lip service to religious authorities to overtly criticizing the conundrums of Christian sexual morality, which ultimately increase the urge of desire and multiply the occasions to sin.

Although Bernard did not deal with whether Adam and Eve had anal intercourse in the Garden of Eden, he asked for the location of the "place where Adam and Eve tasted the first fruit of sin."[39] While these lines refer overtly to the geographical location of the Garden of Eden, they hint at a possible allegorical reading of the terrestrial paradise that opens the door to speculation about other, bodily geographies:

> I leave to the Critics the care of researching which was the place where Adam and Eve tasted the first fruit of sin. This famous place has given rise to thousands of conjectures. Some located it in Asia, others in Africa; some Sages situated it in Europe; still others, finally, interpreted it as an Allegory. Be it as it may, the proper name of this place means *Voluptuousness,* and suffice it to remark that this name is suitable to the *Terrestrial Paradise* in every way possible; since Adam & Eve, who had been immortal before feeling carnal pleasure, opened their eyes to the Mortality of their Nature, as early as they had learned from Voluptuousness to distinguish Good and Evil. It is in this voluptuous place, that they got intoxicated with pleasure and that, swept away by Love, they swore each other an exemplary faithfulness. Once the pleasure went away, the promise disappeared too; because the ardor was a result of Error. Reason regained its place, and showed them that Passion does not promise anything solid and durable.[40]

Bernard immediately shelved the problem of the supposed geographical position of the Garden of Eden, which he clearly felt was irrelevant. What mattered to him was the symbolic meaning that lay beneath the literary meaning of the Scriptures. Here it is fair to imagine that he was indirectly winking at other, more subtle, topographies of desire. The passage moreover contains a not-so-veiled critique of monogamy and lifelong conjugal fidelity. According to Bernard's suggestive prose, fidelity is far from being in accord with sound reason. The knowledge of good and evil is nothing but the awareness of the fallacies of our mental projections while we are in a state of sexual arousal. No one, Bernard suggested, would ever swear an undying allegiance to a partner if not deceived by desire. Desire is, indeed, fleeting and unreliable, as are the promises we utter under its effect.

This is but one example of the vitriolic humor that pervades the *State of Man.* Other passages reveal Bernard's indulgent attitude toward sex. Describing the ubiquity of desire, he rhetorically asks, "If the first man, who was made right away by God's hand, was not able to keep his purity, how would you, miserable sinners, born from a father moved by lust and a mother who was insatiable in her desires, dare say that you can absolutely resist concupiscence, and that you are pure like angels?"[41] Bernard's critique did not spare those who pretended to be saints: "How many people who pass for saints," he asked, "in their rooms sin in more positions than Aretino has described in his book?"[42]

The reference is clearly to the *I Modi* (The positions), a popular pornographic book that consisted of a series of engravings by Marcantonio Raimondi representing different sexual positions commented on through lascivious sonnets authored by Pietro Aretino.[43] Bernard pretended to be unwilling to go into the details of the many ways to indulge in sexual pleasure, but in fact he provided the reader with a list of authors whom he rhetorically condemned as "those infamous Masters of libertinage," which can be read "to learn how we take each other then." Alongside classical authors Petronius and Ovid, Italian erotica, including by the ever-present Aretino and Giovanni Della Casa, plays a crucial role.[44] Bernard also quoted Johannes van Meurs (Meursius, 1579–1639), the sixteenth-century Dutch humanist and alleged coauthor of the notorious *Aloisiae Sigaeae, Toletanae, Satyra sotadica de arcanis Amoris et Veneris* (The Sotadic satire on the mysteries of love and Venus by Aloisia Sigea from Toledo).[45]

After confirming that "the tree of knowledge and its fruit are nothing but the Matrimonial act and the parts [of the body] that are the instrument of this act," Bernard explored the origins of religious feelings in the passage, anticipating the theoretical core of his future endeavors. In his opinion, original sin was, indeed, the reason for our dystonic perception of our own sexual organs: "Without an extraordinary sin that makes these parts infamous . . . , what in them would be more shameful, ridiculous or abnormous than in the other limbs of the human body?" This shame around genitals is so widespread among human beings from every part of the world that Bernard believes we can consider it one of humanity's "inborn ideas." He here abandons the Judeo-Christian tradition and embraces a wider, comparativist approach: "All the Ancient and Modern Nations, at least those that possess an idea of Divinity, agree in deeming obscene the names that designate the body parts that serve to Marriage."[46] He later pushes this comparativist approach even further, diminishing the supposed superiority of Christianity: "I don't know if we, the Christians, would dare boast of measuring up to this Pagan and Muhamaddan baseness. We all have Aretino on our snuffbox, on protective screens, and in our rooms. Our Carnival is not more chaste nor more religious than the Saturnalia, the Lupercalia, the Floral Games [*Ludi Floreales*], and the mysteries of Adonis and of the Good female Deity etc."[47] Bernard eventually extended his criticism of the supposed superiority of Christian societies to condemn the evils of the European colonial enterprise: "The Christians yoked the people of the New World; every year, they go buy and sell men whom they treat like beasts, and whose life is less expensive than that of dogs."[48]

Bernard's reflection on sexual themes set the foundations for a less rigid approach to non-Christian religions, a theme that we saw emerging in Italian inquisitorial trials centuries earlier. Bernard anticipated the enraged critiques it would raise. Some people, he wrote, would not understand "a certain cheerfulness widespread in this dissertation"; they would treat it as a "pamphlet against the good manners" and its author as "a libertine and a heretic." To these anticipated enemies he provocatively replied with a blunt "The joke's on you."[49]

Bernard's *The State of Men* represents the culmination of the long itinerary that this book has attempted to reconstruct across two centuries of dissent and irreligion in Italy and beyond: the belief that anal sex was the forbidden fruit. The fact that this theme was alluded to but not mentioned directly in Bernard's extremely free rendition of *On Original Sin* heralds an important change. As religious and sexual criticism came to be part of political agendas that aimed at triggering social change, caustic irreverence of sixteenth- and seventeenth-century irreligiousness faded from view. The belief that the forbidden fruit was anal sex eventually disappeared, to be reabsorbed in the more generic idea that the Fall consisted of sexual knowledge in general.

CHAPTER EIGHT

Original Sin, Sexuality, and Female Independence

THE AUTHORS and trial defendants we have examined thus far have all been male, yet we know that women were also reflecting on sex and original sin, as we can see in the cases of two female enclosures in eighteenth-century Italy. Their emergence was likely influenced by the circulation of forbidden books, some of which can be ascribed to the cultural milieus that we have analyzed in earlier chapters. One case concerns a Venetian nun, Maria Teresa Garzi, whose deposition seems to allude to a passage of Beverland's *On Original Sin.* Another revolves around five girls housed in Rome's Conservatory of Saint John Lateran, a female boarding school for orphaned and abandoned young women. The transcripts for this second case explicitly refer to a mysterious book that had already disappeared by the time the inquisitorial proceedings began, leaving its title unknown. Both cases give insight into how we might explore women's reading strategies in early modern Italy. The defendants read texts brimming with misogynist stereotypes but interpreted them according to their needs. These women elaborated their own views about bodies and sexual pleasure, which they jealously protected from the interference of their male tutors, thus claiming a degree of independence from Church hierarchies shaped by patriarchal authority.

At the same time, these cases suggest that while the belief that sex constituted the first infraction of God's command was gaining momentum in the eighteenth century, the more radical view that it was specifically sodomitic sex that Adam and Eve enjoyed in the Garden of Eden was fading from this broader cultural construct. The archival holdings of the Roman Holy Office of the Inquisition, where these cases are preserved, testify to the progressive decline of the belief that sodomy constituted Adam and Eve's original act of disobedience. What gradually took its place was the belief that sex more generally caused the Fall, a view that the Inquisition duly condemned formally in 1701. This was probably due to the rising notoriety of Beverland's treatise. While we do not know much about the circulation of *On Original Sin* in Italy, we know that it came to the attention of the Congregation of the Index thanks to Leonard van Rijssen's *On the Just Abhorrence of Hadriaan Beverland's Most Wicked Book.* The cardinals gathered to discuss this merciless review of Beverland's work on February 7, 1693, and this indirect testimony allowed them to reconstruct it enough that they decided to put Beverland's work on the index. Yet they never actually implemented the decision, perhaps because they could not get hold of Beverland's infamous treatise.[1] Eight years later, the Holy Office gathered an ad hoc commission that categorized this opinion as a "heretical statement."[2] Their decision was filed in the same archival fonds that held the cases regarding sodomy as the forbidden fruit, and the fact that they were preserved together in the same folders suggests that the Inquisition considered these two unorthodox opinions to be closely related.[3]

When did this conflation occur? The Holy Office's archives were sorted in a systematic manner after an Apostolic Visitation of 1701 that triggered a complete inventory of the archive that was finished in 1710 and updated in 1745. Another Apostolic Visitation of 1735 led to the appointment of an archivist to reorganize the doctrinal and jurisdictional material. Giuseppe Maria Lugani held this position from 1762 to 1798, having indexed the archival files up to 1775 by the time he died.[4] Lugani organized the doctrinal and criminal matters of the archives in the form that they still have today. The emphasis on sodomy as the original sin that we have analyzed thus far then progressively faded in the sources of the Roman Holy Office, until it apparently disappeared completely during the first half of the eighteenth century. By that point, inquisitors were concerned with the widespread idea that original sin was more simply the discovery of sex.

The first case to demonstrate this is the trial of a priest called Domenico De Marchis, which took place in 1700. He was the rector of a church in Alba, in the territory of the Langhe. The inquisitorial tribunal of Casale Monferrato[5] sent several witnesses and denunciations to the Congregation of the Holy Office in Rome to report that De Marchis had given this provocative opinion in several public spaces and also from the altar during Mass. A forty-year-old peasant called Sorisio di Pietro said that De Marchis told people that Adam sinned "*pro concionationem*," an obscure definition that was explained soon after as a Latinization of a vernacular term meaning "carnal copulation." The Casale inquisitors expressed concern about De Marchis's mental stability. They may have been saying this to protect him from a harsh conviction, but they certainly thought he was capable of "getting out of mind, and doing weird things," including committing suicide. De Marchis confessed that he had held this belief for about ten years, during which time he had become convinced that it was a truth of Catholic doctrine, even though many warned him of the contrary. He denied that he had ever professed this opinion from the altar. The inquisitors opted for a mediating approach, adopting the abbreviated procedure for those who spontaneously confessed (though De Marchis had not) and sentencing him to a formal abjuration followed by a "healthy penitence."[6]

The same series of documents does include cases that emphasize sodomy: Giovanni Leonarducci, a twenty-seven-year-old first-tonsure cleric from Aquileia, accused himself before the inquisitors on June 10, 1727, stating that he first learned about what he called "this dogma" when he was about sixteen years old. Two older clerics introduced him to the mystery, using gestures—a "sign with the hands"—to allude to sodomy. The young ecclesiastic believed that the Catholic Church had purposely covered this truth beneath metaphoric language for the sake of decency, implying that he believed that the opinion was orthodox. Nevertheless, he was condemned to a "vehement abjuration" (*de vehementi*).[7] Later cases in the fonds center on the broader opinion that original sin was sexual intercourse. Two of them involved female defendants exclusively. The following pages will be devoted to analyzing these occurrences.

Sister Maria Teresa Garzi

On February 24, 1714, the Venetian Inquisition took a statement spontaneously offered by Sister Maria Teresa Garzi, who was a professed nun at the Franciscan monastery of Saint Mary Major in the district of Santa Croce in Venice. During Lent of 1710, Sister Maria Teresa declared that "while discussing the original sin with Sister Maria Eugenia Borelli, Sister Maria Soave Borelli, and Sister Maria Perpetua Manfrotti"—who were also nuns in the same monastery—"the abovementioned Maria Eugenia told her that, as far as the original sin was concerned, Adam transgressed the divine precept not by eating the fruit that God had forbidden him, but sinning in his senses . . . that is, that Adam and Eve had sinned in the terrestrial paradise by knowing each other carnally against God's command, who since then prohibited that act."[8]

Assailed by doubt, Sister Maria Teresa Garzi asked her confessor for clarification. She admitted to the judges that she had found his response totally unsatisfactory and lacking "frankness," and it thus confirmed her "in this error." Sister Maria Eugenia Borelli, who was allegedly the first to spread this belief in the monastery, went to the sisters who were present that day to recant her previous statement, under the pressure of her confessor. Indeed, he had "instructed and undeceived her," clarifying the orthodox opinion that the original sin was simply eating the fruit of the Tree of Knowledge of Good and Evil. This only increased Sister Maria Teresa Garzi's doubts. She was skeptical of the reliability of Sister Eugenia and of her male tutors and came to believe that the confessors "wanted to conceal the truth to [the nuns], because [they were] consecrated, women, and uncultivated." Eager to know more, she was unwilling to comply with her guides' injunctions to drop the matter. As her curiosity grew, she turned again to the confessor, who argued that her interpretation of the Scriptures was incorrect. "More stubborn than ever," she said, describing herself in the statement, "I believed what I had believed before, thinking that the abovementioned confessor did not want to tell the truth" and that "not even he knew it." Her inner convictions were more certain than the theological knowledge flaunted by her male guide, but as she shared her views with her fellow sisters, their response became less indulgent. Maria Eletta Lamberti told her that she had already heard this interpretation of original sin from "morbid people," while Sister Maria Cecilia Vernizzi preferred not to respond at all. A third, Sister Francesca Zerbina, noted that she had even heard someone saying that Christ paid for this sin by suffering circumcision, but she soon added that none of these things were true because the Sacred Scriptures said otherwise.[9]

The allusion to the circumcision of Christ as a remedy for Adam and Eve's sexual sin probably refers to a learned source. Beverland's *On Original Sin* explains circumcision as an effort by the Jews to restrain the grip of concupiscence that originated from Adam and Eve's surrender to lust; it "was therefore a type of rejection of carnal desires."[10] Agrippa's *Declamation* had already dealt with this subject, noting that when "the merciful God concluded a covenant with his people," to make sure that "the covenanters would remember their depraved nature," he commanded them to be circumcised "so that the part which had sinned and through which the original sin is transfused would serve as a sign of the covenant. He extended this into metaphor, noting that removing the foreskins of their hearts would remove that depraved concupiscence."[11] Beverland distanced himself from Agrippa's antecedent and claimed that in his sacrifice for the salvation of humankind, Christ voluntarily let his body be wounded by the mark of sexual debauchery: "The immaculate virgin bore him with her virginity intact and without toil and she freed this burden of her chaste womb in a pure delivery as a generous mother. The wounded enemy favoured the offspring of the first semen, which Christ as the semen of the blessed little virgin, the Messiah or Michael destroyed, crushed, and subdued."[12] Despite his virginal conception, however, Christ had to suffer the same fate as every Jewish child: "He suffered circumcision for us and He commanded us to purify ourselves through baptism, because, innocent, He suffered an affliction in the flesh for us, to make himself indebted to always observe the laws."[13]

Sister Maria Teresa Garzi was willing to pursue an inner conviction that she described as coming exclusively from an independent inspiration. She declared that, soon after her discussion with Sister Francesca Zerbina, she decided to go back to her confessor with the explicit intent of "making him believe what [she] believed, because [she] thought he did not know the truth about this issue." Along with this proud claim for independence, Sister Maria Teresa insisted that she had never thought that "the Catholic Roman Church maintained or believed the contrary of what [she] believed." It was probably less risky for her to convince the judges that she had deceived herself into believing something to be orthodox and true when it was not than to admit that she was familiar with something that had been formally declared to be heretical. She claimed that her belief that Christ was circumcised to clean the stain of Adam and Eve's sexual infraction was something that she had "invented in her own head." The confessor was not as easily manipulable as she hoped, and he warned her that "this was a rotten heresy" and that she was obliged to denounce herself to the inquisitor.[14]

Even when she described to her judges the conversion that ultimately led her to repent, she diminished the contribution of her male confessor in this process. She took her time to think about the matter, and, "rather dubious about what was the truth," she turned inward, "thinking about her business, and eventually enlightened by God," she declared, "I realized my error, which I detest, and I firmly believe in all the things, that are reported in the Holy Scripture, how it is thought and considered by the Holy Roman Church." Sister Maria Teresa Garzi thus depicted her return to orthodoxy as depending on direct divine inspiration, as if to diminish her dependence on her confessor's authority until the end of the judicial proceedings.[15] She was vehemently condemned to abjure on March 20, 1714, and given an unspecified spiritual penance.[16]

The Girls of Saint John Lateran

Between April and May 1756, the confessors of the Conservatory of Saint John Lateran in Rome, also known as the "Ospizio Angelico" (the Angelic Nursing Home), encouraged several young women to appear before the judges of the Roman Holy Office and denounce themselves. They were Antonia Andreozzi, Gertrude Rosi, and Maria Angela Azzolini, who were eighteen, and Giulia Invernizzi and Barbara Domenichini, who were twenty-one and seventeen, respectively. They appeared individually and in random order, reporting themselves and accusing the others.[17]

The conservatory was one of the many foundations devoted to the containment of poverty, particularly female poverty, in Rome. A great number of these institutions were founded to assist beggars, homeless people, and a wide range of socially fragile subjects, including elders, lonely girls and children, orphans, widows, separated or abandoned wives, and repentant prostitutes. Conservatories protected the honesty of poor girls by keeping them off the streets and out of sex work and providing them with a Catholic education.[18] While conservatories were usually founded and supported by a multiplicity of institutional, religious, and private patrons, the enclosure dedicated to Saint John the Lateran was directly dependent on papal initiative. It was founded in 1692–1693 by Pope Innocent XII (1691–1700) and was associated with the Apostolic Hospice of San Michele in Ripa, where it was physically transferred in 1779.[19]

Some female conservatories patrolled the streets for poor girls or took them from prisons, where they were often detained under the charge of vagrancy. Others encouraged voluntary requests and carefully reviewed applications, as was probably the case for Antonia, Giulia, Barbara, Gertrude, and Maria Angela at Saint John Lateran. Those seeking to enroll were required to submit a memorial of their individual and familial history, which had to be accompanied by a certificate signed by a parish priest attesting to the trustworthiness of the report.[20]

As far as the inquisitors could later reconstruct the details, these girls' discussion about original sin was initiated by Antonia Andreozzi. When she told some others that she had read somewhere that Adam's sin was in violating God's command to not eat the apple, the girls began debating what kind of fruit God had forbidden. Some argued that it was a fig, an allusion that harked back to the long-standing popular metaphor for the genitals. They "urged each other to debate the issue day by day, sometimes collectively, others singularly with one or another." One of them eventually declared that she had read that "this transgression did not consist in eating an apple or a fig, but in having Adam and Eve commit the sin of impurity." They confessed that they then persisted in this conviction for some time, until one day they decided to turn to their confessors, who finally led them back to orthodoxy.[21]

On June 3, 1756, Antonia Andreozzi was interrogated individually. She declared that the book she mentioned was an honest one dealing with the Sacred Scriptures and that she did not know who brought it into the conservatory. As far as she knew, the volume had already disappeared during the time of her questioning, and she had no idea what had happened to it. She insisted that it was her own idea to believe that Adam's sin had been not eating the fruit but committing dishonest acts and that her conviction was unrelated to the content of the book. She assumed that the Scriptures used the fruit as a metaphor for the sake of modesty—that is, so as not to scandalize readers. In a later questioning on September 13, 1756, she confirmed that she and her friends believed that the sacred text used the symbolic image of the fruit "in order to use more [decent] and modest words." Antonia Andreozzi concluded by solemnly stating that she was available for further interrogation if the judges found it necessary. She reassured the inquisitors that she had seriously regretted this "very foolish thinking of [hers]" and added that "she only believed and professed what the Holy Mother Church believed."[22]

If we go back to Antonia's first voluntary confession, which opened the trial, we get a much more vivid description than the one she provided in her formal questioning. The original self-denunciation depicts the internal motions of her soul, her curiosity, the exciting experience of the discovery, the pleasure of investigating with her own, independent mind truths that she thought had been kept secret from the faithful. The process titillated her fantasies and provoked strong emotional responses: "Being in the infirmary of the Conservatory for a very minor illness, I found a book on a bed, whose title I don't know, and I took it to read it a bit, and I found myself reading about the history of the Fall from Grace and Adam's sin in the terrestrial paradise. And given that we cannot be sure which fruit Adam had eaten in sinning, I then said it was a fig. While I was saying that, there were in my company two maids who heard me, one named Anna Roveri, the other Anna Vittoria Federici, and they replied saying 'Oh you simpleton!'" Their response triggered Antonia's curiosity. The girls were bragging about some knowledge she was apparently excluded from. She realized that there was a hidden truth to be sought and intuitively thought that this secret must have something to do with sex: "From that word I started to bear some malice, suspecting that Adam's sin was not having eaten the fruit, but having committed impurity with Eve." She shared her thoughts with the other girls, and on November 23, 1755, while they were in the middle of Ignatius of Loyola's

Spiritual Exercises, Antonia again began talking about original sin in the company of Agata Rezzoli and Giulia Invernizzi. They too believed that Adam's sin was not eating the fruit but having sexual intercourse, and the two told her that they had already confessed this belief to their instructors.[23]

In her self-denunciation, Antonia went on to say that after this exchange of ideas with her companions she felt progressively more intrigued about the possible truth of this interpretation ("I very nearly believed it").[24] She started bringing it into arguments with other girls although, as she said in her deposition, she was more moved by the desire to impress her audience than by a real conviction in what she said. One day while listening to a sermon of her confessor, she realized that she had made a serious mistake, which she refers to as a "foolishness" (*sciocсheria*), and she immediately repented. She disclosed her mind to her confessor, who then helped restore her to the "orthodox" view about this controversial issue.[25]

The other girls confirmed the broad strokes of Antonia Andreozzi's deposition, although with some inconsistencies. Giulia Invernizzi, who appeared before the judges on March 20, 1756, declared that she once noticed that some of the girls of the school had been sent back from confession without being granted absolution. Wanting to know more, she interrogated some of her companions, who told her that those girls believed that Adam's sin consisted in an act of impurity. Probably to exonerate herself, she stated that she knew that they wanted to accuse her and some companions of having been the first ones to spread this opinion in the conservatory. She admitted that she had often talked about this matter with her friends but swore that she had always believed that original sin consisted in the eating of the fruit. Soon after, however, she admitted that she could have also said otherwise, which was possible "because [she didn't] remember well." Yet in that case, she would "loathe and abominate this, now and forever."[26]

Women's Writings, Women's Readings

These reports read very differently from the dry style that characterized the other documents on original sin in these two fonds within the archives of the Roman Holy Office. The notary captured the defendants' emotional reactions and retraced the complex psychological dynamics that helped shape their unorthodox beliefs. This attention to detail might reflect a site-specific tactic that the judges adopted to get the most from the defendants' confessions. Communication was different inside enclosed spaces like a Venetian monastery or Roman conservatory. In many of the cases we saw earlier, male protagonists overtly boasted of their opinions in public arenas. In enclosed female institutions, dissimulation and deception were more necessary to convey sensitive contents, prompting inquisitors to adopt policies of control and scrutiny that required attention to the subtlest details. The nuances in the notaries' writing style reflected both the two-way relationship between female defendants and inquisitors and also the three-way oral and written exchanges between confessors, female penitents, and inquisitors in these institutions.

The first self-denunciation that Antonia Andreozzi gave to the inquisitors was countersigned by her confessor Francesco Maria Lattanzi, who was also interrogated by the judges. Together with another priest, Clemente Giorgi, who supervised the girls, he pleaded for mercy on their behalf.[27] This male intervention is not out of the ordinary. While some conservatory girls were clearly able to read, they did not necessarily develop adequate writing skills, and so male tutors helped them write down their confessions. But there was more involved than the practicalities of literacy. The male scribe who helped their mentee draft a judicial statement was also a priest who was supposed to respect the sacramental secrecy of penance, yet the testimony he wrote down probably repeated the contents of the confession he had just administered. These intricate relationships intersected the internal sacramental forum of confession and the external, judicial forum of the Inquisition in Tridentine Catholicism. Reconceiving the confessor-penitent relationship was, indeed, one of the critical elements in the reorganization of Catholic society pursued by the ecclesiastic hierarchies during the Catholic Reformation. From the foundation of the Roman Holy Office, the inquisitors used confessors as their informants about the social ferment that followed the spread of religious dissent. Confessors were forbidden to absolve sins belonging to the so-called reserved cases—that is, those infractions that implied heresy and apostasy. The list of these was established by papal decree through the bull "*In coena domini.*" In such cases, the confessor was obliged to send the penitents to authorities entitled to dissolve the excommunications. Only after a secret and private abjuration were penitents reintroduced into the community of the faithful, provided that they had cooperated with the inquisitorial justice by denouncing their accomplices.[28]

If confession was a powerful tool to prosecute dissent once it spread, it also became the cornerstone of the Church's renewed endeavor to prevent it before it began. Believers were pressured to regularly engage in the practice of the sacrament. Confession was no longer considered an occasional undertaking, mainly relegated to the Paschal obligation. After the Council of Trent, it became a periodic recurring step within an everlasting process of self-examination that was meant to foster the internalization of the teachings of the Church, in a progressive "turning inward" of the spiritual path of the faithful.[29] Confessors became key figures in the life of Catholic Christians aspiring to live an honest life and navigate the struggles of spiritual improvement. The spiritual direction of women raised specific concerns. The close relationships between women and confessors were constantly scrutinized by the Inquisition, for they often resulted in illicit affairs.[30] With the strict reinforcement of female enclosure came increased control over the vow of chastity, which contributed to the intensification of anxieties that already surrounded the male confessor–female penitent relationship in these secluded environments.[31] In this context, this relationship became a site of contrasting conflicts: while male guides were encouraged in order to discipline female spirituality in the strictures of enclosure, female denunciations of seduction and sexual abuses were also encouraged in order to keep the overbearing licentiousness of the male clergy under control.[32]

Enclosure complicated the close bonds between women and their male confessors. Although the adolescent girls of Saint John the Lateran cannot be equated with ordained nuns, there are clear common features in the ways in which the Roman and the Venetian cases were handled by both the inquisitors and the confessors. Since convents had frequently engaged in the recovery of "lost girls," the establishment of conservatories altered the institutional containment of female vagrancy.[33] Yet the model of female monastic discipline continued to shape the ways in which male tutors controlled the behaviors and thoughts of the subjects housed in these institutions.

In one of her depositions, Antonia stated that in the conservatory the girls were required to practice Ignatius of Loyola's *Spiritual Exercises.* Loyola's method encouraged the practice of periodic and daily writings and constituted the main model for the examination of conscience in early modern Catholic Europe.[34] The depositions of the Roman lay adolescent Antonia and the Venetian adult nun Sister Maria reveal a common training in the refined technique of self-inspection that Ignatius called "spiritual discernment." It is very likely that Antonia, Sister Maria, and all the women in their enclosures negotiated with their confessors what they subsequently repeated to the inquisitors. Their depositions were a form of autobiographical writing "in which either the marks of control and coercion, or those of collaboration and mutual legitimation and promotion" might prevail but whose final aim was "never the 'neutral' transmission of a subjective point of view."[35] We may wonder whether the carefully selected vocabulary that emphasized Antonia's insatiable curiosity and titillating fantasy reflected her own feelings or the stereotypes about women held by her male tutors, which she may have decided to embrace to satisfy the judges' expectations. The women involved in these trials may have played the card of the inopportunely curious, malicious, emotional, and deceiving woman to appease their male prosecutors and guides. Yet they also frequently countered the interpretations of their spiritual directors, claiming the right to interpret what they believed to be the truth of sex in their own terms.

Women's reading strategies kept these apparently contradicting attitudes together. We know that religious contexts were privileged places for women to engage with the written page. The girls of the Roman Conservatory of Saint John the Lateran often pointed to a mysterious book that inspired their beliefs. According to their depositions, it had appeared in different times and places in the conservatory before disappearing once the judicial machine was set in motion. One of the girls' statements provides us with an extremely rare early modern description of the act of reading by a girl who was not part of the learned elites and who did not leave written traces of her intellectual activities. Mariangela Azzolini described being alone in the conservatory's church at a quiet time of the day:

> I saw on a bench a book, whose title I do not know, and I got it, and started reading it, and I came across a passage that described Adam's sin and Fall from the terrestrial paradise, and I heard that that sin was Adam eating the fruit that Eve had handed him, and I started doubting about this thing, believing to myself that that sin had been a sin of impurity committed among them by Adam and Eve themselves; while I was turning to this thought, I came across a maid of the same Conservatory, whom I knew, called Apollonia Domenichini, who has now left the School and got married in Rome (although I do not know precisely where she lives). The two of us left the church and reached a room, and we started discussing that book about Adam's sin. And I realized that she held my same opinion that this sin was other than the eating of a fruit, which is what it was reported in the book, but rather a sin of impurity. I started scrupling about it, and confessed; the confessor told me that this was a blunder, and instructed me to believe, as I do, that that sin was actually the eating of the fruit and not something else, as the Sacred Scripture and the Holy Church teach.... In addition, the same Father confessor told me that I was obliged to denounce the abovementioned Apollonia to the Holy Office too, as I gladly execute, in order to show that I am a real and obedient daughter of the Holy Church and that I want to live and die in the Holy Roman Faith.[36]

Whom this book belonged to and what its contents were is unknown. Yet the act of reading was the starting point of an autonomous, and critical, process of thinking for Mariangela Azzolini. Left alone with the written page, she used it as a stepping stone for accessing a universe of meanings that belonged to her alone. It also seems that Sister Francesca Zerbina and Sister Maria Teresa Garzi were acquainted with some of the ideas found in Beverland's *On Original Sin*. We don't know what may have circulated in the Franciscan monastery of Saint Mary Major in Venice, whether a copy of the book or transcripts from the text or secondhand opinions shared by some rather sophisticated interlocutors. Although Latin was the language of liturgy, it was not usually taught to nuns, and

Beverland's extremely cumbersome Latin baroque prose would create problems even for the most cultivated readers.[37]

In light of these considerations, both the Venetian and the Roman cases seem to confirm that the Church hierarchy was right to fear that reading was a source of corruption for women. Ever since 1559, confessors had not been allowed to absolve penitents who possessed forbidden books, although we know that this resolution was not applied uniformly. Very few women were prosecuted in Rome and Venice for reading heterodox books of humanistic and theological origins. Women were believed to be too ignorant and temperamental to be responsible for their actions and convictions. Since the key in heresy trials was to establish the defendant's voluntary adoption of dissenting beliefs, women were often considered less liable than their male counterparts. Yet other sorts of readings were deemed extremely dangerous; erotic literature, novels, epic poems, and translations of Greek and Latin classics were particularly threatening as they fed the flaws of frivolity, emotional instability, and sensuality that moralists attributed to women. Literacy as a threat to women's morality became a trope that gained increasing circulation.[38] That said, it is not easy to tell how women consumed erotic literature. Very few women, and usually only those among the cultivated elites, have left written traces of their reading experience. The cases analyzed here therefore represent an important opportunity to formulate a tentative interpretation of how women readers could reappropriate an autonomous discourse on eroticism. We have seen how the rhetoric that these women defendants deployed in describing their experiences might be interpreted as a form of "obedient writing"—that is, a way to embody a script palatable to their male interlocutors and guardians. Yet this attitude was also part of a concealment strategy that allowed them to claim an independent knowledge of sexual matters despite their tutors' control. By meeting the expectations of their male protectors and guides about their supposed maliciousness and proclivity for lascivious thoughts, they would be able to open a space of freedom where they could elaborate a personal discourse on sexual desire that explored the role played by lust in the foundational myth of the Fall from Grace.[39]

Conclusion

THIS BOOK has explored how the belief that Adam and Eve committed sodomy in the Garden of Eden circulated from the second half of the sixteenth century to the mid-eighteenth century. It was discussed in shops and taverns by workers and artisans, spread from pulpits by some rogue clerics, and written up in treatises by highly educated Latinists. They had little in common socially. What some shared was the conviction that by enjoying anal sex, Adam and Eve were laying claim to something that God meant to keep to himself. That made them disobedient; it was their original sin and Fall from Grace. But the ones telling this story shared more: they believed that the cover-up—the denial that the act of sodomy was the act of rebellion—that began in the book of Genesis and continued on through all the Abrahamic traditions and institutions simply proved that religion itself was a fraud. That made their story all the more radical, outrageous, and popular—and all the more compelling as it traveled through various underground routes through the centuries.

We began by looking at how this belief spread orally among shopkeepers, pharmacists, jurists, and artisans, analyzing hundreds of folios of trial records from inquisitorial archives dispersed across the Italian peninsula and Spain. These inquisitorial records testify to the oral transmission of this belief, as we have demonstrated by reconstructing the complex interplay between prosecutors, witnesses, and defendants in the frame of the inquisitorial procedure. But this belief did not just emerge in judicial records. We can find it in seventeenth- and eighteenth-century printed and manuscript works written by more educated authors who were often associated in some way with the movement known as libertinism. Both in the judicial records and in these literary expressions, the idea that sodomy was the first act of human disobedience to God's commands intersected with a cluster of beliefs that leaned toward radical skepticism and atheism. We see their dynamic coupling in various manifestations of dissent, which often extended to the opinion that institutionalized faiths (and Christianity in particular) were political devices fabricated by the ruling classes to keep the unlearned masses under control. In this reading, all religion was a fraud.

We see these two apparently disjointed beliefs emerging clearly in two inquisitorial cases in Italy. One involved the apothecary Marcello Impicciato (1598) and the other the Minor Observant friar Giovan Battista d'Antrodoco (1662), both of whom were tried—respectively—in Naples and Rome. They claimed that God forbade sodomy because he deemed it a "celestial pleasure" that he wanted to keep for himself alone. What Genesis described as a fruit hanging on the Tree of the Knowledge of Good and Evil was not the apple that many thought. In fact, it was not fruit at all but a metaphor for the buttocks. "Taking the apple" was just a decorous way of saying that Adam had taken Eve sexually from behind. When God forbade them taking the apple, he was really forbidding sodomy, and so in transgressing the precept, Adam and Eve dared to make themselves like gods, an act of insubordination that God punished by expelling them from the Garden of Eden.

This account of the expulsion of Adam and Eve from Eden constitutes a radicalization of a trope that was widely used in libertine circles across Italy and Europe to criticize the unfair social order maintained by the clerical and political elites. Libertines argued that the ruling classes invented the prohibition of sodomy to reserve this celestial pleasure for themselves alone, keeping the populace in check with the threat of eternal damnation. We find this reading in two of the most daring libertine texts circulating in the sixteenth and seventeenth centuries, Antonio Vignali's *The Tangle of Pricks* and Antonio Rocco's *Alcibiades the Schoolboy.* By projecting onto God the deception perpetuated by the upper classes, our dissenters radicalized this libertine argument and made God himself the father of all earthly frauds. Their stance proves that, when these ideas were put into writing, they often gained a more refined theoretical background while losing some of their unapologetic radicality.

We see this further when we compare the trials of our Neapolitan apothecary Marcello Impicciato and the famous Dominican friar and philosopher Tommaso Campanella. Campanella was prosecuted in Naples for his part in an attempted coup against the Spanish monarchy in southern Italy in precisely the same years that Impicciato was facing inquisitorial justice. Most of Campanella's charges overlapped with the accusations leveled against Impicciato, and the judges' harshness toward the apothecary was likely due to their anxiety about how ideas like Campanella's could become dangerous for the political stability of the state. By comparing the documentation from Campanella's trial and the evidence from Impicciato's proceedings, we can better understand the wider context in which they took place. This comparison sheds light on both the societal impact of the spread of religious dissent and the ways in which authorities attempted to frame and control it. Reading the two cases together clarifies Impicciato's case and also highlights some previously overlooked aspects of Campanella's trial, particularly regarding what I take to be his views connecting sex with original sin.

Campanella was also accused of having authored a version of the *Treatise on the Three Impostors,* a notorious and elusive compendium of atheism that was widely discussed in the late Middle Ages and the early modern period, despite the fact that a copy of it had never been found. Attributed to various authors back as far as the court of the thirteenth-century Holy Roman Emperor Frederick II, it surfaced only when a published version in French was printed at The Hague in 1719. This ephemeral book condensed the theory of the fraudulence of religions into a clear statement: Moses, Jesus, and Muḥammad were tricksters who deceived humanity with their lies for the sake of power and honors. The accusation that Campanella authored this book was probably specious, but we have shown that the belief that sodomy was the original act of disobedience to God's commands circulated in the cultural milieu from which the first print version of this work later emerged. The evidence we have collected seems to suggest that the association between the oral circulation of this belief and the long-term genesis of the theory of the fraudulence of religion was far from accidental.

It was the seventeenth-century Dutch humanist and author Hadriaan Beverland who gave the theme of Adam and Eve's sodomy its most brazen expression in his scandalous treatise *On Original Sin* (1678 and 1679). The book's main argument is that sex was the original sin. In this context, the reference to Adam and Eve's sodomy played a crucial role in explaining the genesis of "deviant" sexual desires after the Fall. Various extraliterary sources suggest that Beverland credited Italian ecclesiastical environments as the seedbed for this belief, and the inquisitorial testimonies considered here certainly seem to confirm that. Like Campanella, Beverland was accused of authoring a version of the *Three Impostors.* Although the accusation was most likely false, we know that Beverland's critical approach to the Scriptures was clearly indebted to Spinoza's rational exegesis of sacred texts. Spinoza's philosophy was widely discussed by Dutch radical dissenters, who trivialized its complex metaphysics and bent it toward an explicitly atheistic reading. Their simplified version of Spinoza's philosophy became one of the pillars of a rapidly expanding structure of radical unbelief, which took print form in *The Life and Spirit of Mr. Baruch Spinoza* (1719) and contained the first systematic presentation of the legend of the three impostors ever to appear in print. This text was presented as a transcription of a medieval original supposedly written by Frederick II's chancellor Pier della Vigna, who in 1239 was accused by Pope Gregory IX of having written the polemical pamphlet together with his emperor. In reality, the eighteenth-century *Treatise* was a collection of excerpts from Spinoza, Hobbes, and various libertine thinkers. One of them, François de La Mothe Le Vayer, had written earlier about Adam and Eve enjoying anal sex in the Garden of Eden. He revived the Italian erotic theme of sodomy as a pleasure reserved for the ruling classes, which we have seen emerging in a number of the inquisitorial cases analyzed here. Le Vayer also mentioned both Italian popular culture and a rabbinic source as further inspirations for this heterodox opinion.

While the evidence is scattered, enough of it connects and suggests that a strand in popular opinion representing sodomy as the first act of disobedience against God probably originated as a humorous story in Italian ecclesiastical circles before circulating orally in environments where it became connected to the broader theory that all religious were essentially fraudulent. As with all cases of oral transmission, we have individual cases, hints, and suggestions. Given its heretical nature, this explanation of the Fall and its extension into the claim that Christianity was fraudulent shows that there are currents within the larger stream of radical dissent that need further investigation, above all in the kinds of judicial sources that testify to its oral circulation.

We should not be surprised that opinions that were spreading by word of mouth could provide the breeding ground for the subsequent philosophical elaboration of radically atheistic stances. Our close reading of the trial reports has also shown that this oral circulation was not without a certain degree of theoretical speculation. In some instances, the documents reported lists of books read by the defendants. While some dissenters read them as manuals of magic, they also had philosophical content, and it is worth noting that some of the authors mentioned in the inquisitorial proceedings have been recognized as early spreaders of the theory of religious fraud. Girolamo Cardano, who influenced the Sicilian jurisconsult Ludovico Garrano, was accused by Marchand of spreading the ideas contained in the *Treatise on the Three Impostors*. He was suspected of Averroistic leanings, which Church authorities took as code for atheism. The Arab philosopher Ibn Rushd, known in the West as Averroes, was falsely accused of having been the earliest author to ever characterize Moses, Jesus, and Muḥammad as the deceivers of humankind. While Cardano recanted his suspected Averroism by writing a treatise on the immortality of the soul, some passages of his *On Subtlety* resonated with Averroistic ideas widely discussed in radical circles. He also constituted an important source of transmission of the idea of great astrological conjunctions, often used in libertine circles as an argument to substantiate the hypothesis that religious phenomena were mere human fabrications, influenced by the stars and destined to follow one another like historical political regimes. This thesis had been popularized in the Middle Ages by Pietro d'Abano, another author whom our dissenters read and commented on.

By analyzing the networks across which this unorthodox opinion spread, we can appreciate how reflections on sex and the body were crucial to undermining that broad system of beliefs that projected happiness into the afterlife at the expense of the embodied experience of pleasure in the here and now. Asserting that sodomy was as natural as any other type of sex was a powerful means of defending the importance of sexual gratification against those moralizing approaches that limited intercourse to procreation. At the same time, the fact that these dissenters depicted God as both a jealous sodomite and the first trickster of humankind makes the link between religious and sexual criticism more explicit and subversive than any contemporary and later expressions of learned unbelief.

Besides helping restore the relevant role played by sex in the development of radical religious dissent, the cases examined in this book also reveal the extent to which dissenting opinions were often shaped against the backdrop of the interconfessional and interreligious clashes that pervaded Christianity at that time. Some of the opinions held by our dissenters referred to the ongoing polemics between Catholics and Protestants, while others originated in debates that took place at the intersection of the three main Mediterranean monotheistic religions. Among them stood out the belief that all faiths equally led to the eternal salvation, a claim that resonated with widespread feelings among both the learned and the unlearned in the early modern world. This idea was often used to criticize any form of religious fundamentalism, by proving that, in fact, the ultimate truth about religion was unknown and unknowable. In these instances, mocking the tenet of original sin had a twofold result. On the one hand, it undermined centuries of condemnations of lust, which, according to the Augustinian account of the Fall, was the main consequence of original sin. On the other, it disproved the opinion that Catholic baptism was the only remedy to the sinfulness inherited by humankind, an idea that was further reinforced in post-Tridentine Catholic society to stiffen the boundaries dividing Catholics from Protestants, Muslims, Jews, and followers of any other world religions.

I have deliberately avoided fashioning these manifestations of heterodoxy as a formalized and coherent "heresy" because that would reproduce the strategy often adopted by the inquisitors to make intelligible and controllable what they were unable to decipher and understand. The apothecaries, oarsmen, friars, and nuns considered here were clearly unsystematic experimenters. Yet they were also capable of reframing feelings that were widespread across the social spectrum and that had gained renewed currency in the Renaissance elite intellectual culture: naturalism; materialistic and skeptical views that often originated in classical texts or at the intersection of faiths; interconfessional conflicts after the Reformation; political theories that vulgarized, simplified, and popularized Machiavelli's thought; arguments in favor of sodomy discussed in sixteenth- and seventeenth-century Italian academies; reflections of libertine thinkers from across Europe about sex and religion; and new philosophical approaches to science, human history, religion, and society that began emerging in the seventeenth century. None of these varied expressions of dissent took place by canceling what had come before. Rather, the dissenters who held the opinion that Adam and Eve disobeyed God by enjoying anal sex demonstrated an incredible capacity to hold together disparate sources of knowledge, which they creatively adapted to challenge established systems of belief. Such complexity warn us against the temptation to construct an idealized genealogy of western European values and identities that emphasizes concepts like tolerance and secularization. These dissenters referred to tropes and strategies of communication that were clearly at odds with any ideal "modern" or progressive approach advocating sexual and religious "freedom." Rather than reinforcing "Western modernity," this book aims to soften the edges of the myth by restoring the complexity of this hidden past of dissent and radical irreligiousness.

The very male-centered approach that comes from reviewing opinions that surfaced in judicial and literary sources should put paid to any idea of a "presentist" or "progressive" interpretation. The defendants analyzed here celebrated pleasure exclusively from the perspective of the insertive partner. It is true that some literary works like *The Tangle of Pricks* and *Alcibiades the Schoolboy* deemed anal sex to be morally acceptable only if it was consensual and ensured the mutual pleasure of both partners. This deserves attention. Although the predominance of pederastic relationships is still disconcerting for present-day readers, we should not forget that the age gap in premodern homosexual relationships, which we can reconstruct from many studies of male homosexuality in Renaissance Italy and Europe, was not in fact wider than the gap separating heterosexual couples. Moreover, many moral and legal treatises of the time deemed the heterosexual rape of a child a minor offense if compared with consensual homosexual intercourse, even among peers. Reading these authors together allows us to understand how these reflections, by putting consensus in the foreground, challenged contemporary moral standards. That said, literary works like those of Vignali and Rocco could also be frankly exploitative, and we know that they were influential. The behaviors captured in the judicial sources clearly depicted brutal attitudes that often resulted in abusive relationships with both women and boys.

Women's encounters with the belief that Adam and Eve enjoyed sodomy in the Garden of Eden is harder to trace. The evidence we have is later. The women prosecuted in these later trials mobilized heterodox readings of the myth of the Fall to claim interpretive autonomy and independence from their male tutors, particularly in contexts shaped by religiously enforced segregation. It is not surprising that, in these instances, the theme of sodomy faded into the background, and reflections on it seem to have been blended with the wider opinion that the cause of the Fall was the discovery of sex by the first couple. Indeed, at the end of the seventeenth century, Inquisitors began paying attention to this broader belief, which was progressively gaining momentum in public opinion. We can confirm this trend by analyzing Jean-Frédéric Bernard's 1714 French adaptation of Beverland's *On Original Sin.* Bernard was an intellectual who clearly gravitated toward the cultural environment of radical Dutch atheists and dissenters that generated the first print edition of the *Treatise on the Three Impostors.* Yet his *State of Man* neglected the theme of prelapsarian sodomy, except for a possible veiled allusion in a passage devoted to discussing the geographical location of the Garden of Eden. Bernard's treatise set the foundation for a reading of religious feelings as mere psychological phenomena. This new understanding fostered a comparative protoanthropological approach to religions that found its maturest expression in his subsequent work, *Religious Ceremonies and Customs of all the People of the World.* Bernard discussed sexual matters overtly in contexts where religious beliefs were subjected to a new rational analysis. This process progressively pushed out of the closet themes that had long circulated exclusively in a more or less clandestine form, whether orally or in print. Co-opting these expressions of radical religious dissent for the purposes of a more explicit political program of reforms had an impact on their contents. When sexual themes rooted in radical dissent merged with the explicit fight against Catholic obscurantism, they gained some momentum as transformative political tools, but they also lost some of their obscene radicality. This book has aimed to recover that radical obscenity, voiced by artisans, shopkeepers, friars, and schoolgirls in trials, recorded and preserved in transcripts, but lost in the silence of the archives for centuries.

ABBREVIATIONS

MANUSCRIPT SOURCES

ACDF	Archivio della Congregazione della Dottrina della Fede
AHNM	Archivo Histórico Nacional de Madrid
ASDN	Archivio Storico Diocesano di Napoli
ASDPi	Archivio Storico Diocesano di Pisa
ASV	Archivio di Stato di Venezia

PRINTED SOURCES

AT	Tommaso Campanella, *L'ateismo trionfato, ovvero riconoscimento filosofico della religione universale contra l'antichristianesimo machiavelliano,* ed. Germana Ernst (Pisa: Scuola Normale Superore, 2004).
CD	*The Canons and Decrees of the Sacred and Œcumenical Council of Trent,* trans. James Waterworth (London: C. Dolman, 1848).
CN	Piet Steenbakkers, Jetze Touber, and Jeroen van de Ven, "A Clandestine Notebook (1678–79) on Spinoza, Beverland, Politics, the Bible and Sex: Utrecht UL, ms. 1284*," *LIAS* 38 (2011): 225–365.
DPO	Hadriaan Beverland, *Hadrian Beverland's "De peccato originali" (On Original Sin 1679),* ed. and trans. Karen E. Hollewand and Floris Verhaart (Leiden: Brill, 2023); orig. ed.: Hadrian Beverland, *De Peccato originali, κατ' ἐξοχὴν sic nuncupato, dissertatio* (Ex Typographeio, 1679).
EH	Jean Frederic Bernard, *Etat de l'homme dans le peché originel, où l'on fait voir quelle est la source, quelles les causes et les suites, de ce peché dans le Monde* (Printed in the World, 1714).
PROCESSI	Luigi Amabile, *Fra Tommaso Campanella. La sua congiura, i suoi processi e la sua pazzia,* vol. 3, *Documenti e illustrazioni* (Naples: A. Morano, 1882).

TTI — *Trattato dei tre impostori. La vita e lo spirito del signor Benedetto de Spinoza,* ed. and trans. Silvia Berti (Turin: Einaudi, 1994).

REFERENCE WORKS

DBI — *Dizionario biografico degli italiani* (Rome: Istituto della Enciclopedia italiana, 19612020).

DSI — Adriano Prosperi, dir., Vincenzo Lavenia and John Tedeschi, eds., *Dizionario storico dell'Inquisizione* (Pisa: Edizioni della Normale, 2010).

NOTES

INTRODUCTION

1. For a discussion of this scholarship, see Chapter 1 and Chapter 6.
2. On the Middle Ages, see Michael Goodich, *The Unmentionable Vice: Homosexuality in the Later Medieval Period* (Santa Barbara: ABC-Clio, 1979); John Boswell, *Christianity, Social Tolerance, and Homosexuality: Gay People in Western Europe from the Beginning of the Christian Era to the Fourteenth Century* (Chicago: University of Chicago Press, 1980), 269–332. On the transfer of old stereotypes to the native population during the conquests, see Rudi C. Bleys, *The Geography of Perversion: Male-to-Male Sexual Behaviour outside the West and the Ethnographic Imagination, 1750–1918* (New York: New York University Press, 1995); Carmen Nocentelli, *Empires of Love: Europe, Asia, and the Making of Early Modern Identity* (Philadelphia: University of Pennsylvania Press, 2014); Valerie Traub, "Sexuality," in *A Cultural History of Western Empires in the Renaissance*, ed. Ania Loomba (London: Bloomsbury Academic, 2019), 147–180.
3. Helmut Puff, *Sodomy in Reformation Germany and Switzerland, 1400–1600* (Chicago: University of Chicago Press, 2003).
4. Federico Barbierato, *The Inquisitor in the Hat Shop: Inquisition, Forbidden Books, and Unbelief in Early Modern Venice* (Farnham: Ashgate, 2012), 102; Stuart B. Schwartz, *All Can Be Saved: Religious Tolerance and Salvation in the Iberian Atlantic World* (New Haven, CT: Yale University Press, 2008), 31–33; Giovanni Romeo, *Amori proibiti. I concubini tra Chiesa e inquisizione: Napoli, 1563–1656* (Rome and Bari: Laterza, 2008), 86, 104–105; Romano Canosa, *Sessualità e inquisizione in Italia tra cinquecento e seicento* (Rome: Sapere 2000, 1994), 15–24, 123–130.
5. This opposition was mostly due to a crystallized interpretation of Michel Foucault's and John Boswell's contributions to this field of research. More recent research has proved this opposition to be specious when one returns to the roots of Boswell's and Foucault's original positions: Carolyn Dinshaw, "Touching on the Past," in *The Boswell Thesis: Essays on Christianity,*

Social Tolerance, and Homosexuality, ed. Mathew Kuefler (Chicago: University of Chicago Press, 2006), 57–73; Michel Foucault, *The Will to Knowledge*, trans. Robert Hurley (London: Penguin, 1998; orig. ed. 1976); Boswell, *Christianity, Social Tolerance, and Homosexuality*. See also Scott Spector, Helmut Puff, and Dagmar Herzog, eds., *After the History of Sexuality: German Genealogies with and beyond Foucault* (New York: Berghahn Books, 2012); Howard Chiang, ed., "Revisiting the History of Sexuality: Thinking with Foucault at Forty," special issue, *Cultural History* 5, no. 2 (2016).

6. After Foucault, historians who refused to use contemporary categories contrasted previous constructs with a supposedly "modern" homosexual identity. Queer theorists overturned this question by deconstructing the latter. See Teresa de Lauretiis, ed., "Queer Theory: Lesbian and Gay Sexualities," issue, *Differences: A Journal of Feminist Cultural Studies* 3, no. 2 (1991); Eve Kosofsky Sedgwick, *Epistemology of the Closet* (Berkeley: University of California Press, 1990). David Halperin attempted to integrate Sedgwick's insights into a historicist approach: David Halperin, *How to Do the History of Homosexuality* (Chicago: University of Chicago Press, 2002). His attempt raised many criticisms: Jonathan Goldberg and Madhavi Menon, "Queering History," *PMLA* 120, no. 5 (2005), 1608–1617; Carla Freccero, *Queer/Early/Modern* (Durham, NC: Duke University Press, 2006), 31–50. But it also inspired substantial critical defense: Valerie Traub, "The New Unhistoricism in Queer Studies," *PMLA* 128, no. 1 (2013): 21–39.
7. See below, Chapter 1.
8. Judith M. Bennett, *History Matters: Patriarchy and the Challenge of Feminism* (Philadelphia: University of Pennsylvania Press, 2006). The centrality of penetration has been particularly explored in relation to the invisibilization of lesbian desire. See Valerie Traub, "The (In)Significance of 'Lesbian' Desire," in *Queering the Renaissance*, ed. Jonathan Goldberg (Durham, NC: Duke University Press, 1994), 61–83.
9. This issue will be deeply discussed throughout the book. I refer the readers to the bibliographic references contained in the individual chapters.
10. In particular, see Chapter 1.
11. Although some dissenters attributed sodomitic preferences to Jesus. See Chapter 1.
12. Interactions between oral and written transmission have been largely debated: Robert Darnton, "History of Reading," in *New Perspectives on Historical Writing*, ed. Peter Burke (University Park: Pennsylvania State University Press, 1992), 140–167; Roger Chartier, *The Order of Books: Readers, Authors, and Libraries in Europe between the Fourteenth and Eighteenth Centuries*, trans. Lydia G. Cochrane (1992; repr., Stanford, CA: Stanford University Press, 1994); Guglielmo Cavallo and Roger Chartier, eds., *A History of Reading in the West*, trans. Lydia G. Cochrane (1995; repr., Amherst:

University of Massachusetts Press, 1999). On literacy, readership, and the nature of reading in its impact on popular culture, see Armando Petrucci, ed., *Libri editori e pubblico nell'Europa moderna. Guida storica e critica* (Rome: Laterza, 1977). Particularly relevant for the cross-fertilization of oral and written culture is Peter Burke, *The Art of Conversation* (Ithaca, NY: Cornell University Press, 1993). On the Italian Renaissance, see Brian Richardson, *Print Culture in Renaissance Italy: The Editor and the Vernacular Text, 1470–1600* (Cambridge: Cambridge University Press, 1994); Richardson, *Printing, Writers and Readers in Renaissance Italy* (Cambridge: Cambridge University Press, 1999); Richardson, *Manuscript Culture in Renaissance Italy* (Cambridge: Cambridge University Press, 2009). See also Paul Grendler, "Form and Function in Italian Renaissance Popular Books," *Renaissance Quarterly* 46 (1993): 451–485; James K. Coleman, *A Sudden Frenzy: Improvisation, Orality, and Power in Renaissance Italy* (Toronto: University of Toronto Press, 2022). The relationship between oral and written culture is crucial to the history of religious radical dissent. The terms of the question were set by Carlo Ginzburg's *The Cheese and the Worms: The Cosmos of a Sixteenth-Century Miller,* trans. Anne C. Tedeschi and John Tedeschi (Baltimore: Johns Hopkins University Press, 2013). Ginzburg's notion of "peasant culture," however, has been subject to criticism: see Giorgio Spini, "Noterelle libertine," *Rivista storica italiana* 88 (1976): 792–802; Paola Zambelli, "From Menocchio to Piero della Francesca," *Historical Journal* 28 (1985): 983–999. On the use of inquisitorial sources as testimonies to early modern oral cultures, see Carlo Ginzburg, *Clues, Myths, and the Historical Method,* trans. John Tedeschi and Anne C. Tedeschi (Baltimore: Johns Hopkins University Press, 2013); Andrea del Col, "I processi dell'Inquisizione come fonte: Considerazioni diplomatiche e storiche," *Annuario Istituto Storico Italiano per l'età moderna e contemporanea* 35 (1984): 3–51.

13. See Jean-Pierre Cavaillé, *Les déniaisés. Irréligion et libertinage au début de l'époque moderne* (Paris: Classiques Garnier, 2013), 9–18.

14. Elizabeth Horodowich, "Introduction: Speech and Oral Culture in Early Modern Europe and Beyond," *Journal of Early Modern History* 16, no. 4–5 (2012): 301–313.

15. Filippo de Vivo, *Information and Communication in Venice: Rethinking Early Modern Politics* (Oxford: Oxford University Press, 2007), 12.

16. De Vivo, *Information and Communication in Venice,* 9. See also Brendan Dooley, "News and Doubt in Early Modern Culture: or, Are We Having a Public Sphere Yet?," in *The Politics of Information in Early Modern Europe,* ed. Brendan Dooley and Sabrina A. Baron (London: Routledge, 2001), 275–290; Mario Infelise, *Prima dei giornali. Alle origini della pubblica informazione (secoli XVI e XVII)* (Rome: Laterza, 2002).

17. Alec Ryrie, *Unbelievers: An Emotional History of Doubt* (Cambridge, MA: Harvard University Press, 2019), 3–7. For a lengthier discussion of the historiography on late medieval and early modern atheism, see Chapter 1.
18. Barbierato, *Inquisitor in the Hat Shop,* 290–291.
19. Mercedes García-Arenal, ed., *After Conversion: Iberia and the Emergence of Modernity* (Leiden: Brill, 2016). This book challenges Richard Popkin's analysis of early modern skepticism as a result of the influence of Pyrrhonian skepticism. Richard H. Popkin, *History of Scepticism: From Savonarola to Bayle* (1960; repr., Oxford: Oxford University Press, 2003). On the revision of Popkin's paradigm, see also Yosef Kaplan, "Richard Popkin's Marrano Problem," in *The Legacies of Richard Popkin,* ed. Jeremy D. Popkin (Dordrecht: Springer, 2008), 197–212. For a recent reassessment, see Stefania Pastore, "Doubt and Unbelief in the Early Modern Era: Diego Hurtado de Mendoza and the Spanish Tradition," in *Formations of Belief: Historical Approaches to Religion and the Secular,* ed. Philip Nord, Katja Guenther, and Max Weiss (Princeton, NJ: Princeton University Press, 2019), 67–84; "From 'Marranos' to 'Unbelievers': The Spanish Peccadillo in Sixteenth-Century Italy," in *Dissimulation and Deceit in Early Modern Europe,* ed. Miriam Eliav-Feldon and Tamar Herzig (Houndmills, Basingstoke, Hampshire: Palgrave Macmillan, 2015), 79–93. More on this in Chapter 4.
20. See Patricia Crone, "Oral Transmission of Subversive Ideas from the Islamic World to Europe: The Case of the Three Impostors," in *Islam, the Ancient Near East and Varieties of Godlessness: Collected Studies in Three Volumes* (Leiden: Brill, 2016), 3:200–238. On the Islamic genesis of skepticism and unbelief, see also Sarah Stroumsa, *Freethinkers of Medieval Islam: Ibn al-Rāwandī, Abū Bakr al-Rāzī, and Their Impact on Islamic Thought* (Leiden: Brill, 1999), which also contains a section devoted to the transmission of radical ideas beyond the Islamic world (214–238).
21. On toleration as a result of concrete practices of coexistence, see Benjamin J. Kaplan, *Divided by Faith: Religious Conflict and the Practice of Toleration in Early Modern Europe* (Cambridge, MA: Belknap, 2007); Schwartz, *All Can Be Saved.*
22. Among others, see Wilbur K. Jordan, *The Development of Religious Toleration in England from the Accession of James I to the Convention of the Long Parliament, 1603–1640* (Cambridge, MA: Harvard University Press, 1936); Joseph Lecler, *Histoire de la tolérance au siècle de la Réforme,* 2 vols. (Paris: Aubier, 1955); Henry Kamen, *The Rise of Toleration* (London: Weidenfeld and Nicolson, 1967); Cary J. Nederman and John Christian Laursen, eds., *Difference and Dissent: Theories of Toleration in Medieval and Early Modern Europe* (Lanham, MD: Rowman & Littlefield, 1996); Nederman and Laursen, eds., *Beyond the Persecuting Society: Religious Toleration before the Enlightenment* (Philadelphia: University of Pennsylvania Press, 1998); Ole Peter Grell and

Robert W. Scribner, eds., *Tolerance and Intolerance in the European Reformation* (Cambridge: Cambridge University Press, 2002); Perez Zagorin, *How the Idea of Religious Toleration Came to the West* (Princeton, NJ: Princeton University Press, 2003); Benjamin J. Kaplan and Jaap Geraerts, eds., *Early Modern Toleration: New Approaches* (London: Routledge, 2024). This historiography has evolved from a traditional Whiggish approach that attributed the rise of tolerance to seventeenth- and eighteenth-century northern European intellectual elites to concrete practices of toleration in Reformation Europe and the Middle Ages.

CHAPTER ONE ~ ATHEISM AND SODOMY IN THE GARDEN OF EDEN

1. Naples had been under the control of the crown of Aragon since 1442 and had been a viceroyalty of the Spanish monarchy since 1503. Nevertheless, unlike any other of the crown's territories, the city managed to avert the control of the Spanish Inquisition. Popular resistance prompted Emperor Charles V to adopt a new strategy of control. Rather than calling an inquisitor from Spain, Charles asked the Holy See to extend its authority over the city by sending a delegate inquisitor on behalf of the pontiff. Despite the turmoil, Paul III, pope from 1534 to 1549, succeeded in introducing a "vicar" of the chief inquisitor (in Italian, a "commissario"), who acted as a de facto inquisitor. Giuseppe Fonseca, "Napoli," in *Dizionario storico dell'Inquisizione,* dir. Adriano Prosperi, ed. Vincenzo Lavenia and John Tedeschi (Pisa: Edizioni della Normale, 2010), 2:1097–1099 (hereafter cited as *DSI*).
2. Archivio Storico Diocesano di Napoli, SU, 249 (hereafter cited as ASDN). The document is not currently available for consultation because of its bad state of conservation. I would like to thank Professor Giovanni Romeo for sharing his summary of the trial with me. In the inquisitorial practice, defendants could be sentenced to abjuration "de levi" (moderate) either if the matter was irrelevant or the evidence was insufficient. Conversely, the abjuration "de vehementi" (vehement) was meted out for serious offences against the faith that were supported by consistent evidence.
3. ASDN, SU, 756, c. 2r. Quote by Romeo, *Amori proibiti,* 106. All translations are mine unless otherwise indicated.
4. ASDN, SU, 1067, f. 10v.
5. ASDN, SU, 1067, f. 14r.
6. ASDN, SU, 1067, f. 75v.
7. Pierroberto Scaramella, *Lettere della congregazione del Sant'ufficio ai tribunali di fede di Napoli, 1563–1625* (Milan: Università Di Trieste, 2002), 335.
8. Scaramella, *Lettere,* 336.

9. ASDN, SU, 1067, f. 101r.
10. ASDN, SU, 1067, ff. 49r, 102r (formal accusation), 143r, 176r.
11. ASDN, SU, 1067, ff. 102r, 43v.
12. ASDN, SU, 1067, f. 102v.
13. ASDN, SU, 1067, f. 10v (emphasis added).
14. ASDN, SU, 1067, ff. 11v, 15v (emphasis added).
15. Lucien Febvre, *The Problem of Unbelief in the Sixteenth Century: The Religion of Rabelais,* trans. Beatrice Gottlieb (Cambridge, MA: Harvard University Press, 1982).
16. See David Wootton, "Lucien Febvre and the Problem of Unbelief in the Early Modern Period," *Journal of Modern History* 4 (1988): 695–730. Recently, Michael Hunter, *Atheists and Atheism before the Enlightenment: The English and Scottish experience* (Cambridge: Cambridge University Press, 2023).
17. Paul O. Kristeller, "The Myth of Renaissance Atheism and the French Tradition of Free Thought," *Journal of the History of Philosophy* 6, no. 3 (1968): 233–243. Similar conclusions in Michael J. Buckley, *At the Origins of Modern Atheism* (New Haven, CT: Yale University Press, 1987); Alan Charles Kors, *Atheism in France, 1650–1729* (Princeton, NJ: Princeton University Press, 1990). For an analysis of anti-atheistic rhetoric, see Kenneth Sheppard, *Anti-atheism in Early Modern England, 1580–1720: The Atheist Answered and His Error Confuted* (Leiden: Brill, 2015).
18. Nicholas Davidson, "Unbelief and Atheism in Italy: 1500–1700," in *Atheism from the Reformation to the Enlightenment,* ed. Michael Hunter and David Wootton (Oxford: Oxford University Press, 1992), 55–86 (85).
19. Gianluca Mori, *Early Modern Atheism from Spinoza to d'Holbach* (Oxford: Voltaire Foundation, 2021). For Mori, we can speak of atheism when the belief in a first cause was conflated with a materialistic understanding that made this same cause mechanistically subject to its own laws, without implying the exercise of free will, which is the main attribute of the personal God worshipped in monotheistic religions.
20. ASDN, SU, 1067, f. 101v (formal accusation).
21. ASDN, SU, 1067, ff. 14r, 22v, 143v.
22. Crone, "Oral Transmission of Subversive Ideas," 202.
23. While Robert Bader has pointed out Origen's omissions, Origen's reproduction of *Alethes Logos* has been considered reliable by others. Bader, *Der Alethes Logos des Kelsos* (Stuttgart: Kohlhammer, 1940), 10–24; Karl J. Neumann, "Celsus," in *Realencyclopadie fur Protestantische Theologie und Kirche,* ed. Johann Jakob Herzog and Albert Hauck (Leipzig: Hinrichs, 1910), 3:772–775; Henry Chadwick, introduction to *Contra Celsum,* by Origen, trans. and ed. Henry Chadwick (Cambridge: Cambridge University Press, 1980), xxii–xxiii.
24. Some scholars have hypothesized that this Jew was not a fictional character but a mid-second-century Alexandrian Jewish writer: Maren R. Niehoff,

"A Jewish Critique of Christianity from Second-Century Alexandria: Revisiting the Jew Mentioned in Contra Celsum," *Journal of Early Christian Studies* 21, no. 2 (2013): 151–175.

25. Celsus, *On the True Doctrine: A Discourse against the Christians*, trans. and ed. Joseph Hoffmann (New York: Oxford University Press, 1987), 57–59, 66–65.

26. Yaacov Deutsch, "The Second Life of the Life of Jesus: Christian Reception of Toledot Yeshu," in *Toledot Yeshu ("The Life Story of Jesus") Revisited: A Princeton Conference*, ed. Peter Schäfer, Michael Meerson, and Yaacov Deutsch (Tübingen: Mohr Siebeck, 2011), 283–295.

27. This work circulated only in manuscript form until it was eventually edited and printed by Joseph de Voisin in 1651: Ramón Martí, *Pugio Fidei Raymundi Martini Ordinis Praedicatorum Adversus Mauros et Iudæos* [. . .] *Cum obseruationibus Domini Iosephi De Voisin* (Paris: apud Ioannem Henault, 1651); Görge K. Hasselhoff, "The Projected Edition of Ramon Martí's *Pugio Fidei*: A Survey and a Stemma," in *Ramon Martí's "Pugio fidei": Studies and Texts*, ed. Görge K. Hasselhoff and Alexander Fidora (Santa Coloma de Queralt: Obrador Edèndum, 2017), 23–38 (23).

28. Deutsch, "Second Life of the Life of Jesus," 288. See also Riccardo di Segni, "La tradizione testuale delle Toledòth Jéshu: manoscritti, edizioni a stampa, classificazione," *La rassegna mensile di Israel* 50 (1984): 83–100. See also Daniel Barbu, "The Case about Jesus: (Counter-)History and Casuistry in *Toledot Yeshu*," in *A Historical Approach to Casuistry: Norms and Exceptions in a Comparative Perspective*, ed. Carlo Ginzburg and Lucio Biasiori (London: Bloomsbury, 2019), 65–97. With specific reference to the history of sexuality, see Natalie E. Latteri, "Playing the Whore: Illicit Union and the Biblical Typology of Promiscuity in the Toledot Yeshu," *Shofar* 33, no. 2 (2015): 87–102.

29. Deutsch, "Second Life of the Life of Jesus," 290, 294.

30. Ruth Mazo Karras, "The Aerial Battle in the Toledot Yeshu and Sodomy in the Late Middle Ages," *Medieval Encounters* 19 (2013): 493–533 (501–503).

31. Karras, "Aerial Battle," 506–507.

32. Thomas Ebendorfer, *Das jüdische Leben Jesu Toldot Jeschu: Die älteste lateinische Übersetzung in den Falsitates Judeorum von Thomas Ebendorfer*, ed. Brigitta Callsen, Fritz Peter Knapp, Manuela Niesner, and Martin Przybilski (Vienna: R. Oldenbourg, 2003), 56. Translated by Ruth Mazo Karras in "The Aerial Battle," 507–508.

33. ASDN, SU, 1067, f. 49r.

34. The trial of Francesco Calcagno was transcribed and analyzed by Giovanni Dall'Orto: "Il processo a un libertino omosessuale: Francesco Calcagno [1550]," *Sodoma* 5 (1993): 43–55. For a recent interpretation, see Lucia Felici, "A Sixteenth-Century Libertine Priest: Francesco Calcagno," in

Cursed Blessings: Sex and Religious Radical Dissent in Early Modern Europe, ed. Umberto Grassi (New York: Routledge, 2024), 22–39.

35. Millar Maclure, ed., *Christopher Marlowe: The Critical Heritage* (London: Routledge and Kegan, 1979), 37; Gilberto Sacerdoti, *Saggi libertini* (Macerata: Quodlibet, 2020), 175. I found this information in Vittorio Frajese, "The Disciple Whom Jesus Loved," in Grassi, *Cursed Blessings,* 40–55 (41).
36. Dalma Frascarelli and Laura Testa, *La casa dell'eretico. Arte e cultura nella quadreria romana di Pietro Gabrielli (1660–1774) a palazzo Taverna di Monte Giordano* (Rome: Istituto nazionale di studi romani, 2004), 176. See Frajese, "Disciple Whom Jesus Loved," 41. On Bianchi's ideas, see also Vittorio Frajese, *Dal libertinismo ai Lumi. Roma 1690–Torino 1727* (Rome: Viella, 2016), 79–87.
37. See Frajese, "The Disciple Whom Jesus Loved."
38. ASDN, SU, fasc. 143/107C. I thank Professor Giovanni Romeo for this reference.
39. Scaramella, *Lettere,* 39–40.
40. Father Pedro Chirico: Archivo Histórico Nacional de Madrid, Inq. 898 (Sicilia), ff. 47v–48r (hereafter cited as AHNM); Juan [unreadable surname]: Inq. 898 (Sicilia), f. 356v; Octavio de Verardo: Inq. 899 (Sicilia), f. 37r.
41. AHNM, Inq. 899 (Sicilia), *Auto da fé* of May 5, 1601.
42. AHNM, Inq. 899 (Sicilia), ff. 74r–v.
43. AHNM, Inq. 899 (Sicilia), ff. 37r–v.
44. Archivio della Congregazione della Dottrina della Fede, SO, M 5-P, last file, f. 752r (hereafter cited as ACDF).
45. ACDF, SO, M 5-P, last file, f. 752r–v.
46. ACDF, SO, M 5-P, last file, ff. 752v, 753r.
47. ACDF, SO, M 5-P, last file, f. 753r–754r.
48. ACDF, SO, M 5-P, last file, f. 754r.
49. ACDF, SO, M 5-P, last file, f. 755r.
50. ACDF, SO, M 5-P, last file, f. 755v. For a reflection on this lenience toward ecclesiastics, see below, Chapter 3.
51. Jean Toscan, *Le carnaval du langage: le lexique érotique des poètes de l'équivoque de Burchiello à Marino* (XVe–*XVIIe siècles)* (Lille: Presses Universitaires de Lille, 1981), 195.
52. Antonio F. Grazzini detto Il Lasca, *Le rime burlesche edite e inedite di Antonfrancesco Grazzini detto Il Lasca,* ed. Carlo Verzone (Florence: Sansoni, 1882), 616, quoted in Toscan, *Le carnaval du langage,* 197.
53. Alessandro di Rinaldo Bracci, *Canto della trippa e centopelle,* in *Tutti i trionfi, carri, mascherate o canti carnascialeschi andati per Firenze dal tempo del Magnifico Lorenzo de' Medici fino all'anno 1559* (Lucca: Benedini, 1750), 2:553, quoted in Toscan, *Le carnaval du langage,* 197.

54. Francesco Berni, *Capitolo delle pesche,* in *Poesie e prose,* by Francesco Berni, ed. Ezio Chiorboli (Geneva: Olschki, 1934), 54, quoted in Toscan, *Le carnaval du langage,* 210.

55. Toscan, *Le carnaval du langage,* 210–214.

56. Antonio Vignali, *La Cazzaria: The Book of the Prick,* ed. and trans. Ian Frederick Moulton (New York: Routledge, 2003), 93. I checked the translation against the Italian transcription edited by Pasquale Stoppelli: Antonio Vignali (Arsiccio Intronato), *La Cazzaria,* ed. Pasquale Stoppelli (Rome: Edizioni dell'elefante, 1984), 61.

57. See Jane E. Everson, Denis Reidy, and Lisa Sampson, eds., *The Italian Academies 1525–1700: Networks of Culture, Innovation and Dissent* (Abingdon: Routledge, 2016); Simone Testa, *Italian Academies and Their Networks, 1525–1700: From Local to Global* (New York: Palgrave Macmillan, 2015).

58. Ian Frederick Moulton, "Introduction: The Greatest Tangle of Pricks That Ever Was; Knowledge, Sex, and Power in Renaissance Italy," in Vignali, *Book of the Prick* (2003), 1–70.

59. See Nino Borsellino, introduction to Vignali, *La Cazzaria* (1984), 7–27; Lucia Felici, "A Sixteenth-Century Libertine Priest: Francesco Calcagno."

60. See Maria Teresa Ricci, "Antonio Vignali e la Cazzaria," in *Extravagances amoreux. L'amour au de là de la norme à la Renaissance. Actes du colloque international du groupe de recherche Cinquecento plurale Tours 2008,* ed. Elise Boillet and Chiara Lastraioli (Paris: Champion, 2008), 181–190.

61. Moulton, "Introduction," 23.

62. Borsellino, introduction, 24–25; Fabian Alfie, "Arsiccio's Commune: The History and Culture behind Antonio Vignali's *La Cazzaria,*" in *La Cazzaria: Manoscritto K: da una copia ottoencetesca dell'edizione di Napoli (1530 ca.),* by Antonio Vignali (Arisccio Intronato), ed. Fabian Alfie (Florence: Franco Cesati, 2022), 15–53 (31–45).

63. Vignali, *Book of the Prick* (2003), 75–76; Vignali, *La Cazzaria* (1984), 42.

64. Vignali, *Book of the Prick* (2003), 99–100; Vignali, *La Cazzaria* (1984), 67–68. I have slightly modified Moulton's translation by referring, in the first line, to "human beings" rather than "men" because, in my opinion, in this passage Vignali is not referring exclusively to homosexual intercourse but to anal sex in general.

65. Moulton, "Introduction," 51–65.

66. Laura Coci, introduction to *L'Alcibiade fanciullo a scola,* by Antonio Rocco, ed. Laura Coci (Roma: Salerno editore, 1988), 27–28.

67. On Cremonini, see Maria Assunta Della Torre, *Studi su Cesare Cremonini. Cosmologia e logica nel tardo aristotelismo Padovano* (Padua: Antenore, 1968); Antonino Poppi, *Cremonini, Galilei e gli inquisitori del Santo a Padova* (Padua: Centro Studi Antoniani, 1993). On the Aristotelian tradition in

Renaissance Italy, see Charles B. Schmitt, *The Aristotelian Tradition and Renaissance Universities* (London: Variorum, 1984).

68. Rocco, *Alcibiade,* 51–52.
69. Paolo Fasoli, "Bodily 'Figurae': Sex and Rhetoric in Early Libertine Venice, 1642–51," *Journal for Early Modern Cultural Studies* 12, no. 2 (2012): 97–116; Jean-Pierre Cavaillé, "Alcibiade enfant à l'école. Clandestinité, irréligion et sodomie," *Tangence* 81 (2006): 15–38.
70. Cavaillé, "Alcibiade enfant," 36.
71. Rocco, *Alcibiade,* 62.
72. Rocco, *Alcibiade,* 63.
73. Cavaillé, "Alcibiade enfant," 34–38.
74. Rocco, *Alcibiade,* 63.
75. Rocco, *Alcibiade,* 50.
76. Rocco, *Alcibiade,* 61. See also Armando Maggi, "The Discourse of Sodom in a Seventeenth-Century Venetian Text," *Journal of Homosexuality* 33, no. 3-4 (1997): 25–43 (31–34).
77. The *Enfer* is a collection of erotic works gathered together by the librarians of the National Library of France sometime between 1836 and 1844. See Robert Darnton, "Sex for Thought," in *Sexualities in History: A Reader,* ed. Kim M. Philipps and Barry Reay (New York: Routledge, 2002), 203–221.
78. Fabian Alfie, "Introduction: Ms C 113 of La Cazzaria at the University of Kansas Spencer Research Library," in Vignali, *La Cazzaria: Manoscritto K,* 10–13; Alfie, "Arsiccio's Commune," 15–16; Pasquale Stoppelli, "Nota al testo," in Vignali, *La Cazzaria* (1984), 153–162 (155).
79. Tommaso Scaramella, "'La sodomia è boccone da principi.' Voci libertine fuori dall'Accademia: il caso veneziano del Sei e Settecento," in *Tribadi, sodomiti, invertite e invertiti, pederasti, femminelle e ermafroditi. Per una storia dell'omosessualità, della bisessualità e delle trasgressioni di genere in Italia,* ed. Umberto Grassi, Vincenzo Lagioia, and Gian Paolo Romagnani (Pisa: ETS, 2017), 111–128 (115–116).
80. AHNM, Inq. 898 (Sicilia), ff. 64r–v.
81. AHNM, Inq. 898 (Sicilia), ff. 54r–v.
82. AHNM, Inq. 988 (Zaragoza), f. 21r. On sexual heresies in the Hispanic world, see Stuart B. Schwartz, "Pecar en las colonias. Mentalidades populares, Inquisición y actitudes hacia la fornicación simple en España, Portugal y las colonias americanas," *Cuadernos de Historia Moderna* 18, no. 51 (1997): 51–67.
83. AHNM, Inq., 898 (Sicilia), ff. 415v–416r, 426r–v.
84. AHNM, Inq., 898 (Sicilia), f. not readable.
85. AHNM, Inq. 899 (Sicilia), f. 227r.

86. AHNM, Inq. 898 (Sicilia), f. 523v.

CHAPTER TWO ~ TOMMASO CAMPANELLA IN NAPLES

1. Luigi Amabile, *Fra Tommaso Campanella. La sua congiura, i suoi processi e la sua pazzia,* vol. 3, *Documenti e illustrazioni* (Naples: A. Morano, 1882), 3:421, 426–431, 433–434, 436–437, 438–442 (hereafter cited as *PROCESSI*).
2. Luigi Amabile, *Fra Tommaso Campanella. La sua congiura, i suoi processi e la sua pazzia,* 3 vols. (Naples: A. Morano, 1883), 2:119–121.
3. Luigi Amabile, *Il Santo Officio della Inquisizione in Napoli* (Città di Castello: Lapi, 1892), 1:339.
4. C.E., "Nuovi documenti sui processi di Tommaso Campanella," *Giornale Critico della Filosofia Italiana* 8, no. 5 (1927): 321–359 (343).
5. "Essempio agli altri, acciocché si astenghino da simili eccessi": ASDN, f. 144v.
6. On Campanella in Naples, see Headley, *Tommaso Campanella and the Transformation of the World* (Princeton, N.J.: Princeton University Press, 1997), 19–25; Germana Ernst, *Tommaso Campanella: The Book and the Body of Nature,* trans. David Marshall (Dordrecht: Springer, 2010), 15–21.
7. Amabile, *Fra Tommaso Campanella,* 2:24–25.
8. Luigi Firpo, *I processi di Tommaso Campanella*, ed. Eugenio Canone (Rome: Salerno, 1998), 45–54.
9. Firpo, *I processi,* 45–54.
10. *PROCESSI*, 332.
11. Firpo, *I processi,* 52.
12. Germana Ernst, introduction to *L'ateismo trionfato, ovvero riconoscimento filosofico della religione universale contra l'antichristianesimo machiavelliano,* by Tommaso Campanella, ed. Germana Ernst, 2 vols. (Pisa: Scuola Normale Superore, 2004), 1:vii–lv (xxi).
13. Ernst, introduction, xxi–xii.
14. Germana Ernst, "Premessa," in *Atheismus Triumphatus,* by Tommaso Campanella (Pisa: Fabrizio Serra, 2013), xi–xxx (xi–xv).
15. Germana Ernst, "Tommaso Campanella tra censura e autocensura. Il caso dell'Atheismus triumphatus," in *Praedicatores, Inquisitores,* ed. C. Longo (Rome: Istituto Storico Domenicano, 2008), 499–525.
16. Ernst, *Book and the Body of Nature,* 77.
17. Tommaso Campanella, *L'ateismo trionfato, ovvero riconoscimento filosofico della religione universal contra l'antichristianesimo machiavelliano*, ed. Germana Ernst, 2 vols. (Pisa: Scuola Normale Superiore, 2004), 1:22 (hereafter cited as *AT*).
18. Frajese, *Profezia e Machiavellismo. Il giovane Campanella* (Rome: Carocci, 2002), 100–105.

19. Luca Addante, "Campanella et l'*Ateismo trionfato*: du paradigme au texte original," *Les Dossiers du Grihl* 3 (2022), Online since 21 August 2009.
20. *PROCESSI,* 3:422–423.
21. ASDN, SU, 1067, ff. 2r, 6r, 8r, 11r, 13v, 21r, 24r, 27r, 29v, 43v, 63r, 101r, 107r, 110r, 122v, 123r, 126r, 132r, 140v, 163v, 176v.
22. See below, Chapter 4 and Chapter 5.
23. *PROCESSI,* 3:423.
24. *PROCESSI,* 3:444.
25. On the earlier reception of Machiavelli and the condemnation of his work, see Sydney Anglo, *Machiavelli—the First Century: Studies in Enthusiasm, Hostility, and Irrelevance* (Oxford: Oxford University Press, 2005), 164–181. On the complexity of Machiavelli's relations to Christianity, see Ronald Beiner, *Civil Religion: A Dialogue in the History of Political Philosophy* (New York: Cambridge University Press, 2011), 17–45.
26. *AT,* 1:5. Despite Campanella's condemnation of Machiavelli in *AT,* his relation to the Florentine thinker is complex, and his influence persisted in Campanella's subsequent works: Headley, *Tommaso Campanella,* 180–196; Frajese, *Profezia e Machiavellismo.* See also Friedrich Meinecke, *Machiavellism: The Doctrine* of Raison d'Etat *and Its Place in Modern History* (New Haven, CT: Yale University Press, 1957), 98; John M. Headley, "On the Rearming of Heaven: The Machiavellism of T. Campanella," *Journal of the History of Ideas* 49 (1988): 387–404; Germana Ernst, "La mauvaise raison d'Etat: Campanella contre Machiavel et les Politiques," in *Raison et Déraison d'Etat. Théoriciens et Théories de la Raison d'Etat aux XVIe et XVIIe siècles,* ed. Yves-Charles Zarka (Paris: Presses Universitaires de France, 1994), 121–149; Luca Addante, "Campanella e Machiavelli: Indagine su un caso di dissimulazione," *Studi storici* 45 (2004): 727–750.
27. *AT,* 1:9.
28. Firpo, *I processi,* 6.
29. Firpo, *I processi,* 67.
30. Firpo, *I processi,* 65.
31. *AT,* 1:10–11.
32. On Campanella and *On the Three Impostors,* see Germana Ernst, "Campanella e il De tribus impostoribus," *Nouvelles de la République des lettres* 2 (1986): 144–170.
33. *AT,* 1:182–183.
34. *PROCESSI,* 3:262.
35. Amabile, *Fra Tommaso Campanella,* 1:273.
36. Ernst, *Book and the Body of Nature,* 105–106.
37. See Petrolo's sentence and abjuration: *PROCESSI,* 540–541.
38. *PROCESSI,* 3:438, 3:272.

39. Jean Toscan, *Le carnaval du langage,* 3:1436–1442.
40. ASDN, SU 1067, f. 75v.
41. Jean Toscan, *Le carnaval du langage,* 3:1436–1442.
42. Francesco Berni, Francesco Maria Molza, et al., *Il secondo libro dell'opere burlesche di M. Francesco Berni. Del Molza, di Bino, di M. Lodouico Martelli. Di Mattio Francesi, dell'Aretino, et di diuersi auttori. Ammendato, e ricorretto, e con somma diligenza ristampato* (Venice: Dominico Giglio, 1566), f. 19v.
43. ACDF, Stanza Storica, 0 1-h, archival subunit 8, ff. 294r–v.
44. Firpo, *I processi,* 59.
45. Ernst, *Book and the Body of Nature,* 24–25.
46. Firpo, *I processi,* 59.
47. Ernst, *Book and the Body of Nature,* 25.
48. Firpo, *I processi,* 217–218.
49. *PROCESSI,* 3:434.
50. *PROCESSI,* 3:434–435.
51. Headley, *Tommaso Campanella,* 13–14.
52. Sodomy was, indeed, a stable element in the stereotypical representations of Muslims that were circulating in Europe at that time. For a lengthier discussion of this topic, see Chapter 4.
53. *AT,* 1:122. Historical studies have already shown how the argumentative arsenal displayed in anti-Muslim propaganda had meaningful points of convergence with the successive rhetoric developed by the conquerors in the process of European, and especially Iberian, violent geographical expansion that began in the fourteenth century. The process of othering non-Christians drew on the established set of arguments that had already been developed to confront the rise of Islamic countries in the Mediterranean. Traub, "Sexuality."
54. *PROCESSI,* 3:442.
55. *PROCESSI,* 3:444.
56. *AT,* 1:117.
57. *AT,* 1:136–137.
58. *AT,* 1:84.
59. *AT,* 1:84–85.
60. *AT,* 1:40–41.
61. *AT,* 1:180.
62. *AT,* 1:228–229; the last quote is from Eccles. 1:2, 12:9.
63. *AT,* 1:227.
64. *AT,* 1:73.
65. On Campanella, sex, and gender relations, see also Lina Bolzoni, "Tommaso Campanella e le donne: fascino e negazione della differenza," *Annali d'Italianistica* 7 (1989): 193–216.

CHAPTER THREE ~ SEXUAL MORALITY IN POST-TRIDENTINE CATHOLICISM

1. Gianpaolo Angelini, "I collegi della riforma cattolica. L'architettura e la committenza," in *Almum Studium Papiense. Storia dell'Università di Pavia,* ed. Dario Mantovani (Milan: Cisalpino, 2013), 1.2:925–932. For a recent reassessment of the figure of Pius V, see Teresa Delgado-Jermann, *Images of Change: Visual Representations of Papal Power in Rome following the Council of Trent* (Abingdon: Routledge, 2023), 93–133. For an introduction to early modern Catholicism, see Nicholas Terpstra, "Early Modern Catholicism," in *The Oxford Handbook of Early Modern European History, 1350–1750,* ed. Hamish Scott (New York: Oxford University Press, 2015), 601–625; John W. O'Malley, *Trent and All That: Renaming Catholicism in the Early Modern Era* (Cambridge, MA: Harvard University Press, 2000).
2. ACDF, SO, Stanza storica, o 1-h, archival subunit 9, ff. 561r–v.
3. ACDF, SO, Stanza storica, o 1-h, archival subunit 9, f. 561r.
4. ACDF, SO, Stanza storica, o 1-h, archival subunit 9, f. 164v.
5. See Michele Mancino and Giovanni Romeo, *Clero criminale. L'onore della Chiesa e i delitti degli ecclesiastici nell'Italia della Controriforma* (Rome: Laterza, 2013).
6. "Bossi, Egidio," in *Dizionario biografico degli italiani* (Rome: Istituto della Enciclopedia italiana, 1961–), online at http:www.treccani.it/enciclopedia/egidio-bossi_(Dizionario-Biografico)/ (hereafter cited as *DBI*).
7. Egidio Bossi, *Criminalem materiam* (Basel: Sebastianum Henricpetri, 1580), 298.
8. Erick L. Saak, *Creating Augustine: Interpreting Augustine and Augustinianism in the Later Middle Ages* (Oxford: Oxford University Press, 2012), 83.
9. Giovanni Pozzi, "Roberto de' Bardi e S. Agostino," *Italia Medievale e Umanistica* 1 (1958): 139–153; Pozzi, "Il Vat. Lat. 479 ed altri codici annotati da Roberto de' Bardi," *Miscellanea del Centro di Studi Medievali* 2 (1958): 125–165. The collection of sermons is the result of a cumulative process: Saak, *Creating Augustine,* 112–116.
10. Augustine of Hippo, *Opera Omnia,* ed. Jacques-Paul Migne (Paris: Migne, 1841), 6: col. 1326–1327; "Sodomitis non procurabat resistere," col. 1328.
11. See Robert Mills, *Seeing Sodomy in the Middle Ages* (Chicago: University of Chicago Press, 2015), 175–183.
12. "O mulieres luxuriae matres, nonne sufficiebat primum hominem decepisse?": Augustine, *Opera Omnia,* 6: col. 1328.
13. Roberto Bellarmino, *De scriptoribus ecclesiasticis* (Colonia: Bernardo Gualtieri, 1631), 135–136.
14. Augustine, *Opera Omnia,* 6: col. 1234; Jesús Martínez De Bujanda, ed., *Index de l'Université de Louvain: 1546, 1550, 1558* (Sherbrooke: Edition de l'Université de Sherbrooke, 1986).

15. Ambrosiaster, *Ambrosiatri qui dicitur commentarius in epistulas Paulinas,* ed. Heinrich Joseph Vogels (Vienna: Holder-Pichler-Tempsky, 1966), ix.
16. *New American Bible* (2002); Bossi, *Criminalem materiam,* 298.
17. Theodore de Bruyn, "Ambrosiaster's Interpretations of Romans 1:26–27," *Vigiliae Christianae* 65, no. 5 (2011): 463–483.
18. De Bruyn, "Ambrosiaster's Interpretations," 477. On female homoeroticism in ancient Rome, see Bernadette J. Brooten, *Love between Women: Early Christian Responses to Female Homoeroticism* (Chicago: University of Chicago Press, 1996).
19. For a reconstruction of the autographs, see Bruyn, "Ambrosiaster's Interpretation," 478–483 (with English translation). I consulted the following sixteenth-century editions: *Secunda pars operum beati Ambrosii* (Basel: Petri, 1506, f. 185v); *D. Ambrosii Episcopi Mediolanensis, Commentarii in omnes Divi Pauli Epistolas, ex restitutione D. Erasmi Roterodami diligenter recogniti* (Paris: Badio Ascenio, 1534), f. 4v.
20. *Secunda pars operum beati Ambrosii* (Basel: Petri, 1506), f. 185v; De Bruyn, "Ambrosiaster's Interpretations," 469–470.
21. *Secunda pars operum beati Ambrosii,* f. 185v. On Eve and original sin in others of Ambrosiaster's works, see Marie-Pierre Bussières, "Ambrosiaster's Second Thoughts about Eve," *Journal of Early Christian Studies* 23, no. 1 (2015): 55–69.
22. See below, Chapters 6 and 7.
23. Mathijs Lamberigts, "Original Sin," in *The Oxford Guide to the Historical Reception of Augustine,* ed. Karla Pollmann and Willemien Otten (Oxford: Oxford University Press, 2013), 3:1472–1478 (1472).
24. Karla Pollman, "The Proteanism of Authority: The Reception of Augustine in Cultural History; Mapping an International and Interdisciplinary Investigation," in Pollmann and Otten, *Oxford Guide,* 3–14 (3).
25. One of the most obvious examples is Elaine Pagels, *Adam, Eve, and the Serpent* (New York: Random House, 1988).
26. Mathijs Lamberigts, "A Critical Evaluation of Critiques of Augustine's Views of Sexuality," in *Augustine and His Critics: Essays in Honour of Gerald Bonner,* ed. Robert Dodaro and George Lawless (New York: Routledge, 2000), 176–197.
27. Kathy L. Gaca, *The Making of Fornication: Eros, Ethics, and Political Reform in Greek Philosophy and Early Christianity* (Berkeley: University of California Press, 2003), 82–93. See also Aline Rousselle, *Porneia: On Desire and the Body in Antiquity,* trans. Phelicia Pheasant (1983; repr., Cambridge, MA: Blackwell, 1988).
28. *De bono coniugali,* 3.3; *De sancta virginitate,* 10.9, 12.12, 21.21, cited in Anthony Dupont, Wim François, Paul Van Gest, and Mathijs Lamberigts, "Sex," in Pollmann and Otten, *Oxford Guide,* 1726–1737 (1727). See also Augustine of Hippo, *St. Augustine on Marriage and Sexuality,* ed. Elizabeth A. Clark (Washington, DC: Catholic University of America Press, 1996), 5–6;

Peter Brown, *The Body and Society: Men, Women, and Sexual Renunciation in Early Christianity* (New York: Columbia University Press, 1988), 400.

29. *De bono coniugali,* 5.5, cited in Lamberigts, "Critical Evaluation," 181.
30. Lamberigts, "Critical Evaluation," 185.
31. Richard Sorabji, "Augustine on Lust and the Will," in *Emotion and Peace of Mind: From Stoic Agitation to Christian Temptation* (Oxford: Oxford University Press, 2000), 400–418.
32. Lamberigts, "Critical Evaluation," 178–179.
33. For an overview, see Arnoud S. Q. Visser, *Reading Augustine in the Reformation: The Flexibility of Intellectual Authority in Europe, 1500–1620* (Oxford: Oxford University Press, 2011).
34. Alister E. MacGrath, *Iustitia Dei: A History of the Christian Doctrine of Justification* (New York: Cambridge University Press, 2019), 308–344. The term "Pelagianism" identifies an approach that emphasizes the capacity of human beings to attain salvation by their own effort, without the cooperation of divine grace. Scholars are still debating whether this view reflected the real convictions of Pelagius, a British theologian who lived in Rome throughout the fourth and fifth centuries. See Ali Bonner, *The Myth of Pelagianism* (Oxford: Oxford University Press, 2018).
35. For an updated discussion on the bibliography on the Council of Trent, I refer the reader to Nelson H. Minnich, ed., *The Cambridge Companion to the Council of Trent* (Cambridge: Cambridge University Press, 2022); in particular, see Michael Root's contribution, "Original Sin and Justification," 97–121.
36. The decree established that, even after having received the sacrament, "in the baptized there remains concupiscence, or an incentive (to sin); which, whereas it is left for our exercise, cannot injure those who consent not, but resist manfully by the grace of Jesus Christ; yea, he who shall have *striven lawfully shall be crowned*": *The Canons and Decrees of the Sacred and Œcumenical Council of Trent,* trans. James Waterworth (London: C. Dolman, 1848), 24 (hereafter cited as *CD*). The decree on original sin was approved by the fifth session of the council, celebrated on June 17, 1546.
37. *CD,* 24.
38. *Catechismus ex Decreto Concilii Tridentini ad Parochos* (Rome, 1566), 268.
39. Romano Canosa, *La restaurazione sessuale. Per una storia della sessualità tra Cinquecento e Settecento* (Milan: Feltrinelli, 1993), 117.
40. M. Wiesner-Hanks, *Christianity and Sexuality in the Early Modern World: Regulating Desire, Reforming Practice* (London: Routledge, 2000), 62–63.
41. Heide Wunder, "Marriage in the Holy Roman Empire of the German Nation from the Fifteenth to the Eighteenth Century: Moral, Legal, and Political Order," in *Marriage in Europe, 1400–1800,* ed. Silvana Seidel Menchi (Toronto: University of Toronto Press, 2016), 61–93 (68–75). See also Marjorie E. Plummer, *From Priest's Whore to Pastor's Wife: Clerical Marriage and the*

Process of Reform in the Early German Reformation (Burlington: Ashgate, 2012); John Witte Jr., "Sex and Marriage in the Protestant Tradition, 1500–1900," in *The Oxford Handbook on Theology, Sexuality, and Gender*, ed. Adrian Thatcher (Oxford: Oxford University Press, 2014), 204–223.

42. *CD,* 195. For an overview of the decree and its impact, see Gabriella Zarri, "The Decree on Marriage," in Minnich, *Cambridge Companion,* 242–260.
43. *CD,* 195.
44. Wiesner-Hanks, *Christianity and Sexuality,* 60–140; Daniela Lombardi, *Storia del matrimonio. Dal medioevo a oggi* (Bologna: Il Mulino, 2008), 83–171.
45. Diarmaid MacCulloch, *Reformation: Europe's House Divided, 1490–1700* (London: Allen Lane, 2003), 613.
46. Aristocratic marriages had to obey the families' networking strategies; artisans had to wait for their apprenticeship to be concluded; peasants often did not have the means to start a new family: David Herlihy and Christiane Klapisch-Zuber, *Tuscans and Their Families: A Study of the Florentine Catasto of 1427* (New Haven, CT: Yale University Press, 1985), 202–231.
47. Elizabeth Crouzet-Pavan, "The Flower of Evil: Young Men in Medieval Italy," in *A History of Young People,* vol. 1, *Ancient and Medieval Rites of Passage,* ed. Giovanni Levi and Jean-Claude Schmitt (Cambridge, MA: Harvard University Press, 1997), 173–221. See also Konrad Eisenbichler, ed., *The Premodern Teenager: Youth in Society, 1150–1650* (Toronto: Centre for Reformation and Renaissance Studies, 2002); Eleonora Canepari, "Civic Identity, 'Juvenile' Status and Gender in Sixteenth-Century Italian Towns," in *The Routledge History Handbook of Gender and the Urban Experience,* ed. Deborah Simonton (London: Routledge, 2017), 182–194.
48. Michael J. Rocke, *Forbidden Friendships: Homosexuality and Male Culture in Renaissance Florence* (New York: Oxford University Press, 1996), 148–191; Umberto Grassi, *Bathhouses and Riverbanks: Sodomy in a Renaissance Republic* (Toronto: Centre for Renaissance and Reformation Studies, 2021), 59–68.
49. Wiesner-Hanks, *Christianity and Sexuality,* 67–72.
50. Wiesner-Hanks, *Christianity and Sexuality,* 86–87, 124–126. This also occurred in England: MacCulloch, *Reformation,* 634–635.
51. Death penalty rates increased in Spain and Portugal: Rafael Carrasco, *Inquisición y represión sexual en Valencia. Historia de los sodomitas (1565–1785)* (Barcelona: Laertes, 1985); Luiz Mott, "*Justitia et misericordia*: The Portuguese Inquisition and the Repression of the Nefarious Sin of Sodomy," in *Pelo Vaso Traseiro: Sodomy and Sodomites in Luso-Brazilian History,* ed. Harold Johnson and Francis A. Dutra (Tucson, AZ: Fenestra Books, 2006), 63–104. In Italy, the number of trials quantitatively decreased, but qualitatively the crime was, overall, treated more harshly. On Venice, see Gabriele Martini, *Il "vitio nefando" nella Venezia del Seicento. Aspetti sociali e repressione di giustizia* (Rome: Jouvence, 1988), 56. On Lucca, see Grassi, *Bathhouses and*

Riverbanks, 173–202. In Florence, severe legislation was approved but apparently not enforced: Rocke, *Forbidden Friendships,* 233–235.

52. On the Protestant world, see Puff, *Sodomy in Reformation Germany and Switzerland,* 75–104. On this shift toward intention, see Terpstra, "Early Modern Catholicism," 617–621. See also John Bossy, *Christianity in the West, 1400–1700* (Oxford: Oxford University Press, 1985). The implications of this turn for the history of sexuality have been explored by the seminal work of Michel Foucault, *The Will to Knowledge,* trans. Robert Hurley (London: Penguin, 1998), 43; originally published as *Histoire de la sexualité.* I: *La volonté de savoir* (Paris: Gallimard, 1976).
53. See Alan Bray, *Homosexuality in Renaissance England* (London: Gay Men's Press, 1982), 63–80.
54. Archivio della Curia Arcivescovile di Udine, 1318, Inquisizione, fasc. 358, act of May 9, 1659, cited in Flavio Rurale, *Ecclesiastico e gentiluomo. Clero, sesso e politica nella prima età moderna* (Viterbo: Sette città, 2018), 169–170. See also Grassi, *Bathhouses and Riverbanks,* 213.
55. Barbierato, *Inquisitor in the Hat Shop,* 103.
56. Barbierato, *Inquisitor in the Hat Shop,* 104. See also Grassi, *Bathhouses and Riverbanks,* 213.
57. AHNM, Inq. 898 (Sicilia), f. 113.
58. On this case, see Chapter 4.
59. Archivio di Stato di Venezia, SU, B. 132, April 8, 1705, f. 8v (hereafter cited as ASV). Although it has not been the subject of a specific analysis, Partenio's case is mentioned several times in Barbierato, *Inquisitor in the Hat Shop*, 46-47, 101, 115, 180, 210, 280. Here, Partenio's case will be analyzed in Chapter 5.
60. Archivio Storico Diocesano di Pisa, Inquisizione, Atti dal 1596, f. 608r–609r (hereafter cited as ASDPi).
61. ASDPi, Inquisizione, Atti dal 1596, f. 613r.
62. The letter was, however, subsequently recovered and attached to the trial report: ASDPi, Inquisizione, Atti dal 1596, f. 620r–v.
63. ASDPi, Inquisizione, Atti dal 1596, f. 618r–v.
64. ASDPi, Inquisizione, Atti dal 1596, f. 619r–v.
65. See Mancino and Romeo, *Clero criminale.*
66. AHNM, Inq. 899 (Sicilia), Auto da Fé of February 25, 1600.
67. On Canatta's case, see Chapter 4.
68. AHNM, Inq. 899 (Sicilia), Auto da Fé of December 14, 1603.

CHAPTER FOUR ~ SEX AND CROSS-CULTURAL INTERACTIONS

1. Schwartz, *All Can Be Saved,* 242–255.
2. ASDPi, Inquisizione, Atti dal 1596, f. 609v–610r. On the influence of the English community in Livorno and the development of latitudinarian

attitudes, see Stefano Villani, "Religious Pluralism and the Danger of Tolerance: The English Nation in Livorno in the Seventeenth Century," in *Late Medieval and Early Modern Religious Dissents: Conflicts and Plurality in Renaissance Europe,* ed. Federico Barbierato and Alessandra Veronese (Pisa: Arnus University Books, 2012), 97–124. On cultural diversity in Livorno, see Villani, "Livorno: Diversis Gentibus Una," in *Twelve Cities—One Sea: Early Modern Mediterranean Port Cities and Their Inhabitants,* ed. Giovanni Tarantino and Paola Von Wyss-Giacosa (Rome: Edizioni Scientifiche Italiane, 2023), 37–53.

3. Germana Ernst, "Cristianesimo e religione naturale. Le censure all'*Atheismus triumphatus* di Campanella," *Nouvelles de la république des lettres* 1–2 (1989): 139–200 (139–142).
4. Hubert Jedin, *A History of the Council of Trent*, trans. Ernest Graf, 2 vols. (London: Thomas Nelson and Sons, 1958), 2:162.
5. *CD,* 30–31.
6. ASV, SU, B 132, f. 8r.
7. In sixteenth-century Italy, faith in predestination was merged with the belief in the Erasmian notion of the boundless mercy of God. See Lucia Felici, "L'immensa bontà di Dio. Diffusione e adattamenti dell'idea erasmiana in Italia e in Svizzera," in *Religione e politica in Erasmo da Rotterdam,* ed. Enzo A. Baldini and Massimo Firpo (Rome: Edizioni di storia e letteratura, 2012).
8. Felici, "L'immensa bontà di Dio," 129–157.
9. These notions permeated the Italian Reformation: Massimo Firpo, *Juan de Valdés and the Italian Reformation,* trans. Richard Bates (Burlington: Ashgate, 2015).
10. For a recent reassessment of this theme, see Mario Biagioni, *The Radical Reformation and the Making of Modern Europe: A Lasting Heritage* (Leiden: Brill, 2017).
11. B. Kaplan, *Divided by Faith.*
12. Mercedes García-Arenal and Stefania Pastore, eds., *From Doubt to Unbelief: Forms of Scepticism in the Iberian World* (Cambridge: Legenda, 2019).
13. AHNM, Inq. 899 (Sicilia), ff. 231v–232v. Canatta's case has already been briefly summarized in William Monter, *Frontiers of Heresy: The Spanish Inquisition from the Basque Lands to Sicily* (1990; repr., Cambridge: Cambridge University Press, 2002), 165–166.
14. Under the influence of the jurisdictional battles inspired by the Enlightenment, the viceroy Domenico Caracciolo, Marquis of Villamarina, suppressed the Sicilian tribunal on March 16, 1782. He commanded that the archives of the Inquisition be publicly burned on June 27, 1783: Manuel Rivero Rodríguez, "Sicilia," in *DSI,* 3:1421–1423.
15. AHNM, Inq. 898 (Sicilia), f. 257v.
16. AHNM, Inq. 899 (Sicilia), ff. 231v–232v.

17. Francesco Renda, *L'Inquisizione in Sicilia. I fatti. Le persone* (Palermo: Sellerio, 1997), 341–375.
18. AHNM, Inq. 899 (Sicilia), f. 231v.
19. AHNM, Inq. 898 (Sicilia), f. 257v.
20. In inquisitorial practice, the first conviction always resulted in an abjuration and in other more- or less-severe penalties (depending on the gravity of the charges). Only those who were convicted for a second time were sentenced to death.
21. AHNM, Inq. 899 (Sicilia), f. 83r. The act by which the Inquisition readmitted a confessed sinner into the community of believers was called a reconciliation.
22. AHNM, Inq. 899 (Sicilia), ff. 231v–232v.
23. AHNM, Inq. 899 (Sicilia), ff. 231v–232r.
24. Ira Katznelson and Miri Rubin, *Religious Conversion: History, Experience and Meaning* (Farnham: Ashgate, 2014), 12–13. On Muslim-Christian conversions, see Bartolomé Bennassar and Lucille Bennassar, *Les Chrétiens d'Allah* (Paris: Perrin, 1991); Mercedes García-Arenal, ed., *Conversions islamiques. Identités religieuses en Islam méditerranéen* (Paris: Maisonneuve et Larose, 2001); Tijana Krstić, *Contested Conversion to Islam: Narratives of Religious Change in the Early Modern Ottoman Empire* (Stanford, CA: Stanford University Press, 2011); Claire Norton, ed., *Conversion and Islam in the Early Modern Mediterranean: The Lure of the Other* (New York: Routledge, 2017). On early modern Spain, see Trevor J. Dadson, *Tolerance and Coexistence in Early Modern Spain: Old Christians and Moriscos in the Campo de Calatrava* (Suffolk: Tamesis, 2014); James S. Amelang, *Parallel Histories: Muslims and Jews in Inquisitorial Spain* (Baton Rouge: Louisiana State University Press, 2013).
25. Krstić, *Contested Conversions to Islam,* 16. See also Norton, *Conversion and Islam,* 1. On cross-religious interactions in the early modern world, see Nicholas Terpstra, ed., *Global Reformations Sourcebook: Convergence, Conversion, and Conflict in Early Modern Religious Encounters* (London: Routledge, 2021); Kenneth Mills and Anthony Grafton, eds., *Conversion: Old World and New* (Rochester, NY: University of Rochester Press, 2003); Katznelson and Rubin, *Religious Conversion,* 14–15. On multiple conversions, see Michael Heyd, "'Double Conversions' in the Early Modern Period: The Road to Religious Scepticism?," in Katznelson and Rubin, *Religious Conversion,* 233–259.
26. Mercedes García-Arenal, "Religious Dissent and Minorities: The Morisco Age," *Journal of Modern History* 81 (2009): 888–920 (907).
27. Daniele Conti, "Religione naturale e salvezza universale. Appunti sulla fortuna di Ficino e una nota su Agrippa e Camillo Renato," *Rinascimento* 57 (2017): 231–285 (243, 247).
28. AHNM, Inq. 899 (Sicilia), f. 232r.

29. Iris Shagrir, *The Parable of the Three Rings and the Idea of Religious Toleration in Premodern European Culture* (New York: Springer, 2019); Marcel Poorthuis, "The Three Rings: Between Exclusivity and Tolerance," in *The Three Rings: Textual Studies in the Historical Trialogue of Judaism, Christianity and Islam,* ed. Barbara Roggema, Marcel Poorthuis, and Pim Valkenberg (Leuven: Peeters, 2005), 257–285; Iris Shagrir, "The Parable of the Three Rings: A Revision of Its History," *Journal of Medieval History* 23, no. 2 (1997): 163–177.
30. Maurice Kriegel, "Not Scepticism, but Certainty: A Different Plea for Toleration in Late Medieval Spain," in García-Arenal and Pastore, *From Doubt to Unbelief,* 31–45; Eleazar Gutwirth, "The Three Rings: *Shevet Yehuda*-Lessing / Graetz-Fritz Ishaq Baer," in García-Arenal and Pastore, *From Doubt to Unbelief,* 46–64.
31. Shagrir, *Parable of the Three Rings,* 43.
32. Shagrir, *Parable of the Three Rings,* 88–108.
33. Giovanni Boccaccio, *The Decameron,* trans. G. H. McWilliam (London and New York: Penguin, 1995), 176.
34. Shagrir, *Parable of the Three Rings,* 108.
35. Friedrich Niewöhner, *Veritas sive Varietas: Lessings Toleranzparabel und das Buch von den drei Betrügern* (Heidelberg: Schneider, 1988).
36. Guy G. Stroumsa, "Three Rings or Three Impostors? The Comparative Approach to the Abrahamic Religions and Its Origins," in *The Oxford Handbook of the Abrahamic Religions,* ed. Adam J. Silverstein et al. (Oxford: Oxford University Press, 2015), 56–70.
37. Shagrir, *Parable of the Three Rings,* 26–27.
38. See Dorothea Weltecke, "Beyond Exclusivism in the Middle Ages: On the Three Rings, the Three Impostors and the Discourse of Multiplicity," in Silverstein et al., *Oxford Handbook of Abrahamic Religions,* 189–205. On the relationships between tolerance and atheism, see Eric MacPhail, *Religious Tolerance from Renaissance to Enlightenment: Atheist's Progress* (New York: Routledge Taylor & Francis Group, 2020).
39. Pastore, "Doubt in Fifteenth-Century Iberia," in *After Conversion: Iberia and the Emergence of Modernity,* ed. Mercedes García-Arenal (Leiden: Brill, 2016), 283–303 (286). See also John Edwards, "Religious Faith and Doubt in Late Medieval Spain: Soria circa. 1450–1500," *Past and Present* 120 (August 1988): 3–25 (18).
40. Ginzburg, *Cheese and the Worms,* 49–51.
41. Manuel II Palaiologos, *Dialoge mit einem 'Perser,'* ed. Erich Trapp (Vienna: Hermann Böhlaus, 1966), 102:42–104:10, translated in Shagrir, *Parable of the Three Rings,* 117–118.
42. See Shagrir, *Parable of the Three Rings,* 117. On Manuel II, see Adel Théodore Khoury, introduction to *Entretiens avec un Musulman: 7e controverse,* by Manuel II Palaiologus, ed. Adel Théodore Khoury (Paris: Éd. du cerf, 1966),

9–28; Siren Çelik, *Manuel II Palaiologos (1350–1425): A Byzantine Emperor in a Time of Tumult* (New York: Cambridge University Press, 2021), 144.

43. The *cirujanos latinos* (Latin surgeons) were trained in reading Latin medical texts; the *cirujanos romancistas* learned from treatises written in the Romance languages; the *cirujanos barberos* (barber surgeons) and the *barberos-sangradores* or *flebotomianos,* who practiced bloodletting, did not have any theoretical education: José Antonio Rodríguez Montes, "La cirugía en la época de Cervantes," *Anales de la Real Academia de Doctores de España* 6, no. 2 (2021): 341–357 (347–348).
44. Charles-Benoit Hase, "Notice d'un ouvrage de l'Empereur Manuel Paléologue," in *Piissimi et sapientissimi Imperatoris Manuelis Palaeologi Opera omnia, theologica, polemica, panegyrica, paedagogica,* ed. Gēorgios Sfrantzēs, Joannes (Anagnostes), and Jacques Paul Migne (Paris: Migne, 1866), 111–128 (111–112).
45. Giovanna Fiume, *Del Santo Uffizio in Sicilia e delle sue carceri* (Rome: Viella, 2021), 157–161.
46. AHNM, Inq. 899 (Sicilia), f. 31r.
47. Arthur John Arberry's translation.
48. Vincenzo Lavenia, "Between Heresy and 'Crimes against Nature': Sexuality, Islamophobia and the Inquisition in Early Modern Europe," in *Mediterranean Crossings,* ed. Grassi, 65–88 (71–72).
49. Ze'ev Maghen, *After Hardship Cometh Ease: The Jews as Backdrop for Muslim Moderation* (Berlin: De Gruyter, 2006), 187–203.
50. Romeo, *Amori proibiti,* 70.
51. On "maurophilia," see Barbara Fuchs, *Exotic Nation: Maurophilia and the Construction of Early Modern Spain* (Philadelphia: University of Pennsylvania Press, 2009).
52. On the legal meaning of abjuration *de vehementi,* see Chapter 1.
53. AHNM, Inq. 899 (Sicilia), ff. 119r–v.
54. Particularly relevant was the association of Islam with anti-Trinitarian and Anabaptist heresies. See Martin Mulsow, "Socinianism, Islam and the Radical Uses of Arabic Scholarship," *Al-Qantara* 31, no. 2 (2010): 549–586; Gerard A. Wiegers, "Polemical Transfers: Iberian Muslim Polemics and Their Impact in Northern Europe in the Seventeenth Century," in García-Arenal, *After Conversion,* 229–248; Gary K. Waite, "'Turning Turke' the Anabaptist Way: Muslims, Jews, Christian Spiritualists, and Polemical Discourse in the Dutch Republic, c. 1570 to c. 1630," in Terpstra, *Global Reformations.* See also Lucca Addante, *Eretici e libertini nel Cinquecento italiano* (Rome: Laterza, 2010), 76–84.
55. Similar associations were also recorded elsewhere in the Italian peninsula during the fifteenth century. In Naples, the abbot Matteo di Pastena, known as "Monsignor Sodom," was accused of reading the Qur'ān: Romeo, *Amori proibiti,* 106–107.
56. AHNM, Inq. 899 (Sicilia), f. 233r.

57. ASDN, SU, 1067, f. 2r, 6r, 24r, 27r, 29v, 110r, 122v, 126r, 132v, 140v, 163v, 176v, see also f. 43v, 101r (formal accusation).
58. AHNM, Inq. 902 (Sicilia), ff. 126v, 130v, 133r.
59. Andrea Del Col, ed., *Domenico Scandella Known as Menocchio: His Trials before the Inquisition (1583–1599),* trans. John Tedeschi and Anne C. Tedeschi (Binghamton, NY: Medieval & Renaissance Texts & Studies, 1996), 46.
60. *El fiore della bibbia hystoriato et di novo in lingua toscana corretto* (Venice: Bindoni, 1523). On the influence of *El fiore della bibbia* on Menocchio's heretical beliefs, see Ginzburg, *Cheese and the Worms,* 60–62. The other versions I have consulted are *El fiore novello estratto dalla Bibbia* (Milan: Philippus de Lavagnia, ca. 1477; Lucca: Bartolomeo Civitali, 1477). It was printed under the same title in Venice by Mastro Alvise da Salamedico da Padova, 1473; Baptistam de Tortis, 1482; Antonio et Renaldo fr.lli de Trino da Monteferrato, 1493.
61. Ginzburg, *Cheese and the Worms,* 43.
62. Del Col, *Domenico Scandella,* 81, 95, 157.
63. Maria Sofia Messana, *Inquisitori, negromanti e streghe nella Sicilia moderna (1580–1782)* (Palermo: Sellerio, 2007), 456n.
64. Del Col, *Domenico Scandella,* lxvi.
65. Iraeneus of Lyon, *Contro le eresie/1. Smascheramento e confutazione della falsa gnosi,* ed. and trans. Augusto Cosentino (Rome: Città Nuova, 2009), 1:24.4, 155.
66. Del Col, *Domenico Scandella,* 87.
67. Qur'ān, 4:157 (Muhammad Habib Shakir's translation).
68. Todd Lawson, *The Crucifixion and the Qur'an: A Study in the History of Muslim Thought* (Oxford: Oneworld, 2009), 7.
69. Lawson, *Crucifixion and the Qur'an,* 1–25.
70. Lawson, *Crucifixion and the Qur'an,* 148–149.
71. Neal Robinson, "Jesus," in *The Encyclopedia of the Qur'ān,* ed. Jane McAuliffe (Leiden: Brill, 2003), 3:7–21.
72. Pier Mattia Tommasino, *The Venetian Qur'an: A Renaissance Companion to Islam,* trans. Sylvia Notini (Philadelphia: University of Pennsylvania Press, 2018), 34–43, 118.
73. Tommasino, *The Venetian Qur'an,* xviii, 169–184. On the circulation of the Qur'ān in Italy, see also Federico Stella and Roberto Tottoli, eds., *Qur'an in Rome: Manuscripts, Translations, and the Study of Islam in Early Modern Catholicism* (Boston: De Gruyter, 2024).

CHAPTER FIVE ~ ESOTERIC PRIVATE LIBRARIES

1. ASDPi, Inquisizione, Atti dal 1596, ff. 608r, 610v.
2. AHNM, Inq. 902 (Sicilia), f. 125v.
3. ASV, SU, B 132, f. 8v.

4. A detailed report of this case is in AHNM, Inq. 902 (Sicilia), ff. 120r–135v. See also Messana, *Inquisitori, negromanti e streghe,* 456–458; Melita Leonardi, "Inquisizione, sette necromantiche e cabalistiche in Sicilia tra XVI e XVII secolo," *Rivista di storia e letteratura religiosa* 1 (2003): 65–99. On the legal meaning of abjuration *de vehementi,* see Chapter 2.
5. AHNM, Inq. 902 (Sicilia), f. 120r–v; 130v; 133r.
6. AHNM, Inq. 902 (Sicilia), f. 122r. It could be a work by the Italian humanist Polidor Vergil (1470–1555), but it could also refer to a spurious work by Publius Vergilius Maro. Since the late Middle Ages, many traditions have circulated depicting the Latin poet as an omniscient and omnipotent magus: Jan Ziolkowski, "Virgil the Magician," in *Dall'antico al moderno. Immagini del classico nelle letterature europee,* ed. Piero Boitani and Emilia Di Rocco (Rome: Edizioni di Storia e Letteratura, 2015), 59–75.
7. AHNM, Inq. 902 (Sicilia), f. 123r. For further details, see later in this chapter.
8. AHNM, Inq. 902 (Sicilia), f. 123r; Julius Caesar Scaliger, *Exotericarum liber XV, de subtilitate ad H. Cadanum* (Paris: ex officina typographica Michaelis Vascosani, 1557). This book was a detailed critical response to Cardano's *De subtilitate.*
9. AHNM, Inq. 902 (Sicilia), ff. 127r, 133v; Johannes Trithemius, *Polygraphiae libri sex* (Haselberg, 1518).
10. AHNM, Inq. 902 (Sicilia), f. 127r. See later in this chapter.
11. AHNM, Inq. 902 (Sicilia), f. 134r. There are no further hints about Artemidorus's work in the trial transcripts.
12. AHNM, Inq. 902 (Sicilia), f. 125v. It could refer to Paride del Pozzo, *De syndicatu* (Lyon: Giunta, 1548).
13. Leonardi, "Inquisizione," 85–89.
14. Federico Barbierato, *Nella stanza dei circoli. Clavicula Salomonis e libri di magia a Venezia nei secoli XVII e XVIII* (Milan: S. Bonnard, 2002).
15. Zambelli, *White Magic, Black Magic in the European Renaissance* (Leiden and Boston: Brill, 2007), 75–76. The term "Steganographia" indicates the art of concealing a secret message within a nonsecret text. With a key, this concealing technique allowed the recipient of the message to decipher its hidden content, which, in the case of Trithemius, was a treatise on demonic magic.
16. Leonardi, "Inquisizione," 90.
17. AHNM, Inq. 902 (Sicilia), 127v–131r.
18. AHNM, Inq. 902 (Sicilia), ff. 126v, 130v, 133r. See Chapter 5.
19. AHNM, Inq. 902 (Sicilia), f. 133r.
20. AHNM, Inq. 902 (Sicilia), f. 124v. The idea of a secret sect performing illicit sexual acts was a recurring element in Christian antiheretical propaganda: Goodich, *The Unmentionable Vice.* See also Fernanda Molina, "La

herejización de la sodomía en la sociedad moderna. Consideraciones teológicas y praxis inquisitorial," *Hispania Sacra* 62 (2010): 539–562.

21. Federico Barbierato, "Writing, Reading, Writing: Scribal Culture and Magical Texts in Early Modern Venice," *Italian Studies* 66, no. 2 (2011): 263–276 (265).
22. Zambelli, *White Magic, Black Magic,* 87–88.
23. Patricia Crone, "Ungodly Cosmologies," in Crone, *Islam, the Ancient Near East and Varieties of Godlessness,* 118–150.
24. Giorgio Spini, *Ricerca dei libertini; la teoria dell'impostura delle religioni nel Seicento italiano* (Rome: Editrice Universale, 1950), 18–19. Didier Ottaviani, "L'intellectuel laïque: de Siger de Brabant à Pietro D'Abano," in *Les Athéismes philosophiques,* ed. Emmanuel Chubilleau and Eric Puisais (Paris: Kimé, 2001), 13–25. On the "horoscope of religions" in early modern astrology, see Paola Zambelli, *Astrology and Magic from the Medieval Latin and Islamic World to Renaissance Europe: Theories and Approaches* (Farnham: Ashgate, 2012); Eugenio Garin, *Astrology in the Renaissance: The Zodiac of Life,* trans. Carolyn Jackson, June Allen, and Clare Robertson (London: Arkana, 1983). See also Joan DeGuire North, "Astrology and the Fortunes of Churches," *Centaurus* 24, no. 1 (1980): 181–211.
25. On Cardano, see Nancy G. Siraisi, *The Clock and the Mirror: Girolamo Cardano and Renaissance Medicine* (Princeton, NJ: Princeton University Press, 1997); Anthony Grafton, *Cardano's Cosmos: The Worlds and Works of a Renaissance Astrologer* (Cambridge, MA: Harvard University Press, 1999); Germana Ernst, "'Veritatis amor dulcissimus': Aspects of Cardano's Astrology," in *Secrets of Nature: Astrology and Alchemy in Early Modern Europe,* ed. William R. Newman and Anthony Grafton (Cambridge, MA: MIT, 2001), 39–68.
26. On genitures, astrology, and the figure of Christ, see Aaron Adair, "The Star of Christ in the Light of Astronomy," *Zygon* 47, no. 1 (2012): 7–29.
27. Grafton, *Cardano's Cosmos,* 158, 165–166. On Cardano's approach to dreams, see also Siraisi, *Clock and the Mirror,* 174–191.
28. Frajese, *Profezia e Machiavellismo,* 60.
29. *PROCESSI,* 3:589.
30. Spini, *Ricerca dei libertini,* 28.
31. Lorenzo Bianchi, *Naturalismo, scetticismo, politica. Studi sul pensiero rinascimentale e libertino* (Florence: SISMEL, ed. del Galluzzo, 2019), 87–133.
32. The first version, published in Nuremberg in 1550, was heavily reworked by the author and reprinted in Basel in 1554, increasing from an original 371 pages to 561. This second edition was subsequently revised without substantial changes to its structure and outlook and then republished yet again in the same place in 1560, this time with the addition of an apology written in response to Scaliger's *Exotericarum liber XV*: Girolamo Cardano,

De subtilitate (Nuremberg: apud Johannem Petreium, 1550; Basel: per Ludovicum Lucium, 1554; Basel: ex officina Petrina, 1560).

33. Girolamo Cardano, *The "De Subtilitate" of Girolamo Cardano,* ed. John M. Forrester (Tempe: ACMRS, 2013), 16.
34. See Ian Maclean, "The Interpretation of Natural Signs: Cardano's *De subtilitate* versus Scaliger's *Exercitationes,*" in *Occult and Scientific Mentalities in the Renaissance,* ed. Brian Vickers (Cambridge: Cambridge University Press, 1984), 231–252.
35. John Henry and John M. Forrester, introduction to Cardano, *"De Subtilitate" of Girolamo Cardano,* xi–xxxvii (xviii).
36. See Paola Pirzio, "Note sulle tre redazioni del *De subtilitate* di Girolamo Cardano," in *Girolamo Cardano. Le opere, le fonti, la vita,* ed. Maria Luisa Baldi and Guido Canziani (Milan: Franco Angeli, 1999), 169–179.
37. Ian Maclean, introduction to *De libris propriis. The editions of 1544, 1550, 1557, 1562, with supplementary material,* by Girolamo Cardano, ed. Ian Maclean (Milan: Franco Angeli, 2004), 9–39 (38–39).
38. Henry and Forrester, introduction, xix.
39. See Cardano, *"De Subtilitate" of Girolamo Cardano,* books 6 ("On Metals") and 7 ("On Stones"), 335–431; book 19 ("On Demons"), 953–972.
40. Cardano, *"De Subtilitate" of Girolamo Cardano*, 645.
41. This influence is particularly apparent in his *De sapientia libri quinque* (The five books on wisdom, 1554) and in the *Proxeneta* (first print edition 1627): Bianchi, *Naturalismo, scetticismo, politica,* 45–65.
42. Bianchi, *Naturalismo, scetticismo, politica,* 128. Naudé edited and printed for the first time the manuscript of Cardano's autobiography, *De propria vita liber* (*The Book about His Own Life*).
43. Bianchi, *Naturalismo, scetticismo, politica,* 130. On Naudé as an editor, see Paul Oskar Kristeller, "Between the Italian Renaissance and the French Enlightenment: Gabriel Naudé as an Editor," *Renaissance Quarterly* 32, no. 1 (1979): 41–72.
44. AHNM, Inq. 902 (Sicilia), f. 125v.
45. Leonardi, "Inquisizione," 87.
46. Vittorio Frajese, "Machiavelli, Machiavellismo," in *DSI,* 2:951–954 (953).
47. Rocco, *Alcibiade,* 56.
48. Grafton, *Cardano's Cosmos,* 167.
49. Cardano, *"De Subtilitate" of Girolamo Cardano,* 957–958.
50. Guido Giglioni, introduction to *Renaissance Averroism and Its Aftermath: Arabic Philosophy in Early Modern Europe,* ed. Anna Akasoy and Guido Giglioni (Dordrecht: Springer, 2013), 1–34. The term "Averroist" was already in use in the Latin Middle Ages, but the category of Averroism was first coined by the French orientalist historian and philosopher Ernest Renan (1823–1892). For a critical revision of the category of Averroism, see Luca Bianchi, "L'Averroismo di Dante," *Le Tre Corone* 2 (2015): 71–109. On the

legacy of Averroes in the Italian Renaissance, see Paul O. Kristeller, "Paduan Averroism and Alexandrism in the Light of Recent Studies," in *Renaissance Thought and the Arts* (1965; repr., Princeton, NJ: Princeton University Press, 1990), 114–115. See also Kristeller, "Renaissance Aristotelianism," in *Studies in Renaissance Thought and Letters,* 4 vols. (Rome: Edizioni di Storia e Letteratura, 1984–1996), 3:341–357. The stereotype of the "Averroistic" philosopher was ultimately crystallized by the theologian and philosopher from the Kingdom of Majorca Raymond Lull (1232–1316): Ruedi Imbach, "Lulle face aux Averroïstes parisiens," *Chaiers de Fanjeaux* 22 (1987): 261–282; Constantin Teleanu, *Raymundista et Averroista. La réfutation des erreurs averroïstes chez Raymond Lulle* (Paris: Schola Lulliana, 2014).

51. Bianchi, "L'Averroismo di Dante," 76.
52. Giglioni, introduction, 1–2. The edition of Aristotle's work with commentaries by Averroes was published by Giunta in Venice in 1550–1552, and the study of Averroes was firmly established in university curricula: Charles B. Schmitt, "Renaissance Averroism Studied through the Venetian Editions of Aristotle-Averroes," in *The Aristotelian Tradition and Renaissance Universities* (London: Variorum Reprints, 1984), 121–142.
53. See Georges Minois, *The Atheist's Bible: The Most Dangerous Book That Never Existed,* trans. Lys Ann Weiss (Chicago: University of Chicago Press, 2012), 1–9.
54. Benvenuto da Imola, *Benevenuti de Rambaldis de Imola Comentum super Dantis Aldigherii Comoediam,* ed. James Ph. Lacaita, 5 vols. (Florence: Barbèra, 1887), 1:181–182. See also Esposito, "Una manifestazione d'incredulità religiosa nel medioevo: il detto dei 'Tre Impostori' e la sua trasmissione da Federico II a Pomponazzi," *Archivio Storico Italiano* 399 (1931), 3-48(29).
55. See John Marenbon, "Ernest Renan and Averroism: The Story of a Misinterpretation," in Akasoy and Giglioni, *Renaissance Averroism,* 272–283.
56. Alessandro Medico, "Averroismo," in *DSI,* 1:126.
57. José Manuel García Valverde, "Averroistic Themes in Girolamo Cardano's *De Immortalitate Animorum,*" in Akasoy and Giglioni, *Renaissance Averroism,* 145–171.
58. Leen Spruit, "Cardano, Girolamo," in *DSI,* 1:271.
59. ASV, SU, B 132, f. 8r.
60. ASV, SU, B 132, f. 1r.
61. ASV, SU, B 132, f. 1r.
62. ASV, SU, B 132, f. 1r.
63. Alessandro Pratesi, "Barliario, Pietro," in *DBI,* https://www.treccani.it/enciclopedia/pietro-barliario_%28Dizionario-Biografico%29/.
64. Egidio Guidubaldi, "Stabili, Francesco," in *Enciclopedia Dantesca* (1970), https://www.treccani.it/enciclopedia/francesco-stabili_%28Enciclopedia-Dantesca%29/.

65. Villani, *Storie Fiorentine,* x, 39. See Spini, *Ricerca dei libertini,* 19; Esposito, "Una manifestazione d'incredulità," 43–44; Lucio Biasiori, "'Empietà e bestemmie anche alle orecchie dei saraceni infedeli': La condanna di Zanino da Solza tra rafforzamento ecclesiastico e progetti di Crociata (1459)," *Rivista Storica Italiana* 3 (2017): 863–886 (874–875).
66. ASV, SU, B 132, f. 1r. The book was well known in Venice: Simonetta Adorni Braccesi, "Passioni repubblicane, polemiche antinobiliari e inquietudini religiose dei lettori del 'Della vanità delle scienze' di Agrippa nella Venezia del '500," in *Repubblicanesimo e repubbliche nell'Europa di antico regime,* ed. Elena Fasano Guarini, Renzo Sabbatini, and Marco Natalizi (Milan: Franco Angeli, 2007), 61–79.
67. Zambelli, *White Magic, Black Magic,* 138–182. In a later work, *De incertitudine et vanitate scientiarum atque artium declamatio invectiva* (Invective attacking the uncertainty and vanity of the sciences and the arts), Agrippa developed a radically skeptical approach that questioned as transient and unreliable every form of knowledge, including those magical arts to which he had devoted his whole life. On Agrippa's skepticism, see Richard H. Popkin, *The History of Scepticism from Erasmus to Spinoza,* 3rd ed. (Berkeley: University of California Press, 1979), 23–26; Vittoria Perrone Compagni, "'Dispersa Intentio.' Alchemy, Magic and Scepticism in Agrippa," *Early Science and Medicine* 5, no. 2 (2000): 160–177; Charles G. Nauert Jr., "Magic and Skepticism in Agrippa's Thought," *Journal of the History of Ideas* 18, no. 2 (1957): 161–182. In spite of this skeptical turn, Agrippa must have retained some interest in the secret knowledge that he had apparently recanted: Paola Zambelli, "Magic and Radical Reformation in Agrippa of Nettesheim," *Journal of the Warburg and Courtauld Institutes* 39 (1976): 69–103; Zambelli, *White Magic, Black Magic,* 115–188.
68. Simonetta Adorni-Braccesi, "Agrippa von Nettesheim," in *DSI,* 1:25. See Auguste Prost, *Les sciences et les arts occultes au XVIe siècle. Corneille Agrippa, sa vie et ses oeuvres* (Paris: Champion, 1881–1882); Charles Nauert, *Agrippa and the Crisis of Renaissance Thought* (Urbana: University of Illinois Press, 1965); Christopher I. Lehrich, *The Language of Demons and Angels: Cornelius Agrippa's Occult Philosophy* (Leiden: Brill, 2003). Vittoria Perrone Compagni has edited the critical edition of the *De occulta philosophia* (Leiden: Brill, 1992).
69. Antonello Gerbi, *Il peccato di Adamo ed Eva. Storia dell'ipotesi di Beverland* (Milan: La Cultura, 1933). Gerbi called this theory "the Beverland hypothesis," referring to the notorious treatise on original sin by the Dutch humanist Hadriaan Beverland.
70. Cornelius Agrippa von Nettesheim, *Operum pars posterior* (Leiden: Per Beringos fratres, n.d.), 554–555, translated in Marc Van der Poel, *Cornelius Agrippa: The Humanist Theologian and His Declamations* (Leiden: Brill, 1997), 230, 236.

71. On Agrippa's *Declamation,* see Dario Gurashi, "Decoding Adam and Eve: Agrippa on Sexuality and Redemption" in *Cursed Blessings: Sex and Religious Radical Dissent in Early Modern Europe,* ed. Umberto Grassi (New York: Routledge, 2024), 79-95. The sources of the work are discussed in Nauert, *Agrippa and the Crisis of Renaissance Thought,* 58–59; Van der Poel, *Cornelius Agrippa,* 227–229.
72. ASV, SU, B 132, ff. 1v–3v.
73. ASV, SU, B 132, f. 4r.
74. ASV, SU, B 132, ff. 4r–7v.
75. Many inquisitorial sources testify to the spread of theological discussions concerning predestination and salvation in Venice: John Martin, "Salvation and Society in Sixteenth-Century Venice: Popular Evangelism in a Renaissance City," *Journal of Modern History* 60, no. 2 (1988): 205–233.
76. Barbierato, *Inquisitor in the Hat Shop,* xi–xiii.
77. ASV, SU, B 132, f. 8r–9r.
78. ASV, SU, B 132, f. 9r.
79. ASV, SU, B 132, f. 8r.
80. On the relationship between early modern magic and the development of the scientific method, see Lynn Thorndike, *History of Magic and Experimental Science,* 8 vols. (New York: Macmillan, 1923–1958); Daniel P. Walker, *Spiritual and Demonic Magic from Ficino to Campanella* (London: Warburg Institute, University of London, 1958); Eugenio Garin, *Science and Civic Life in the Italian Renaissance,* trans. Peter Munz (Garden City, NY: Anchor Books, 1969); Frances A. Yates, *Astraea: The Imperial Theme in the Sixteenth Century* (London: Routledge & K. Paul, 1975); Yates, *Occult Philosophy in the Elizabethan Age* (London: Routledge & K. Paul, 1979); Yates, *Giordano Bruno and the Hermetic Tradition* (London: Routledge, 1999); Yates, *The Rosicrucian Enlightenment* (London: Routledge, 1999). See also the recent synthesis by Mark A. Waddell, *Magic, Science, and Religion in Early Modern Europe* (Cambridge: Cambridge University Press, 2021). In Venice, the case of the Rosicrucian, Francesco Gualdi, well illustrates these complex interactions: Barbierato, *Inquisitor in the Hat Shop,* 46. On libertinism and science, see also Alain Mothu and Antonella Del Prete, eds., *Révolution scientifique et libertinage* (Turnhout: Brepols, 2000); Edward Muir, *Culture Wars of the Late Renaissance: Skeptics, Libertines, and Opera* (Cambridge, MA: Harvard University Press, 2007), which deals specifically with Venice; Antonio Frajese, *Dal libertinismo ai Lumi.* On medicine and heterodoxy in Venice, see Alessandra Celati, *The World of Girolamo Donzellini: A Network of Heterodox Physicians in Sixteenth-Century Venice* (London: Routledge, 2023).
81. ASV, SU, B 132 (1705), 8r.
82. Barbierato, *Inquisitor in the Hat Shop,* 54–55.

CHAPTER SIX ~ HADRIAAN BEVERLAND'S *ON ORIGINAL SIN*

1. *Hadrian Beverland's "De peccato originali" (On Original Sin 1679),* ed. and trans. Karen E. Hollewand and Floris Verhaart (Leiden: Brill, 2023); orig. ed.: Hadrian Beverland, *De Peccato originali, κατ' ἐξοχὴν sic nuncupato, dissertatio* (Ex Typographeio, 1679), 163 [28] (hereafter cited as *DPO*). The page number within brackets refers to the original edition.
2. *DPO,* 165–166 [29–30].
3. *DPO,* 185 [44].
4. See especially chapter 7: *DPO,* 169–177 [33–39].
5. *DPO,* 169–171 [33–34].
6. *DPO,* 201 [56]. I changed Hollewand and Verhaart's translation of "culum angustum" from "narrow buttocks" into "narrow asshole," which in my opinion better renders Beverland's unapologetic and scurrilous style.
7. *DPO,* 201 [57].
8. *DPO,* 201 [57–58].
9. Giovanni Dall'Orto, "Della Casa, Giovanni," in *Who's Who in Gay and Lesbian History: From Antiquity to World War II,* ed. Robert Aldrich and Garry Wotherspoon (London: Routledge, 2002), 143–144.
10. Karen E. Hollewand, *The Banishment of Beverland: Sex, Sin and Scholarship in the Seventeenth-Century Dutch Republic* (Leiden: Brill, 2019), 31–32, 269.
11. *DPO,* 193 [50–51].
12. *DPO,* 197–199 [54–55].
13. *DPO,* 199 [56]; Catullus, *Carmina,* 64:405.
14. *DPO,* 167 [30–31] (emphasis added).
15. Beverland lost his father in 1653, when he was only three years old. His mother married again to de Gomme, a Zeelander working for the British army: Hollewand, *Banishment of Beverland,* 20–22.
16. Hollewand, *Banishment of Beverland,* 23–26.
17. *DPO,* 121 [second preface, B1r] (emphasis added).
18. Hollewand, *Banishment of Beverland,* 223. The categories of "libertine" and "libertinism" are controversial. In the 1960s, Alberto Tenenti distinguished between a first wave of libertinism (sixteenth century), assimilated to a Christian heresy, and a second wave (seventeenth century), eminently philosophical: "Milieu XVIe siècle. Libertinisme et hérésie," *Annales ESC* 18, no. 1 (1963): 1–19. Now, a third stage has been included, identified with loose moral conduct, especially in matters of sexual habits (eighteenth century): Renée Pintard, *Le libertinage érudit dans la première moitié du XVIIe siècle* (Paris: Boivin et cie, 1943); Gerhard Schneider, *Der Libertin: zur Geistes- und Sozialgeschichte des Bürgertums im 16. und 17. Jahrhundert* (Stuttgart: J. B. Metzler, 1970); Tullio Gregory, "'Libertinisme érudit' in Seventeenth-Century

France and Italy: The Critique of Ethics and Religion," *British Journal for the History of Philosophy* 6, no. 3 (1998): 323–349; Françoise Charles-Daubert, *Les Libertins érudits en France au xvii*[e] *siècle* (Paris: PUF, 1998); Didier Foucault, *Histoire du libertinage. Des goliards au marquis de Sade* (Paris: Perrin, 2007). Recent scholars have softened the edges of this partition: Jean-Pierre Cavaillé, *Les Déniaisés: irréligion et libertinage au début de l'époque modern* (Paris: Garnier, 2013), 382–383. Cavaillé identifies libertinism with a radical quest for freedom: of thought against orthodoxies; from the concept of sin (ethical); from the constraints imposed by institutionalized religions (373–414). On concealment as a communication strategy, see Cavaillé, *Les Déniaisés*; Isabelle Moreau, *"Guérir du sot." Les stratégies d'écriture des libertins à l'âge classique* (Paris: Honoré Champion, 2007).

19. *DPO*, 327 [163 (153)].
20. *DPO*, 333 [N3v].
21. Hollewand, *Banishment of Beverland*, 28–40.
22. Hollewand, *Banishment of Beverland*, 228–240.
23. Hollewand, *Banishment of Beverland*, 73.
24. Prosper Marchand, "IMPOSTORIBUS (LIBER DE TRIBUS) sive Tractatus de Vanitate Religionum," in *Dictionnaire historique, ou Memoires critiques et litteraires, concernant la vie et les ouvrages de divers personnages distingues, particulierement dans la republique des lettres* (The Hague: Pierre de Hond, 1758), 1:312–329. I refer to the critical edition of this entry by Jeffrey Dean, "Marchand's article IMPOSTORIBUS," in *Heterodoxy, Spinozism, and Free Thought in Early-Eighteenth-Century Europe: Studies on the Traité des trois imposteurs,* ed. Silvia Berti, Françoise Charles-Daubert, and Richard H. Popkin (Dordrecht: Reidel, 1996), 477–524, 522.
25. Beverland probably named his imaginary friend after the nickname of the Italian painter Pietro Buonaccorsi (1501–1547), which was Perino dal Vaga: Hollewand, *Banishment of Beverland*, 270.
26. Hollewand, *Banishment of Beverland*, 237–238.
27. Marchand, "IMPOSTORIBUS," 522.
28. Martin Mulsow, "Freethinking in Early-Eighteenth-Century Protestant Germany: Peter Friedrich Arpe and the Traité des trois imposteurs," in Berti, Charles-Daubert, and Popkin, *Heterodoxy, Spinozism, and Free Thought*, 193–239 (215).
29. On Vanini, see Francesco Paolo Raimondi, *Giulio Cesare Vanini nell'Europa del Seicento* (Pisa and Rome: Istituti editoriali e poligrafici internazionali, 2005); Didier Foucault, *Un philosophe libertin dans l'Europe baroque: Giulio Cesare Vanini (1585–1619)* (Paris: Garnier, 2003); Cesare Vasoli, "Vanini e il suo processo per ateismo," in *Atheismus in Mittelalter und in der Renaissance,* ed. Friedrich Niewöhner and Olaf Pluta (Wiesbaden: Harassowitz, 1999), 129–144. On

Gabriel Naudé, see Cavaillé, *Les Déniaisés,* 195–217. On Naudé's relationship with Cardano's work, see Bianchi, *Naturalismo, scetticismo, politica,* 107–134.

30. Marchand, "IMPOSTORIBUS," 496.
31. *DPO,* 149 [16].
32. *DPO,* 131–133 [3–5]. The quote is in Horatius, *Carmina,* book 1, *Carmen* 3.
33. *DPO,* 253 [105].
34. *DPO,* 277 [124].
35. *DPO,* 259 [110].
36. *DPO,* 293 [136]; *CD,* 16–17.
37. *DPO,* 293–309 [137–150].
38. Jonathan Israel, *Radical Enlightenment: Philosophy and the Making of Modernity, 1650-1750* (Oxford: Oxford University Press, 2001), 87–88; Wiep van Bunge, *From Stevin to Spinoza: An Essay on Philosophy in the Seventeenth-Century Dutch Republic* (Leiden: Brill, 2001), 158–159; Van Bunge, *Spinoza Past and Present: Essays on Spinoza, Spinozism, and Spinoza Scholarship* (Leiden: Brill, 2012), 155–156. See Hollewand, *Banishment of Beverland,* 6–7.
39. Jetze Touber, *Spinoza and Biblical Philology in the Dutch Republic, 1660–1710* (Oxford: Oxford University Press, 2018), 158.
40. Touber, *Spinoza and Biblical Philology,* 175–176.
41. See Hollewand, *Banishment of Beverland,* 82–108.
42. *DPO,* 134–135 [5]. The passage contains a quote from Jer. 2:13, 17:13.
43. *DPO,* 209 [64].
44. *DPO,* 217 [73–74]; Gen. 3:25.
45. *DPO,* 223 [78]. A paraphrase of Cic., *Rep.* 3:1.1. (ed. Ziegler) from Aug., *C. Iul.* 4.12.60.
46. *DPO,* 213 [68]. See Prop., *Eleg.*, 3:9.20.
47. *DPO,* 205 [61]; Ov., *Am.* 3.4.9.
48. *DPO,* 163 [27].
49. *DPO,* 165 [30] (emphasis added).
50. *DPO,* 169 [33].
51. Touber, *Spinoza and Biblical Philology,* 164.
52. The manuscript is preserved in the Special Collections of the Utrecht University Library.
53. Touber, *Spinoza and Biblical Philology,* 165–168.
54. Piet Steenbakkers, Jetze Touber, and Jeroen van de Ven, "A Clandestine Notebook (1678–79) on Spinoza, Beverland, Politics, the Bible and Sex: Utrecht UL, ms. 1284*," *LIAS* 38 (2011): 291 (hereafter cited as CN).
55. CN, 269.
56. CN, 287. Other passages on Beverland's opinions about original sin correspond to the entries 88, 89, 90, 91, 98, 103, 145, 156 in the transcription and translation of the manuscript.

57. CN, 289.
58. CN, 339.

CHAPTER SEVEN ⁓ FRENCH TRANSLATIONS

1. François de La Mothe Le Vayer, *L'Antre des nymphes,* ed. Jean-Pierre Cavaillé (Toulouse: Anacharsis, 2004). I thank Jean-Pierre for introducing me to this extraordinary document.
2. Homer, *Odyssey,* trans. Emily Wilson (New York: W. W. Norton, 2020), book 13, 95–112.
3. Cavaillé, *Les Déniaisés,* 78–82.
4. Le Vayer, *L'Antre des nymphes,* 84–85.
5. Le Vayer, *L'Antre de nymphes,* 85–86. Seneca the Elder's *Controversy II,* in Lucius Annaeus Seneca, *Elder Seneca Declamations,* trans. M. Winterbottom, 2 vols. (Cambridge, MA: Harvard University Press, 1974), 1:58–89. The quotation "inepta loci" belongs to the third carmen of the *Carmina Priapeia.*
6. See Pietro Capitani, *Erudizione e scetticismo in François de La Mothe Le Vayer* (Florence: Olschki, 2009).
7. José R. Maia Neto, *Academic Skepticism in Seventeenth-Century French Philosophy: The Charronian Legacy, 1601–1662* (New York: Springer, 2014), 82–91; Daniel R. Brunstetter, "La Mothe Le Vayer and Political Skepticism," in *Skepticism and Political Thought in the Seventeenth and Eighteenth Centuries,* ed. John C. Laursen and Gianni Paganini (Toronto: University of Toronto Press, 2015), 36–54. Popkin's opinion is still of considerable relevance: *The History of Scepticism: From Savonarola to Bayle* (Oxford: Oxford University Press, 2003), 84.
8. Cavaillé, *Les Déniaisés,* 77–90.
9. Jean-Pierre Cavaillé, "Sodomy and Irreligion in the Culture of the Déniaisés (17th Century)," in Grassi, *Cursed Blessings,* 145–154 (147); with reference to François de La Mothe Le Vayer, *Le Banquet sceptique*, in *Dialogues faits à l'imitation des Anciens,* ed. André Pessel (Paris: Fayard, 1988), 101.
10. Silvia Berti, *Anticristianesimo e libertà. Studi sull'illuminismo radicale europeo* (Bologna: Il Mulino, 2012), xvi–xvii. Winfrid Schröder emphasizes the *Traité*'s innovativeness, but he also recognizes that it simplified the Spinozian system by shifting it toward a radical materialism: Schröder, "Panthéisme—spinozisme—matérialisme athée: La métaphysique du Traité des trois imposteurs," *La Lettre clandestine* 24 (2016): 133–140, 137–139. Jonathan Israel has dismissively qualified the *Traité* as "being little more than a crude vulgarization of Spinoza supplemented by a collage of additional matter drawn from several writers": Israel, *Radical Enlightenment,* 695. Conversely, other authors emphasize the influence of libertine currents on the text: Silvia Berti, introduction to *Trattato dei tre impostori. La vita e lo spirito del signor Benedetto de Spinoza,* ed. and trans. Silvia Berti

(Turin: Einaudi, 1994), xviii–xix; Jean-Pierre Cavaillé, "Libertinage ou Lumières radicales," in *Qu'est-ce que Lumières "radicales"? Libertinage, athéisme et spinozisme dans le tournant philosophique de l'âge Classique,* ed. Catherine Secrétan, Tristan Dagron, and Laurent Bove (Paris: Éditionis Amsterdam, 2007), 61–74.

11. Richard H. Popkin, foreword to Berti, Charles-Daubert, and Popkin, *Heterodoxy, Spinozism, and Free Thought,* vii–xix, ix. The legend of the three impostors circulated in two distinct forms, one in Latin (*De tribus impostoribus*) and the other in French (*Traité des trois imposteurs*). The known copies of the Latin version, which at least in its manuscript version chronologically precedes the French one, are today mainly concentrated in libraries and archives located in the German territories and their borders: Miguel Benitez, "La diffusion du *Traité des trois imposteurs* au XVIIIe siècle," *Revue d'histoire moderne et contemporaine* 40–41 (1993): 137–151; Benitez, "Une histoire interminable: Origines et développement du *Traité des trois imposteurs,*" in Berti, Charles-Daubert, and Popkin, *Heterodoxy, Spinozism, and Free Thought,* 53–74. The Latin version was eventually printed in 1753 by the publisher Straub in Wien with a false date (1598): Minois, *Atheist's Bible,* 136–137.
12. See Bertram Eugene Schwarzbach and A. W. Fairbarn, "History and Structure of Our *Traité des trois imposteurs,*" in Berti, Charles-Daubert, and Popkin, *Heterodoxy, Spinozism, and Free Thought,* 75–129 (78–79); Margaret Jacob, *Radical Enlightenment: Pantheists, Freemasons, and Republicans* (London: Allen & Unwin, 1981), 217–225; Richard H. Popkin, "Spinoza and the Conversion of the Jews: Spinoza's Political and Theological Thought," in *Spinoza's Political and Theological Thought: International Symposium Commemorating the 350th Anniversary of Spinoza: Amsterdam, 24–27 November 1982,* ed. Cornelius de Deugd (Amsterdam: North Holland, 1984), 171–183, (176–177); de Deugd, "Some New Light on the Roots of Spinoza's Science of Bible Study," in *Spinoza and the Sciences,* ed. Marjorie Green and Debra Nail (Dordrecht: Reidel, 1986), 171–188; Charles-Daubert, "Les principales sources de *L'Esprit de Spinoza,* traité libertin et pamphlet politique," in *Travaux et documents 1: Lire et traduire Spinoza,* Groupe de recherches spinozistes (Paris: Presses de l'Université de Paris Sorbonne, 1989), 61–108.
13. Marchand, "IMPOSTORIBUS," 510; Silvia Berti, "Jan Vroesen, autore del 'Traite des trois imposteurs,'" in *Rivista Storica Italiana* 103, no. 2 (1991): 283–298; Silvia Berti, "*L'Esprit de Spinosa*: ses origines et sa première édition dans leur contexte spinozien," in Berti, Charles-Daubert, and Popkin, *Heterodoxy, Spinozism, and Free Thought,* 3–51, 30. See also Berti, *Anticristianesimo e libertà,* xix.
14. Berti, introduction, xx–xxvii.

15. Berti, introduction, xxvi–xxvi. It was not until 1985 that Silvia Berti discovered the first print edition of the work in the Special Collections of the Los Angeles University Research Library. There are currently four surviving exemplars of the book, including the one discovered by Berti. See Berti, introduction, xxvii–xxxiii.
16. Berti, introduction, xxxiv.
17. Minois, *Atheist's Bible,* 144–149.
18. *Trattato dei tre impostori. La vita e lo spirito del signor Benedetto de Spinoza,* ed. and trans. Silvia Berti (Turin: Einaudi, 1994), notes 265–270, 274–277 (hereafter cited as *TTI*); Berti, introduction, lviii.
19. *TTI,* notes 282–284. On the legacy of Celsus's *On the True Doctrine* in anti-Christian polemics and its importance for our cases, see Chapter 1.
20. The *Traité,* however, forces Le Vayer's interpretation; the redactors quoted Celsus's passages through the mediation of *On the Virtue of the Pagans,* ignoring Le Vayer's critical remarks about this author: *TTI,* 136–138, 286.
21. *TTI,* 136; François La Mothe Le Vayer, *De la Vertu des Payens* (Paris: Targa, 1642), 117–118.
22. Lynn Hunt, Margaret C. Jacob, and Wijnand Mijnhardt, *The Book That Changed Europe: Picart & Bernard's "Religious Ceremonies of the World"* (Cambridge, MA: Harvard University Press, 2010), 16–17.
23. Hunt, Jacob, and Mijnhardt, *Book That Changed the World,* 119.
24. On Picart's biography and his intellectual relationships, see Hunt, Jacob, and Mijnhardt, *Book That Changed the World,* 25–70.
25. Hunt, Jacob, and Mijnhardt, *Book That Changed the World,* 102.
26. Hunt, Jacob, and Mijnhardt, *Book That Changed the World,* 123–124, 272.
27. Hunt, Jacob, and Mijnhardt, *Book That Changed Europe,* 121.
28. Jean Frederic Bernard, *Etat de l'homme dans le peché originel, où l'on fait voir quelle est la source, quelles les causes & et les suites, de ce peché dans le Monde* (Printed in the World, 1714), 5–6 (hereafter cited as *EH*).
29. *EH,* 8–10.
30. *EH,* 12.
31. *EH,* 16–18.
32. *EH,* 20–21.
33. *EH,* 25.
34. *EH,* 35.
35. *EH,* 48.
36. *EH,* 51.
37. *EH,* 53.
38. *EH,* 54.
39. *EH,* 57.
40. *EH,* 57–58.
41. *EH,* 83.

42. *EH,* 84–85.
43. See Paolo Fasoli, "Body Language: Sex Manual Literature from Pietro Aretino's *Sixteen Positions* to Antonio Rocco's *Invitation to Sodomy,*" in *Sex Acts in Early Modern Italy: Practice, Performance, Perversion, Punishment,* ed. Allison Levy (London: Routledge, 2016), 27–42.
44. *EH,* 85.
45. The work, published around 1659 or 1660, was in fact written by the French author Nicholas Chorier (1612–1692). Chorier passed it off as van Meur's Latin translation of an alleged Spanish original supposedly written by Louise Sigée (the Aloisia Sigea of the title), a female poet who was born of a Spanish noblewoman and an expatriated French man and who lived and wrote in Toledo during the sixteenth century (1522–1560): James Turner, *Schooling Sex: Libertine Literature and Erotic Education in Italy, France, and England, 1534–1685* (Oxford: Oxford University Press, 2003).
46. *EH,* 109–110.
47. *EH,* 187.
48. *EH,* 191.
49. *EH,* 206.

CHAPTER EIGHT ~ ORIGINAL SIN, SEXUALITY, AND FEMALE INDEPENDENCE

1. Karen E. Hollewand and Floris Verhaart, introduction to *DPO,* 1–91 (54).
2. ACDF, Stanza storica (hereafter cited as SSto), O 1-h, archival subunit 9, July 18, 1700. The commission was composed of the master of the Sacred Palace, the commissioner general of the Holy Office (Tommaso Maria Bosi), and two theological consultors (the Minor Conventuals Paolino Bernardini and Giovanni Damasceno Bragaldi).
3. ACDF, SSto, O 1-h, archival subunits 8, 9.
4. Andrea Del Col, "Archivi e serie documentarie: Vaticano," in *DSI,* 1:89–91 (90).
5. Their jurisdiction also included the Alba's bishopric. See Albrecht Burkardt, "Casale Monferrato," in *DSI,* 1:228.
6. ACDF, SSto, O 1-h, archival subunit 9, ff. 76r–77v.
7. ACDF, SSto, O 1-h, archival subunit 9, f. 154r–v, 157v.
8. ACDF, SSto, O 1-h, archival subunit 9, f. 119r.
9. ACDF, SSto, O 1-h, archival subunit 9, ff. 119v–120r.
10. *DPO,* 231–233 [85–86].
11. Agrippa von Nettesheim, *Agrippae [. . .] operum,* 560.
12. *DPO,* 235 [88–89].
13. *DPO,* 237 [90].
14. ACDF, SSto, O 1-h, archival subunit 9, f. 120r–v.
15. ACDF, SSto, O 1-h, archival subunit 9, f. 120v.
16. ACDF, SSto, O 1-h, archival subunit 9, f. 132v.

17. ACDF, SSto, O 1-h, archival subunit 9, f. 232r.
18. On female conservatories, see Nicholas Terpstra, "Mothers, Sisters, and Daughters: Girls and Conservatory Guardianship in Late Renaissance Florence," *Renaissance Studies* 17, no. 2 (2003): 201–229; Terpstra, *Abandoned Children of the Italian Renaissance* (Baltimore: Johns Hopkins University Press, 2005); Terpstra, *Lost Girls: Sex and Death in Renaissance Florence* (Baltimore: Johns Hopkins University Press, 2010).
19. On the Conservatory of Saint John the Lateran, see Angela Groppi, *I conservatori della virtù. Donne recluse nella Roma dei papi* (Rome Bari: Laterza, 1994), 19, 22.
20. Groppi, *I conservatori della virtù,* 68; Terpstra, *Abandoned Children.*
21. ACDF, SSto, O 1-h, archival subunit 9, ff. 232r–v.
22. ACDF, SSto, O 1-h, archival subunit 9, f. 232v–233v.
23. ACDF, SSto, O 1-h, archival subunit 9, ff. 235r–v.
24. ACDF, SSto, O 1-h, archival subunit 9, f. 235v.
25. ACDF, SSto, O 1-h, archival subunit 9, f. 235v.
26. ACDF, SSto, O 1-h, archival subunit 9, ff. 236r–v.
27. ACDF, SSto, O 1-h, archival subunit 9, f. 234r.
28. On the Tridentine reform of the sacrament, see Roberto Rusconi, "The Sacrament of Penance at the Council: Innovation as a Confirmation of the Centuries-Old Tradition of Confession," in Minnich, *Cambridge Companion,* 139–155. On the sixteenth-century shift, see John Bossy, "The Social History of Confession in the Age of the Reformation," *Transactions of the Royal Historical Society* 25 (1975): 21–38; Adriano Prosperi, *Tribunali della coscienza. Inquisitori, confessori, missionari* (Turin: Einaudi, 1996), 513–548.
29. Terpstra, "Early Modern Catholicism," 617–621.
30. Among the sexual infractions, the "solicitatio ad turpia" (solicitation to turpitudes), otherwise called "solicitation in the confessional," was the one that kept the inquisitorial tribunals busiest between the late fifteenth and the eighteenth centuries. See Stephen Haliczer, *Sexuality in the Confessional: A Sacrament Profaned* (New York: Oxford University Press, 1996).
31. The Tridentine decree *On Female Regular Clergy and Nuns* (1563) reestablished strict enclosure for female monasteries. On involuntary female monastic vows, see Anne Jacobson Schutte, "Between Venice and Rome: The Dilemma of Involuntary Nuns," *Sixteenth Century Journal* 41, no. 2 (2010): 415–439; Giovanna Paolin, *Lo spazio del silenzio: monacazioni forzate, clausura e proposte di vita religiosa femminile nell'età moderna* (Monreale Valcellina: Centro studi storici Menocchio, 1996). For an overview of female monastic life, see Gabriella Zarri, "The Third Status," in *Time, Space, and Women's Lives in Early Modern Europe,* ed. Anne J. Schutte, Thomas Kuehn, and Silvana Seidel Menchi (Kirksville, MO: Truman State University Press, 2001), 181–199; Silvia Evangelisti, *Nuns: A History of Convent Life, 1450–1700* (Oxford:

Oxford University Press, 2007). On resistance to monastic discipline, see Craig A. Monson, *Nuns Behaving Badly: Tales of Music, Magic, Art, and Arson in the Convents of Italy* (Chicago: University of Chicago Press, 2010). On sex and sodomy, see Judith C. Brown, *Immodest Acts: The Life of a Lesbian Nun in Renaissance Italy* (New York: Oxford University Press, 1986). On Venice, see Anne Jacobson Schutte, *Aspiring Saints: Pretense of Holiness, Inquisition, and Gender in the Republic of Venice, 1618–1750* (Baltimore: Johns Hopkins University Press, 2001); Jutta G. Sperling, *Convents and the Body Politic in Late Renaissance Venice* (Chicago: University of Chicago Press, 1999).

32. Prosperi, *Tribunali della coscienza,* 520–542. See also Jodi Bilinkoff, *Related Lives: Confessors and Their Female Penitents, 1450–1750* (Ithaca, NY: Cornell University Press, 2005).
33. Terpstra, *Lost Girls,* 3–4; Groppi, *I conservatori della virtù,* 16–18.
34. See Terence W. O'Reilly, *Spiritual Exercises of Saint Ignatius of Loyola: Contexts, Sources, Reception* (Leiden: Brill, 2021).
35. Adelisa Malena, "Ego-Documents or 'Plural Compositions'? Reflections on Women's Obedient Scriptures in the Early Modern Catholic World," *Journal of Early Modern Studies* 1 (2012): 97–113 (105). On autobiographical writings as a source for historians, see Dekker Rudolf, ed., *Egodocuments and History: Autobiographical Writing in Its Social Context since the Middle Ages* (Hilversum: Verloren, 2002). Women's autobiographical writings in religious contexts have been widely studied. On Italy, among others, see Elena Bottoni, *Scritture dell'anima. Esperienze religiose femminili nella Toscana del Settecento* (Rome: Edizioni di Storia e Letteratura, 2009); Adriano Prosperi, "Diari femminili e discernimento degli spiriti. Le mistiche della prima età moderna in Italia," in *America e Apocalisse e altri saggi* (Pisa: Istituti editoriali poligrafici internazionali, 1999), 343-365. Anne J. Schutte has dealt with this issue in *Aspiring Saints: Pretense of Holiness, Inquisition and Gender in the Republic of Venice, 1618–1750* (Baltimore: Johns Hopkins University Press, 2001). On Spain, see Isabelle Poutrin, *Le voile et la plume. Autobiographie et sainteté féminine dans l'Espagne modern* (Madrid: Casa de Velazquez, 1995). On early modern England, see Victoria Van Hyning, *Convent Autobiography: Early Modern English Nuns in Exile* (Oxford: Oxford University Press, 2019).
36. ACDF, SSto, 0 1-h, archival subunit 9, f. 238r–v.
37. On women's literacy in religious orders, see Virginia Blanton, Veronica O'Mara, and Patricia Stoop, eds., *Nuns' Literacies in Medieval Europe: The Antwerp Dialogue* (Turnhout: Brepols, 2017); Elizabeth Clarke, "Women in Church and in Devotional Spaces," in *The Cambridge Companion to Early Modern Women's Writing,* ed. Laura Lunger Knoppers (New York: Cambridge University Press, 2009); Erica Longfellow, *Women and Religious Writing in Early Modern England* (Cambridge: Cambridge University Press, 2004); Denis Renevey and Christiania Whitehead, eds., *Writing Religious*

Women: Female Spiritual and Textual Practices in Late Medieval England (Toronto: University of Toronto Press, 2000).

38. Xenia von Tippelskirch, *Sotto controllo. Letture femminili in Italia nella prima età moderna* (Rome: Viella, 2011), 100–101, 156. For an introduction to women readership, see Belinda E. Jack, *The Woman Reader* (New Haven, CT: Yale University Press, 2012). On reading as a form of subversion, see Frances E. Dolan, "Reading, Writing, and Other Crimes," in *Feminist Readings of Early Modern Culture: Emerging Subjects,* ed. Valerie Traub, Lindsay Kaplan, and Dympna Callaghan (Cambridge: Cambridge University Press, 1996), 142–167. On the British world, see Leah Knight, Micheline White, and Elizabeth Sauer, eds., *Women's Bookscapes in Early Modern Britain: Reading, Ownership, Circulation* (Ann Arbor: University of Michigan Press, 2018); Edith Snook, *Women, Reading, and the Cultural Politics of Early Modern England* (Aldershot: Ashgate, 2005).
39. On "obedient writings," see also Alison Weber, "Autobiografias por mandato: ego-documentos o textos sociales? / Autobiografias por mandato: Ego-documents or Social Texts?," *Cultura Escrita & Sociedad* 1 (2005): 116–118; Massimo Lollini, "Scrittura obbediente e mistica tridentina in Veronica Giuliani," *Annali d'Italianistica* 13 (1995): 351–369.

ACKNOWLEDGMENTS

This book is the result of a long journey. It was 2012 when I first came across some of these cases. At that time, I was working on a project supervised and directed by Giuseppe Marcocci at the Scuola Normale Superiore of Pisa titled "Beyond the Holy War" and jointly coordinated by the Scuola Normale, La Sapienza of Rome, and the University of Palermo. Up to that point, I had mostly worked on the cultural and social history of homoerotic relationships in early modern Italy among the lower ranks of society. I started surveying the Archives of the Spanish Inquisition in Sicily to investigate the homoerotic relationships between Muslims and Christians, firmly convinced that this methodological approach would have brought a fresh new look to this subject. But things did not go as I expected. While I was digging into the archives, I was surprised to see the curious heretical proposition that became the object of this book emerging from the archival material. This fortuitous event makes this book a genuine example of serendipity in research. It took me ages to understand how to frame these cases, and their interpretation required me to explore types of sources, methodologies, and secondary literature that I had never approached before. This adventure lasted almost twelve years, and it would not have been possible if I had not had the support of a number of institutions and research groups that have helped me unravel the tangle, accompanying me through the temporary failures, as well as the successes, of this rocky road.

My first thanks go to Andrew Lynch, director of the Australian Research Council Centre of Excellence for the History of Emotions, and Juanita Feros Ruis, the director of the Sydney node, who gave me the opportunity to set the foundation of this research from 2015 to 2018. I then carried out this work as a Marie Skłodowska-Curie Global Fellow based at the PoliTeSse Research Center at the University of Verona and at the Department of History of the University of Maryland, respectively host and partner institutions of the project SPACES (Sex, disPlacements, and Cross-cultural EncounterS), funded by the European Union Horizon 2020 program from 2018 to 2021. I am immensely grateful to my supervisors Lorenzo Bernini and Philip M. Soergel, who accompanied my training as an early scholar during these formative years of my career.

I am also thankful for the stimulating learning environment of the two research groups I have been part of since the beginning of my investigation: PoliTeSse (Politics and Theories of Sexuality), based at the University of Verona, and the international research network EMoDiR (Early Modern Religious Dissents and Radicalism). In these communities I found food for thought as well as friendship and conviviality, indispensable support through the hardships of research. I am also indebted to the many critiques and insights I received from colleagues and friends from all around the world in the many conferences, workshops, and seminars where I presented the partial outcomes of this work from 2012 to 2020. It would be too long to list all of the organizers, discussants, and speakers, as well as to recall the stimulating and provoking questions raised by the public. You all know how much I owe to each one of you.

Beyond institutions, this work is the result of the constant dialogue with colleagues and friends who have helped me find my bearings in this troubled journey. Among them, I am particularly grateful to Jean-Pierre Cavaillé, Bernard Cooperman, Peter Cryle, Lucia Felici, Vittorio Frajese, Mercedes García-Arenal, Stefano Villani, and Gary K. Waite. With great generosity and spirit of cooperation, Karen E. Hollewand and Floris Verhaart provided me with the drafts of the transcript and translation of their annotated edition of Beverland's *On Original Sin* (published in 2023), and Giovanni Romeo shared with me the archival references of the cases preserved in the Archivio Storico Diocesano of Naples. I have no words to thank the peer reviewers, who saw the potential in my first manuscript and helped me reorganize that rambling stream of thoughts into a coherent whole. This process has been possible thanks to the constant support and supervision of Nicholas Terpstra, who glossed the many redactions of the book repeating the mantra "Less is more" with a patience that I would have never had if I were in his place. Thanks, Nick! Further thanks go to Andrea Wenz, who has helped me "anglicize" my cumbersome English prose throughout the many redactions of this text with diligence and competence. I will always be grateful also to Adriano Prosperi, who was my mentor during graduate school and was the first to open my mind to the understanding of the early modern world. Finally, a heartfelt thank-you to the faculty staff, the librarians, and the archivists of all the institutions I have gone through during this long path of research for their professionalism and care in providing me with all the necessary arrangements for undertaking my work. This would not have been possible without you.

The Introduction touches on ideas I first discussed in "Sexual Nonconformity and Religious Dissent in Early Modern Europe," the introduction to U. Grassi, ed., *Cursed Blessings: Sex and Religious Radical Dissent in Early Modern Europe* (Routledge, 2024). Portions of Chapter 3 were first published in "The Forbidden Fruit: Heresy, Original Sin, and Emotions in Early Modern Italy," in *Infamous Stains: Unbridled Masculine Sexualities in Early Modernity*, ed. F. Alfieri and V. Lagioia (Viella, 2024). This chapter also continues discussions first presented in "Emotions and Sexuality: Regulation and Homoerotic Transgression," in *The Routledge History of Emotions in Europe (1100–1700)*, ed. S. Broomhall and A. Lynch (Routledge, 2020) and in a work I co-authored with Vincenzo Lagioia, "The Papacy, Homosexuality, and Same-Sex Marriage," in *The Cambridge History of the Papacy*, ed. J. Rollo-Koster, R. A. Ventresca, M. H. Eichbauer, and M. Pattenden (Cambridge, 2025), vol. 3 (*Civil Society*). Chapters 4 and 5 build on ideas first discussed in "The Fall from Grace: Religious Skepticism and Sexuality in the Early Modern Mediterranean World," *Journal of Early Modern History* (2021), and "Sex and Toleration: New Perspectives of Research on Religious Radical Dissent in Early Modern Italy," *Intellectual History Review* 29, no. 1 (2019). A portion of Chapter 4 was first published in "Ambiguous Boundaries: Sex Crimes and Cross-Cultural Encounters in the Early Modern Mediterranean World," *Studi e Materiali di Storia delle Religioni* 84, no. 2 (2018), a text that also informs Chapter 5.

INDEX